NOTES FROM
ANOTHER INDIA

Jeremy Seabrook

Pluto  Press

LONDON • EAST HAVEN, CT

First published 1995 by Pluto Press
345 Archway Road, London N6 5AA
and 140 Commerce Street, East Haven,
Connecticut 06512, USA

99 98 97 96 95   5 4 3 2 1

British Library Cataloguing in Publication Data
A catalogue record for this book is available from the British Library

ISBN 0 7453 0840 6 hardback

Library of Congress Cataloging in Publication Data
Seabrook, Jeremy, 1939–
      Notes from another India / Jeremy Seabrook.
         p.   cm.
      Includes index.
      ISBN 0–7453–0840–6
      1. India—Politics and government—1977– 2. India—Description
      and travel. I. Title.
      DS480.853.S43   1995
      954.05'2—dc20   95–5828
                                                             CIP

Typeset from the author's disks in Minster Book
Designed and produced for Pluto Press by
Chase Production Services, Chipping Norton, OX7 5QR
Printed in the EC by WSOY, Finland

Contents

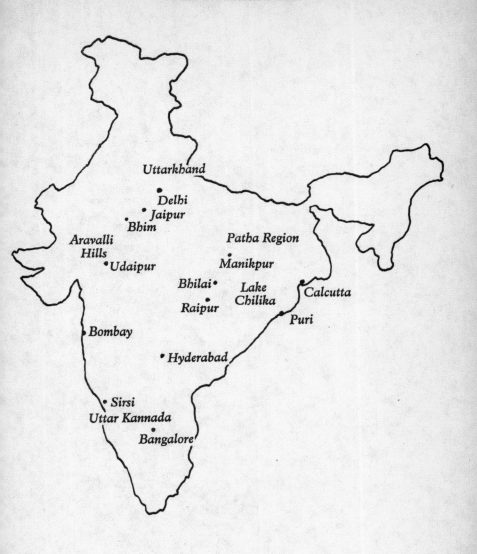

Uttarkhand

Delhi
Jaipur
Bhim

Aravalli
Hills
Udaipur

Patha Region

Manikpur

Bhilai
Raipur

Lake
Chilika

Calcutta

Puri

Bombay

Hyderabad

Sirsi
Uttar Kannada
Bangalore

Guide to principal places mentioned in the text

Introduction

India, like most countries of the South, appears in the Western media principally as pathology: the site of violence, brutality, cruelty, natural and human-made disasters; as fundamentally in need of 'our help'. There is, of course, plenty of evidence for this version of India: the destruction of the mosque at Ayodhya (in Uttar Pradesh, northern India, the most populous state in the country), and the communal violence that ensued in 1992, were the most spectacular manifestation of what is wrong with India.

On the other hand, the West appears to a majority in India as the source of all hope, a place of luxury, affluence and ease. This two-way, one-dimensional exchange reinforces the most simplistic and damaging falsification of the real relationship between North and South. For what is suppressed in this traffic is the endurance, courage, heroism of millions of people in India in their daily survival, and the uncelebrated struggles against injustice and insufficiency, the sacrifice and altruism of popular movements. Similarly, India has little inkling of the true social costs of the Western success story that it now feels constrained to emulate: it knows little of the levels of crime, violence, cynicism, social dislocation and breakdown which afflict the West.

The desire to write this book arose from a sense of the inadequacy of this thin, reduced version of the realities of both India and the West; from a profound irritation at the manipulation by the media of tired clichés and their unexamined acceptance of received ideas and images that bear little relation to the feelings and passions of the people in India. Perhaps the most dramatic opportunity for keeping alive archaic notions of India in recent years occurred with the outbreak of plague in the autumn of 1994: the country was represented as the source of medieval squalor and filth, a place where antique scourges that can nevertheless still frighten the West remain alive. The fact that there were subsequently serious doubts as to whether it was the plague at all did little to repair the damage done to India's exports – especially foodstuffs – and tourist industry; the fragility of two of the major hopes of the country's economic reforms was highlighted at the same time.

Of course there are other subtexts in this representation of India

1

by and to the West. There is always a market for Raj-nostalgia, with its unspoken suggestion that since the country passed from 'our' tutelage, it has gone downhill all the way; there is a ready audience for the eternal spiritual truths of India, many of them packaged and marketed in a form suitable for Western consumption. There is a vigorous tourist industry, which inflames the sense of the exotic, the outlandish, the colourfully bizarre; creates, out of an ancient and profound Indian civilisation, yet another item of consumption for jaded Westerners. Finally, there is approbation of 'the bold and courageous reforms' of the Narasimha Rao Congress government, which has been implementing free market economic policies since 1991, the one positive note as India falls into line with the prescriptions of Western financial institutions and the recommendations and pressures of the G-7 – the world's seven most industrialised countries – to integrate itself into the global economy. We should not be deceived by this approval: it represents the fidelity of the Indian government to policies crafted in Washington, Tokyo and Frankfurt, and if the West applauds these, it is merely another aspect of Western self-congratulation; its benefits to a majority of the people of India have yet to appear.

I had intended to call this book 'A Journey of Hope'. But to return from India brimming with enthusiasm for the signs of hope would also be a little unrealistic. For although there is much to encourage and inspire, there remains a a great deal to deplore: injustice, caste and communal strife, violence against women, child labour, gross social inequalities, abuse of human rights by the State and many of its agencies. Few of these, however, are likely to be mitigated by any Western-style developmental model. On the other hand, there are, literally, hundreds of thousands of individuals, groups, popular movements, committed to a different kind of change; people whose efforts go largely unrecorded, not only in the West, but even within India itself. This book is not about the fatalism of India – which is as nothing compared to the fatalism of the West's assumption that nothing can any longer be done about any social or economic evil – but about some people's dynamic and tenacious efforts to change the current balance of forces in India. Most of these people are not well known, although some have received attention in development circles in the West.

At a time when no alternatives are foreseen in an impoverished, wasting world, India remains the site of much resistance, both to the 'reforms' imposed by the International Monetary Fund/World Bank (IMF/WB) and to the implications of the new World Trade Organisation (WTO) following the conclusion of the General Agreement on Tariffs and Trade (GATT) negotiations. Strong traditions of self-reliance, subsistence and more modest use of resources remain a powerful influence in the villages of India. Furthermore, there are signs that what have always been regarded as the ageless passivity and resignation of the poor are also beginning to change – partly, no doubt, in response to the imposition of an economic order which, in a country of such vast age-old inequalities and social injustice, is bound to exacerbate inequality even further, in accordance with the mysterious principles of Western wealth creation.

This book can show only a fragment of the diversity and richness of India. It is limited by its geographical coverage, by the constraints of space, and by the expense of staying in India for more than the year I spent there. Its principal purpose is to show visitors to India another way of looking at the country; and if it serves to bring to the notice of people in the West something of the courage and moral strength, the endurance and steadfastness of millions of ordinary people, if it begins to combat inherited racist stereotypes, it will have served its purpose.

The book is dedicated to all those in one form of struggle or another who shared with me their time, their hospitality, and in many cases, their lives, in ways that make me feel humble, grateful and as committed as they are in their desire to improve their sometimes splendid, often appalling, country, with its resilience and its admirable capacity to survive.

I am most deeply indebted to Bharat, Madhu and Bharti Dogra, for sharing their insights with me, and for their sustained kindness during my stay in India. Indeed, Bharat Dogra has been a consistent defender of the poor and oppressed throughout his career as writer, journalist and social critic; and I am happy to pay tribute to his tenacity and courage. He has helped and advised me with this book, and without him, it would be even less than the modest contribution to the discussion on the development of India that it now is.

I am grateful also to Vinod Mehta, Raminder Singh, formerly at *The Pioneer* newspaper in New Delhi, who have published some fragments of this book. I would also like to thank Mukul and Charu, Winin and Melanie Pereira, Rajni Kothari, Vandana Shiva, as well as all those named in the book.

The book is for Bharti, Ishan, Asika, Aditi, Nayantara, Nishant, Dhipa, Priyanka, and the better India which will be made by their growing up in it.

I have explained most Hindu phrases and expressions in the text. Their first use is marked by a change of font and they are gathered together in a glossary at the end of the book.

1. Chilika

People's Response to Environmental and Social Degradation

It is a Sunday morning in early December in the village of Vatapada, near Lake Chilika in eastern Orissa. As far as the eye can see, the fields are waterlogged. Here and there, patches of drooping *padi* strain to rise out of the water, and people stand knee-deep, cutting the sodden crop stalk by stalk. Some women and children sit on the raised causeway beside the flooded fields. They are fishing. They cast blue nylon nets into the water, and retrieve a catch of algae, decaying padi and the roots of water-lilies. They turn it out on to the verge of the pot-holed road, and from the mass of vegetation, pick out a few marine creatures – some small silver fish, crabs, a handful of translucent shrimps. Not much, but a little protein to supplement a family diet grown meagre and unnourishing with the drowning of their rice-fields.

The scene has, it must be admitted, a severe beauty. The white elegance of migrant herons is reflected in the serene water; a blue kingfisher flashes through the grasses. The lilies open up their red and white cups to the tepid December sun; at night, they will promiscuously make the same gesture to the almost full moon. But it is a poisonous beauty. For this is just one example of the waterlogging that now affects some 80,000 hectares on the edge of Chilika where 450 villages have been partly or totally flooded, and 280,000 people have suffered some loss of livelihood.

Purna Chandra Pradhan dismounts from the cycle he is riding along the rough causeway. He no longer cultivates his land. He is returning from the nearby town of Puri, where he has sold the few vegetables that he can still grow in the waterlogged ground. Today, he travelled 14 kilometres each way and made Rs50 (US$1.50). Ten years ago he says his 2 acres provided enough rice for his family for the year, with even a little left over to sell in the market. Each year, he saw the yield decrease, as the water from the rains failed to run off. It is good soil, too. Even so, this has not been one of the worst seasons. The rain came late, and there was less than usual, so those who are still taking the trouble to sow were able to salvage something of the crop.

4

This extraordinary stretch of water, Lake Chilika – 1,100 square kilometres in the rainy season, shrinking to about 900 square kilometres as it it dries out in winter – is being degraded in a number of ways, and with it, the self-reliant subsistence life of fishing people and cultivators. About 13 tons of silt are deposited each year from the more than a dozen rivers that flow into the lagoon, and from there into the Bay of Bengal. This siltation is caused partly by deforestation upstream and partly by altered patterns of fishing within the lake, notably prawn cultivation instead of traditional fishing methods. This chain of maldevelopment is a bitter affront to the farmers who have to watch rich productive land become barren, submerged by actions of others over which they have no control.

The seasonal ebb and flow of water in Chilika has been interrupted by the construction of *bunds,* or embankments, around the prawn fields. Those who see only the money to be made out of an apparently insatiable foreign appetite for prawns have not looked at the cost to the people who live on the shores of Chilika. For it means the ruin, not only of their livelihood, but also of the social relationships between cultivators and fishing people.

A few kilometres from Vatapada is the village of Kapileswarpur. This is the second biggest village in Orissa, with 10,000 inhabitants. The disaster that has overtaken both farmers and fishing communities has had a powerful effect upon the people. They have resolved not to remain passive spectators of their own ruin, but have formed the *Chilika Bachao Andolan* (CBA), the Save Chilika Movement.

Both farmers and fishermen have nowhere else to go, no other source of income, no refuge from eco-degradation and social conflict. For them, 'development' means eviction. They, peaceable people, living in calm symbiosis with earth and lake, are being forced to resist. They ask nothing more than to be left alone to pursue their lives in security. Instead, they have been caught up in wars not of their making, the prawn wars.

That weekend in December, we sat in the heart of the village, drinking water from tender coconuts, the palms forming a shady green architecture above the village. The farmers spoke, not only about their immediate problems, but also of the implications of the signing by India in the GATT negotiations of the Dunkel draft, which has become the basis of the WTO. 'We shall become dependent upon the multinational companies for our seeds. We shall become labourers in our own land, beggars in our own country.' They recognise the grip in which the Western financial institutions hold India. It is exactly the same grip that holds many poor farmers: having once contracted a loan to answer some urgent need, they discover they are in the hands of moneylenders, who will take everything for debts that can never be repaid – their crops, fields, even tools and homes. To these farmers, the World Bank is only another moneylender, though on a far bigger scale.

The *Janata Dal* leftist government came to power in Orissa in 1990, promising to halt artificial prawn cultivation and stamp out the prawn mafia who had been seizing the fishing grounds of the local people. The most vital issue was a promise given by the previous Congress(I) government to Tata, one of India's major industrial houses, that they could take some of the shallow waters for intensive prawn cultivation for export. The opposition Janata Dal had campaigned against this, and promised that the agreement between the company and government would be scrapped. But when the Janata Dal came to power, it signed its own deal with Tata, permitting the company to build a huge enclosure, 12 metres high, on the edge of the Lake. The Janata Dal was defeated by Congress(I) in March 1995.

The CBA prevented the scheme from going ahead, and took the issue to the High Court. The Court upheld the right of people who depend on the lake to continue their traditional occupation. Tata finally withdrew from the project. However, prawn mafia groups continue to cultivate prawns artificially and to grab land with the connivance of corrupt officials and politicians. 'The Janata Dal have shown that they are even more venal and anti-people than the Congress', say the CBA activists. 'Politicians are there to dominate and to terrorise. The police are just government *goondas*' (hired thugs).

In the wake of ecological and social degradation, many families see their men migrate in order to earn a livelihood which their own land no longer provides. They go to Puri to work as cycle-rickshaw drivers or in the hotels; some become like those workers on strike outside the Puri Hotel after management cut their wages: one man said bitterly 'You can't imagine how it feels, to have been independent, to have grown your own food, and then to have to eat the remains from a hotel kitchen because you are hungry.' Another said 'What does it do to our dignity, to pedal rickshaws like draught animals, we who have enough land to make us free and independent?'

Others must go even further afield. Recruited by *thikedars*, (contractors), for construction gangs, they are taken to Madras, Calcutta, Delhi, even to Assam. All who have left the village have some story of being cheated or brutalised by contractors and middlemen, or of being abandoned in the city, penniless, when the work has been completed.

For a family to be self-sufficient in padi, 2 acres are enough. To

6

buy padi in the market (that is, husks and stalks) costs Rs270 a quintal, while rice grain is Rs600 a quintal. To buy by the kilo costs a minimum of Rs7. About half the people of Kapileswarpur have a cow, but the milk yield is low.

'Fifty-four *crores* of rupees came from the Canadian International Development Agency for the improvement of Chilika', says Darjaydhan Berik. 'Absolutely nothing reached the people. Every *paise* was siphoned off by the bureaucrats and politicians. On 15 August, Independence Day, we had a meeting to declare that we were still struggling for our freedom. Police came from Puri to arrest us, on the grounds that we were creating "anti-national agitation". An armed police force. They proved the very point we were making. We have to struggle. Our lives are here. This is where our children must live and grow.'

In 1992, 16 temporary migrant labourers from this area were killed by terrorists in Punjab, which has been yet another destination for those forced to move, ousted from their lands by 'development'. Another irony in the long history of forced migration. 'For the sake of Rs15 or 20 a day, they went across the whole country to keep an appointment with violent death.'

Here, there is anger, not apathy; resolution, not resignation. The women say 'To feed a family costs Rs60 a day here. About half the people will have an income which can provide a reasonable diet; the other half are lucky if they make more than Rs20 or 30. There are no rich people in this village. Most are cultivators. A few cut coconuts. Some make tools. In some places, there has been discord between cultivators and fishing people. We see our struggle as theirs: we wish to cultivate our fields, just as they wish to continue to catch fish. The government and the prawn mafia will not allow us to do so. Their development ruins our land. Then when we protest, it is we who are the guilty ones, the criminals. Those who are ruining our country on a huge scale are called businessmen, entrepreneurs; they are praised because they earn foreign exchange at our expense.'

The village is deceptively serene. The houses are solid, well-built, with carved, weathered stone pillars, shading verandas with low roofs of padi straw. Some have paintings in rice powder on earthen or cement walls. The overarching coconut palms form a cool green nave for the long low houses that are built to withstand excessive heat and the storms from the Bay of Bengal.

We go into the house of Laltendu Mohanty, who is 22. He has been in the CBA for two years and stays in the Andolan ashram in Puri. His family has 3 acres of land, but it is now all water-logged. He says that for the young there are three choices: to migrate as labour to West Bengal, to become hired goondas in the employ of the mafia, or to stay and fight with the people. For him, there is only one possible response.

Holy *tulsi* plants stand in stone pots at the door of almost every house. There is a score of temples in the village. For the fishing people and the farmers, water and earth are sacred: they have sustained the people eternally, as the people have sustained the elements that give them life. 'The market economy desacralises everything. It turns forests into timber, streams and lakes into water resources, the harvest of the sea into marine products, and human beings into labour.'

Srimati, who stays in the ashram in Puri, says that the alliance between the struggle for social justice and the people's intense religious spirit is what makes the CBA stronger than the brute force of their opponents. 'The fight is of the people for control of the resource-base. In one way, their adversaries are the most powerful people on earth. Yet paradoxically, those forces are also internally weak, because they are empty of all content except greed. This is why they can only oppress and never liberate.'

'Spirituality', says Chittaranjan, one of the guiding founders of the movement, 'means a disciplined, frugal life; not joyless, but taking seriously the value-based alternative that is emerging from the shadow of a decaying, valueless capitalism. How profoundly sad it is that the Indian government should have committed itself to such a system just as it is entering the terminal throes of moral decrepitude. If the government cannot show a better way, the people will do it; and this is what we, in Chilika, are doing.'

Gopinathpur

In 1993, the migratory birds that overwinter on Chilika arrived early. More than 150 species of birds, from Siberia, the Urals, Lake Baikal, from Ladakh and Tibet, come here each year: egrets, kites, eagles, storks, swans, pelicans, herons. They are part of the great chain of life which exists in delicate balance on the shores of this unique lake, one of the wonders of the world, a chain extending from the plankton in the warm, brackish shallow waters to the 70,000 fishing families who have lived for centuries in frugal harmony with Chilika.

This year, even the birds may have sensed something significant in the air. For in November 1993, the Orissa High Court declared that the traditional fishing methods on the lake should not be disturbed, and that the communities whose livelihood depends upon sustainable fishing – that is, which may be renewed each year for an indefinite future – must be preserved.

This was a remarkable judgment, because it vindicated what the people here had been saying for the past decade, ever since the CBA was formed.

Gopinathpur is a fishing village some 20 kilometres from the holy city of Puri, on the very edge of the lake. Gopinathpur offers a test case of how thoroughly the High Court judgment will be implemented, particularly given the presence of the prawn mafia, with its chain of corruption that includes politicians, bureaucrats, police, business and organised crime. Their network has nothing to do with fish: it is designed to catch the money made out of the taste for prawns in the restaurants of Tokyo, Frankfurt and London. The innocent prawn has probably done more to damage traditional communities worldwide than any other creature, apart, perhaps, from ranched cattle. For here we have the supreme example of a luxury item whose consumers are protected from any awareness of the conditions in which their purchases are produced; they have no idea of the ravages these cause in the lives of others.

This is one of the starkest conflicts confronting the government of India in its development and economic policy. With one breath, they insist that the market economy must be given precedence over everything; export earnings must be maximised to pay back the $90 billion debt. On the other hand, here is a unique tract of water, declared by the Iran Convention in 1972 to be part of the world heritage, which must be protected and conserved. Should the waters of Chilika be mined for their resources and polluted in the process for the sake of the fast money to be made? Or should the traditional inhabitants be permitted to continue undisturbed in their relationship with the water, which they themselves describe as that between a mother and son?

Gopinathpur has a sandy village street, less than 20 metres from the lakeside. The houses are characteristic of Orissa, with pillars and wide verandas on raised platforms, some of which require two or three steps; deep and low rice-stalk thatch, wooden doors, some of the older ones elaborately carved; clothes drying on a bamboo pole; cows tethered to some of the stone pillars. Between the houses, narrow pathways lead to the water; stretches of placid sparkling silver, dotted with green islands linked by long red earthen bunds, and above a deep, wide sky.

The villagers here belong to a fishing co-operative formed long ago, 'in our grandfathers' time', as they say to designate anything of great antiquity. This has remained a collective village enterprise. The members of the co-operative, the Machajibi Mahasangha Gopinathpur, have been totally committed to the struggle to preserve the lake for traditional fishing. They, too, cultivate prawns, but without the use of artificial feed or pesticides. They earn around Rs50 a day, which, although far from making them rich, provides them with a secure sufficiency. They have no other source of income.

Two days after the High Court decision, the fishing grounds of the people of Gopinathpur were attacked by a bomb; a riposte from the prawn mafia. The police came but instead of investigating the incident, they immediately arrested two of the villagers, a man in his fifties and a younger man of 23. They were taken to the police lock-up in Brahmagiri town, about 10 kilometres away.

The following day, we visited Gopinathpur. The people are tense and uneasy. With the defeat of the Tata prawn project, they felt the struggle might be over; and the High Court decision seemed to confirm this. But powerful interests are not constrained by mere High Court judgments.

Beyond the fishing villages is a belt of other villages inhabited by small farmers and cultivators. Until now, both communities had coexisted harmoniously. But the extensive waterlogging of their land has created ill feeling; and many of the frustrated cultivators also want access to what they see as the bounty of Chilika Lake. Some of them are being used by the mafia and prawn cultivators to intimidate the fishing families. This is the one of the social consequences of eco-degradation: quarrels over access to diminishing resources.

'Development', says Satya Pir Behera, president of the fishing co-operative. 'What does it mean? Lalchi.' A word hard to translate: it means unlimited wants, greed, excessive desire, something that destroys order, that unsettles people and disturbs ways of life.

The fishing people sit beneath the sheltering trees, palms, mango, guava and papaya, to discuss the incident. They well understand the nature of the present struggle. 'All we are asking for is livelihood. The prawn owners want money. These are different things.'

The village itself has remained virtually unchanged, little touched by transnational-company consumer goods. There is no shop selling Colgate toothpaste or Lux soap. The people do not use plastic; only nylon has replaced the fibres with which they used to make fishing-nets. The *chaupari* still stands, the traditional village meeting place, where the panchayat formerly settled any disputes that occurred within the village. 'We had no need of police', they say. 'There was no crime, no offence that could not be dealt with in the village itself.' Today, some unemployed youths are playing cards inside the chaupari.

10

On the sandy village thoroughfare, through which nothing more than a bullock-cart passes, some fish are drying in the sun. A finely wrought bamboo cage, used for catching fish in shallow water, is being used to protect a batch of tiny chickens. On the walls and on the earth in front of some of the houses are finger paintings in chalk or rice-paste: a lotus flower, some sheaves of padi, with the footsteps of Laxmi, goddess of wealth, between the flowers. This week is the festival of Laxmi, and by drawing her footprints in the earth, they indicate the path she should follow to their home; although, they say self-deprecatingly, when did wealth ever visit poor fishing people? In the village, there is a large number of temples and shrines, many of them improvised: a large stone is invested with great power, becomes a goddess, smeared with crimson powder, with an offering of red hibiscus flowers and some pieces of coconut. The gnarled branch of a pipal tree is garlanded with marigolds; around the base of a mango tree, a rough platform has been built, and some turmeric paste and tulsi leaves put out as offerings. The struggle of the fishing people is animated by a powerful sense of their stewardship of a sacred heritage; and this informs their fight for social justice.

There are about 2,000 people in Gopinathpur. On the landward side, it is bordered by a cashew-nut plantation. A few people from the village are employed there for a daily wage of Rs15 or 16 a day (50 cents).

As we walk through the street, we meet Gopal Chandra Saringi, the teacher in the school. He has been here for 27 years. They now have 370 children in the school and four teachers. 'We have seven classes and four rooms. The government provides no facilities. Most children leave after the seventh standard, at the age of 12 or 13. No one wants to work with the people. Our intellectuals want to become *sadhus* or engineers.'

We go out to the cool waterside. The light is dazzling. Egrets and herons white as marble, statues mirrored in the still water. Over the earthen bunds that separate the prawn-fields, plankton darkens the water above which skim blue and orange dragonflies. The bunds connect natural islands where cattle browse; stunted castor-oil plants and, everywhere, *chakunda*, which is dried for its fuel, leaves used to heal cuts. On the margins of the waterline, receding now in the dry season, tiny crystals of salt are kindled into silver sparks by the sun.

We walk about 2 kilometres along the bunds, out towards the site where Tata had built a long 12-metre-high rampart in preparation for the aborted prawn development. The structure is being used by the unofficial cultivators of artificial prawns.

The remains of yesterday's bomb – more to intimidate than to injure – are still visible, some charred paper, some gunpowder. This area, which belongs to the Gopinathpur fishing co-operative, has been repeatedly invaded; nets have been cut and stolen, staves driven into the lakebed to keep the nets in place have been uprooted and burnt.

In response to this attack, and the arrest of the two innocent men in the village, the women of Gopinathpur decide to go to Puri, to the Collector's office, and sit there on a *dharna*, until justice is done. In fact, the Collector has just been suspended. The festival at the Jagannath Temple a few days earlier had attracted about 700,000 people. Because the numbers far exceeded expectations, the police had locked the temple doors, and panic followed. The police *lathi*-charged the pilgrims, and three people died. Scores were injured.

The village women sat in the shadow of the yellow-pillared colonial structure through the cold December night. Next morning, the Superintendent of Police came and promised that police would guard their fishing grounds if they would disperse and go home. The women discussed the offer, and decided that it was merely a ploy to get rid of their embarrassing presence. They remained another night. Next day, the Superintendent told them he would appoint a deputy additional *tehsildar* (local official) with the power of magistrate. He would take immediate action if the peaceable work of the fishermen were to be interfered with in any way. One police sub-inspector and one constable would remain on the spot 24 hours a day. The men falsely arrested would be released forthwith.

The women agreed to go home. But, they insist that the questions raised by the CBA remain. Chilika belongs to whom? What, exactly, is the policy of the State in relation to the natural resources of the region?

This, says Chittaranjan, is the time to test the sincerity of the government, to see whether the law of the market is in fact now superior to the laws of India; or whether the rule of the goondas and the mafia is in fact weaker than the rights of the people to protect and conserve what has been in their safekeeping for generations. This conflict of interests will have significance for all people's struggles for resources in the whole of India.

A Day on Chilika

At Satapada, on the south of the lake, there is a ferry-boat to the island of Janikuda, about an hour's journey towards the centre of

Chilika. In the sheltered shallow water at Satapada, an old man, Dukhishyama Jali, is fishing. He uses bamboo fish-traps, cages made by his grandson, to catch crabs and other fish in shallow muddy water. Dukhishyama Jali has grey hair, silver stubble on his face, but vivid dark eyes that dart faster than the seabirds over the water. He says that formerly the fishermen used to take opium while standing for so many hours in the cold water, the kala kanhu, as they called it, the black god that comforted and relieved the pain of standing so long. Jagannath and Krishna are black; they are gods. The sky at night is black, the depths of the sea are black; they are gods. So it is with the kala kanhu.

Dukhishyama Jali says he has no time for cultivating prawns. I know when the shrimps will come, I know when to expect them; they flow with the water, which changes with the wind. He says, 'Life flows like water; sometimes the flow is easy, sometimes it is blocked, but it always flows, like time. Now', he says, 'I am not earning, I am just playing.' His wife is dead, his eyesight is failing. He says, 'My children feed me, nothing else, but what more do I want?'

His small hut is on the foreshore, surrounded by a screen of *jui* trees. He is without fear. 'I stand in the water each day and one day I'll stop. If I have been good in this life, I'll be born again into human society; if not, I'll be born in the jungle.' He says there are 63,000 gods and goddesses. God is everywhere; in the head, the eyes; the beard is a god. Dukhishyama Jali, an old man merging with the sea, with his strong sense of the fluidity, the volatility of things, the profound feeling of a human being whose identity is his place in the landscape which bore him, as it bears the fish and the rocks and the trees; a human life growing like the flowers and reeds, where immortality is visible in the shifting reconstitution of the elements into different forms of life and non-life.

In the nearby bay, some traditional fishermen are preparing to go out deep into the lake. They expect to stay away many days. The men are making their strange preparations in the shallow open boat: a stove, water, vegetables, rice, kerosene. One man is grinding *masala* with a pestle; another is stuffing ganja into his pipe for the same reason that the old man took opium: fishing people endure long monotonous days, extremes of cold and wet. Some fortification against that loneliness under the night sky and the mobile waters is common to all fishing communities, although for most, now, it is alcohol. This is functional; it is not drug abuse.

As the men prepare the boat, their occupations appear oddly domestic, vulnerable, intimate, in full view of the shore. They have a serene sense of the necessity of what they are doing, of what people have always done on these shores. The men are away a long time. The women are always true to us, for we are gods', says one of the fishermen, not boastfully but as explanation. On the front of the boat is a flag, representing Mother Kalijai, a legendary woman married to the son of a king of one of the islands. Wanting to see his daughter-in-law, the king sent for her; on her way to her new family, a storm blew up and she was drowned. She became a goddess, and in spite of her own fate, a protectress of the lives of fishing people.

Satapada is a village whose sand-filled street is one kilometre long, shaded by palms and pulang trees from the fruits of which soap is made. Satapada has a new tourist bungalow (unoccupied), a long jetty into the shallow water, a dozen or so small shops, mainly wooden booths with metal roofs, which sell vegetables, *paan*, foodstuffs, medicines, tea and cooked food. There are 150 families in the village. It is not the poorest, although there are many poor people here. Some own country-boats, the small traditional craft propelled in the water by means of a bamboo pole. The poorest people fish simply by wading into the water, and spreading their nets around bamboo staves. In this, the lean season, they catch only a few kilos a day. They pool the catch, and sell it to middlemen from Bulangao.

Kartik Jali lives in a traditional house away from the main street, within a small compound surrounded by cactus and jui. He works only part-time as a fisherman. He also has a small 'shop', selling rice, dal, *bidis*, sugar, flour and paan. He has taken a loan of Rs8,000 for nets, bamboos and rope from the Fishermen's Cooperative; each net costs Rs350. He says the only thing the men take to resist the cold and discomfort of standing in the water for long hours is bidis. He does not use ganja or liquor. The nylon nets also catch small fish, which means that the future stock of the lake is being increasingly jeopardised. Some fish – jagala, for instance – have almost disappeared from the lake. Kartik Jali is deaf; with his fringe of silver beard, he looks older than his 40 years. He has six daughters. He owns no boat and is philosophical about the dangers of standing in water – leeches, the cold, the poisonous suri or water-snake.

The village street is full of activity. Those who have a little land – in most cases, less than one acre – are threshing padi. The men take a sheaf of padi and beat it vigorously against an inclined red sand-stone slab. As they beat, the ripe grains fall and accumulate in a pyramid at the base of the slab. When all the grains have become detached, the stalks are stacked, ready to renew the roofs of the houses or for sale to others. Outside the houses, pulang berries;

some, like unripe plums freshly harvested from the glossy green trees, others withered and creased. The whole length of the street, padi is laid out on bamboo mats. In Orissa, they boil the rice first, with the husks, and then dry it in the sun. Some ber fruits, golden-brown, sour and rich in vitamin C, lie on a strip of polythene on the verandas: a sense of a vast resourcefulness in people who have nothing.

The village is poor but not squalid. Jhuti-chitra, finger painting, decorates the walls of many houses: bundles of padi or an earth-red frieze around the wall; here and there, a more ambitious design, a lotus flower or peacock, sometimes in colour, or a sun-flower, a cockerel, a tree. Everywhere, red or green tulsi in little stone urns. The main temple is a concrete structure, painted blue, with yellow dragons at the door; offerings of marigolds, blood-red canna lilies and bananas; constructed when the village was more prosperous, and a monument to the declining economic status of the fishing community. There is a bhagavad, a village meeting place, where people also study. There is no government health-post in the village; one man has turned his house – a substantial arcaded building with carved arches – into a clinic for Ayurvedic and homoeopathic medicine.

Dukhishyam Dalai stands on the veranda of his house, while his wife looks cautiously through the grille of the small window. The veranda is about 2 feet off the round, three earthen steps up from street level. He has a country-boat; that is, two halves of weathered wood, hollowed out and clamped together when he goes out fishing. It is propelled by a bamboo pole. He took a private loan to buy the boat. In the high season he takes 10–20 kilograms of fish a day. Today he took only 200 grams, for which he got Rs5. With six children, a loan is necessary in the thin season: Rs5,000, interest 5 per cent a month, that is Rs250. He knows that if he does not pay, the moneylender will take his boat, his nets and, finally, his house. His wife appears, curiosity overcoming her shyness. She says it takes Rs50 a day to feed the family. Dukhishyam says that they pay back the loan when the fish are plentiful, from March to June when, on some days, he can earn up to Rs200. The loan is partly repaid in kind: the moneylenders are also fish-businessmen, and they accept repayment in fish at a very low price, thereby making even bigger profits in the summer season.

Sachinanda Dalai has seven children. She says they eat only twice a day. Her house is smaller, of red earth, unpainted; it stands out against the majority which are colour-washed, green, blue, yellow. Sachinanda pays rent for her house. Her own was seized by moneylenders when she found it impossible to repay a loan of Rs5,000. She says she still owes one *lakh* rupees in interest. She will never repay. All her family's assets have been taken. From nothing, she says, nothing can be taken. Next to her house, there are the remains of a dwelling that has been broken: the bare lattice of a bamboo frame, some crumbled earth. Behind the remaining outer wall a family is living. Whether their house was destroyed as a punishment for unpaid debts, they do not say.

The local fishermen's co-operative also lends money for nets, boats, bamboos. These loans too are repaid in fish on a commission basis – the society takes half the daily catch. Dilip Kumar Shaoo, a young man in yellow-and-green check *lungi*, is the oldest of ten children. He says that people from the village go away as migrant labourers. 'But we are fishing people. This is our life. We have lived beside Chilika for generations. Why should we go?' There is a strong sense of rootedness and belonging, the security of people defined by their social function. If this sense is eroded it will have consequences that cannot be foreseen, while the ruin of livelihood imperils social cohesion. Some young men play cards on a bamboo mat under a makeshift bamboo shelter that protects them against the sun. They say it is not worth going on to the lake in this season, to spend all day for a negligible catch.

Many of the houses are quite extensive: courtyards behind, here and there with a cow or buffalo tethered; a stack of fuel-wood; pots of rice cooking on a *chulha*, which is made of the same earth, hardened by the fires of countless meals.

The people must buy everything in the market, except fish which is always available. No one has enough padi to last the whole year. The village has electricity, but there are frequent and prolonged cuts in the supply. There are several water-pumps which draw fresh water from deep underground; around them grass or moss has grown, a patch of vivid green in the pale, sandy street – not really a street at all but a space between irregularly aligned houses. In the sand is a dishevelled elderly woman in a crumpled red and green saree. She is crying for food. People come to their doors. Some bring her chappatis. She throws them into the sand and continues to cry for food. The children laugh and run away. She chases them and kicks sand into the air.

Bidula Jali, a dignified mature woman, tells of the hardship of her life. She needs at least Rs50 a day for food for her five children. In this season, a good day's income would be Rs40. They never have fruit or milk, but eat rice, dal, some vegetable like potato or aubergine. Her husband has taken a loan of Rs7,000, for a boat and nets. Repayment is at the rate of 5 per cent interest per month. When the season is right, March to July, they pay back; if not, the loan accumulates, and is held over to the next year. What she does not admit is that loans are actually used by many people, not for work, but in order to buy food, the necessities of life. In the small enclosure she has a green coconut palm, which provides nourishment for the children, with three or four harvests a year. Some women dig roots – pithula – to eat which are like sticky potato when cut.

There are four castes among the fishing people. Some of the lower-caste women catch fish – small prawns and shrimps – with their bare hands in the shallow waters; but this is slow, painful work and not very profitable. Most women do not actually fish, but they still perform most of the labour: not only caring for the children, but looking after domestic fowls, goats and cattle. They fetch fodder, fuel and water. Their labour may be less physically arduous than that of the men, but it is more relentless. Women never sit and play cards, says Bidula Jali. She is happy that few of the men in the Chilika villages drink. The culture of the sea-fishing villages is quite different.

Surath Beheri is a worker with the CBA. His father is a fisherman. Surath has nine sisters, and is the only son. His family has no other resource but the sea. He tells how, in November 1993, five children were found begging near his home. They had come from Panda Pokhari village. Their parents had died of hunger, first the mother and then the father, within two days of each other.

The ferry-boat to Janikuda comes. People have been to the small shops to buy basic provisions: at the vegetable stall, potatoes are Rs5 a kilo, cauliflower Rs8, and onions Rs14. The people complain of the scandalous price of onions, which are a basic necessity.

On the ferry, people discuss the merits of prawn cultivation. You get 6 tons of prawns per hectare if you grow them without artificial feed or chemicals. If you do it artificially, you can get 10 tons. But look what happens: you feed them himpid, a mixture of tapioca, prawn heads, shrimp powder, phosphates and calcium. This leaves a permanent residue in the water that damages other creatures. But with natural prawns, you don't pollute the water, you don't poison the other fish.

The mafia are still cultivating: pesticides contaminate the fresh water, the sulphur content has risen. The mafia capture land when the water is low in the dry season, enclose it and then start cultivation in the shallow waters when the rain comes.

It is a warm day in November; a milky sky, green-grey water. Reeds and grasses appear above the water-line, so it looks like a flooded meadow. The fishing people talk of the eternal discrepancy between what they earn and the profits made by middlemen in the market. 'We will get Rs13 or 15 a kilo for *marada,* which is sold in the market at Rs30; Rs10 or 20 for *panu,* according to the season.' The white prawn is the most valuable fish. It is unique to Chilika; the middlemen make Rs15 a piece for the white prawns. The fish available vary, according to the delicately changing salt content of the lake. In April–May, the water becomes saltier, as the area shrinks; and then it becomes fresher with the onset of the rain.

We land on Janikuda Island, at the village of Navpada. Here, the government has broken some of the artificial prawn cultivations. The case is still under dispute in the courts. The people are sceptical, and feel this might just be government electioneering. They doubt whether it is serious about ousting people who have provided them with so much money. There are 80 villages on this island of which 70 per cent are non-fishing communities. They are cultivators, but as their land is increasingly waterlogged, most of them are poor. The young people leave the island, travelling mainly as construction labourers. Many of the impoverished cultivators are recruited by businessmen for prawn fishing. They then become labourers, encroaching upon the rights of traditional fishing families.

'The government speaks with two voices. Give the waters to the fishermen; then they tell their friends they can have contracts for prawn cultivation.'

Rice and fish were formerly both abundant, and people could buy vegetables from outside. Now, the rice harvest is diminished and traditional fish varieties are less plentiful. The fishing-people here say they can make Rs35–50 a day, not enough to eat adequately. They catch panu, *konga,* marada, *bagada, genda, sahb;* and then take their catch the two-and-a-half hour journey to the town of Bulangao on the mainland. We can't depend on our children because they are unemployed. The government is silent. There is no other labour.

'We give our children education', says Dushasan Mohanty, 'yet after graduation, no one wants to do fishing. Things are bad enough without outsiders. There were no quarrels between fishermen and cultivators until the prawn cultivators came in.' On the ferry from Navpada, we meet the son of the teacher and the son of the family planning doctor. Both are studying; both equally adamant they would never live on the island.

We travelled back to the mainland on a motorised boat owned by a prawn dealer, a middleman, who had bought a consignment of natural prawns from Navpada, which he will sell in Bulangao. He has bought 250 kilos at Rs320 a kilo ($10), and says he will sell at Rs335, a profit of Rs15 a kilo (50 cents).

In the shallow part of the lake, a buffalo-cart crosses from one island to another; half the wheel is submerged, the flanks of the buffaloes under water, the load of padi straw half-drowned. The prawn traps have to be negotiated carefully by the boats. The natural traps are very simple. The prawns simply swim into them, and 'not being very clever', as the boat owner tells us, cannot find their way out again.

There are many boats on the lake, some with outboard motors. On the traditional boats, three men, sometimes only adolescents, dark silhouettes against the pale green water and curdled clouds. Late in the afternoon, we reach the busy port. On the waterfront there are fish collection points, buyers, ice-merchants and freezing centres. Outboard-motor vessels fill the small artificial harbour, polluted by oil and noisy with seabirds and the sound of fish catches being sold to the wholesalers and distributors. Many of the middlemen themselves give loans to farmers; and as interest on the loan simply appropriate the whole crop, sometimes even the prawn-field itself.

Our boatman takes his 250 kilos to the merchant's shed – a strange place, with red and green Divali (the festival of light, the most significant festival in the Hindu year) decorations hanging from the ceiling, and ice, dead fish and silver fish-scales on the floor. He actually sold them at Rs360 a kilo – a profit of Rs40 (US\$1.30) a kilo. This trip alone will have earned him a profit of Rs10,000 (about \$320). The prawns will go to Calcutta, packed between layers of crushed ice. There, they will sell for Rs450. If subsequently exported, they will finish up at some restaurant table abroad for Rs900 a kilo.

The Roots of Resistance

Chittaranjan Sarangi lives in a small house not far from the Jagannath Temple in Puri, which has become the ashram of members of the CBA and of some of the young people they are training in Gandhian non-violent struggle. Chittaranjan is from Puri; his father and mother have a small house with a piece of land where they grow vegetables which they give freely to those who live in the ashram.

When he speaks of the Chilika struggle, it is clear that it is a very distinctive and successful crusade against lopsided 'development'. The struggle for the conservation of livelihood is informed by a sense of the sacredness of the earth and water which provide the people with nourishment and life.

Dharma – religion – is a harmonious and spontaneous relationship between people, society and nature. Our leaders no longer feel the spiritual strength of the Indian tradition. Sectarian movements are not dharma. The BJP (Bharatiya Janata Party) is not dharma. Unless our education moves towards that, we will not attain that level of spontaneous harmony. Here, in the ashram, we are living an alternative lifestyle also, that is alternative in practice. It implies discipline and self-restraint that are voluntary, not imposed. It is a joy, not a penance, a pleasure in simple living.

The house is modest: stone floors, camp beds, a kitchen where simple food is prepared, study rooms; some shelves of books and documentation on the Chilika movement. Close to the Jagannath Temple, with its hucksters and religious commerce, its tangle of cycles, rickshaws, vendors and holy men, beggars and flowersellers, it is a place of serene calm and quiet; an ironic comment on the noisy devoutness nearby.

I believe that the present people, the present time, the present circumstances are always the best for work. Whoever you are with, now, wherever you are, under whatever conditions, every moment is joyous. There is no point in waiting for a better time to come, a better job, a better person. Wheresoever you are, concentrate on that. Let us not live on memories of the past, or dreams of the future. That is not to say hedonism, but a sober appreciation of what is. Hedonism is not living in the present: the mind goes to the past and future to think how can I enjoy more and grab more, or what did I miss, what have I not got. Living in the present means concentrating all the faculties of mind and spirit on the here and now.

Tribal and fishing people are joyous, happy with the minimum necessary things. They are less encumbered than rich people, and have an appreciation of the nature of our lives, our human existence. Their culture has grown around this, which is why they have a cultural wealth denied the monetarily rich. Death is natural, therefore grief is not excessive. Birth too: women give birth in the forest, sometimes at their work. There is no anxiety, no display; only the celebration of what is natural. The tribal people adjust to circumstances. If a woman's husband dies, she will find another; but not to feed sexual appetite. The modern world teaches them how to be poor; and how to want. Belongingness and presentness are there, in the tribals, the fishing people, field labourers and marginal farmers. Physical labour, interaction with nature under an open sky – this is not romanticism, their lives are hard, but they have a rootedness which those who have fled to the towns do not.

I asked him about those people considered traditionally 'untouchable', outside the caste system, had they not truly been the custodians of the resource-base? Why were they not elevated and revered for their work, rather than excluded?

Chittaranjan answered, *Social arrangements are made and remade by visionaries. But the management of societies is a different matter. The social management group in any culture is not made up of visionaries and seers. So the contrast lies between understanding and implementation: these things are done by different groups. Those who run society, because of their lack of vision and deep faith, are more concerned with immediate things around them. So they will take what they want from the visionaries, and translate it in such a way that they, the controlling group, retain power, have the upper hand. The same sentences can be translated in a different way, to distort truth. Therefore, those who are vulnerable are looked down upon. The visionaries always give the highest respect to the labouring class because they understand that society is sustained by them; their work is its foundation.*

The young are emotional. And if no deep understanding is cultivated, with age the fear of death comes to our mind, and a feeling of insecurity. Therefore, people cling to wealth and power; so even if, when they are young, they are idealistic and emotional, they become power-crazy in later years. They want to survive death, leave something to posterity, something memorable. They seek 'immortality'. They saw the visionaries, their predecessors, as memorable, so they want to be memorable too. They want fame through power or money, so they can linger, as it were, after their death. That degrades the quality of their lives. Those persons have a sense of their own superiority and the inferiority of others. Even if they are responsible social managers, they are used by kings, by governments, hierarchies, business or other vested interests. In the process social laws change and become inhumanistic. Distortions occur, which are the opposite of what the visionaries said, and run counter to their spirit.

Religion binds, dharma liberates. Religion, from Latin 'religio', I bind. Religion and dharma are opposite things. The scriptures of Indian origin do not instruct or give commandments. They say you should understand.

I commented that this has a particular resonance for the West, which has forfeited understanding by virtue of its universalising thrust, its desire to remake the world in its own image. Its power and strength blind and do not reveal. Locked inside its paradigm of universal values, seeing only hostility in Islam or Confucianism, beset by a sense of superiority, Westerners are destroying, not only themselves, but the world.

Chittaranjan maintained that Indian tradition is to analyse and to present. *It offers liberty to behave as you wish. Even if you kill Jagannath, you will survive. In Islam or Christianity, if you kill a priest, you do not survive.*

Originally, some Brahmins respected and loved sudras as equals.

And the sadhus were never given office, as priests and mullahs were, yet they were more respected than kings, because of their dedication, simplicity and wisdom; not for their authority. Therefore, that openness of thought is still there. Christ and Buddha come from the same level of profundity, but Christ says 'Do as I do, because I say so.' Buddha says 'Don't do it because I am saying, or because you like it, do it, if it is within yourself.' If you feel it right then it should be done; then only you do it. You judge.

Hinduism is not a religion, but a collection of thoughts. It will live and grow if its values are understood. Indian thoughts cannot be erased while humanity exists. The survival of nature, too, lives in the values embodied in the Vedas and Upanishads.

Now, the spiritual sector of experience has become detached from society. Dharma, if it exists, is not with the sadhus. It lies with the common mass of the community of the soil, who are searching silently; those who live not in monasteries but under the open sky, earth beneath their feet, no other support, no other security, that is enough. Then relationships will flow in both directions, between earth and humanity. All searchers lived in nature, from Buddha to Socrates.

Ashrams were laboratories, rooted in the soil. In India, you should show by living what you believe. Experiments in social and religious life – there are so many sects and religions in the country. In the Upanishads, the rishi is saying, 'Even the coming generation will find out the truth in their own way, in a different way'. It is liberating for a younger generation to find new principles, or new examples of old truths.

The Upanishads are the best outcome of the human mind; seers turn over the wisdom of the generations and it re-emerges, appears in a new light. Seers will not have authority, but respect through wisdom, a wisdom which they do not claim as their own. No one claims ownership of thought. There are no intellectual property rights. If I understand something new, it is not because I found it out, it is because it is the wisdom of the ages. I rediscovered it, gave it some final touch. The idea of intellectual property rights is anti-natural, anti-human. No seer claims he has found something new. Some sadhus may become self-important, but that is not the same thing. Gandhi says, 'Non-violence and truth are as old as the Himalayas. I have nothing new to give.'

Criticism is a Western idea. Let us, rather, analyse. Analysis makes humble, and helps understand weakness. Criticism only feeds the ego. In India, there have been visionaries every century, but in Christianity, there has been no visionary for 2,000 years. The successors here bow down before their predecessors; any rishi or seer, before he writes or speaks, bows down before those who went before him. They learn from the disciples of their predecessors, they learn humility. Im-

plementation of knowledge is more important than expressing it. Now action has become divorced from contemplation; the sadhus have deviated from the ideas they preach and do not practise. There are few who practise the values; but if some remain, that force will build up in India, and this is our true tradition.

Nature is complex, yet in it there is unity. Society is complex but impenetrable, opaque. Unity in diversity is nature; only politicians cause discord. That same unity and diversity must be present in social arrangements too; then there would be no repeat of what occurred with the mosque at Ayodhya.

The atmosphere of openness to truth remains in India. The question is, how can we open our doors to the breeze that is blowing? Such work must be built upon dedication and courage. That means facing the situation with full self-confidence and steadfastness of mind. If you lose self-confidence, you will look to the future as a source of hope or seek refuge in the past. If you have self-confidence, it must give this result. Do the action and leave it. Non-attachment should be there, not to the work, but to the fruit of the work. Non-attachment to the fruit of the work must be there, or the quality of the work degrades. Fix a target and run to it. No. Quality is maintained through the movement of the work. Discussion is not to achieve, but to concentrate on the reality. Words are not to convince, but to elucidate. If the self-confidence is there that the work is right, the result must be right.

Gandhi said in 1933, 'I shall die before India is free.' He was going to declare himself no longer with the Congress on 2 February of the year when he was murdered. He was going to dissociate himself from Congress, because it was taking the help of a colonial Constitution. Gandhi could see his country delivered to bondage. He could see his successors, the management group, were not visionaries. Gandhi only realised this at the end. In the same way, he had maintained his faith in the British government until Jallianwala.

In 1946, he urged the dissolution of Congress. He wanted them to go back to the villages. He had not concentrated upon building up visionary successors; that subtle process was elided by Gandhi. Nehru had a great ambition to become something. But being and becoming are different things, and indeed incompatible. Nehru wanted to become something personal and make something of the country. He was not crooked, but he was critical and ambitious. He would do anything. Ruthless, too. He ousted Subhash Bose. After 1937, Gandhi realised that Nehru was not a man of his line. Gandhi said to Nehru, 'Come and prove your thoughts before the people.' Gandhi selected Nehru, but did not build him up. That is one of the principal reasons why we see a spoiled India.

23

In the Independence Treaty signed between Nehru and Mountbatten in 1947, there were three conditions which were secret. The first was to permit British companies to remain as they were; 28 companies, including Brooke Bond and Wheelers: this is why to this day the station bookstalls are all Wheelers. In the sector dominated by those 28 companies no one should be allowed to compete. Second, that the hierarchical, bureaucratic structure should remain in place, the administrative status quo be retained, essentially a colonial situation. The IAS, Indian Administrative Service, would be substituted for the ICS, Indian Civil Service, nothing changed but one letter. Third, the Government of India Acts passed in 1892, 1919 and 1935 would be incorporated, unchanged, in the Constitution of India. Therefore, all Acts remain.

What we have to do is not merely cry out against injustice, but build up our boys and girls; awareness, perhaps, rather than consciousness. Build up the next generation, those who can retrieve a sense of vision with the necessity for management. 'Act from the cosmic end.' That means like Christ, like Buddha, who cannot be challenged by sadhus. They are beyond cause and effect, judgement, reason, intellect.

This is why many of our national leaders are fighting for an alternative. Sunderlal Bahaguna, Medha Patkar; they are good persons, but their effect is slight. I said to B.D. Sharma 'You are a great intellectual, but you do not know how to implement what you know.' As individuals, alone, they will get awards, they will be applauded; and thereby neutralised. Deep struggles must have the mass of people there; if there is not unity between the intellectuals and the mass of the people it will not be an effective struggle.

I don't go to meetings. I am trapped by the depth of the struggle we are waging here in Chilika. When I see people running around the country for meetings and seminars, I say to them 'How come you have time for meetings?'

In India, the sadhus were independent individuals; not now. The country is full of holy men. Lakhs of them. How have they advanced the cause of the poor of India? That separation is there. You cannot divide the struggle for social justice from the spiritual struggle. That is impossible.

2. A Picture of Puri

One of the holiest cities in India and the site of the celebrated Jagannath Temple, Puri is not just one city, but a series of overlapping communities. The holy city is highly visible, in the ubiquitous shrines and temples, some grand and ornate, others homely, around an imposing tree or a powerful rock, the spontaneous expression of the intense spirituality of the people of Orissa. In the street where I stayed, the canopy of a baobab tree sheltered a shrine garlanded with marigolds and rose petals, a painted platform on which reclined sadhus and holy men. They seemed unperturbed by the Western disco music from the Mickey Mouse restaurant next door.

For the people of Orissa, Jagannath is an extraordinarily powerful and familiar presence. The fishing and farming people speak to him as though to a familiar member of the household; he is revered, but also chided, petitioned, consulted; even cursed and abused at times. He is a living force in the lives of the people, one of the most appealing aspects of what being Hindu means, and a far cry from the stark reductive asperities of the BJP. It is no accident that in Orissa the BJP has made little headway: the sacralising of the elements that provide the people with their livelihood, as well as the tutelary presence of Jagannath, make for a subtle and rooted sense of dharma.

There is also, of course, the commerce that thrives in the shadow of the holy places: makers of garlands, sellers of *agarbatti,* the coin-changers who provide the small change for people to make offerings at each temple; the rows of beggars on the roads around the Jagannath Temple, exhibiting their damaged limbs and stumps; bony old men lying in ghost-grey thornbushes to show their imperviousness to suffering. The grand esplanade along which the statue of Jagannath is drawn each July is full of booths and stalls, astrologers, seers, vendors of visions. The entrance to the temple is thronged with sellers of prasad, sweets, and offerings for those visiting the temple, as well as the food vendors who answer the bodily hunger of the pilgrims. There are even entrepreneurs ready to escort foreigners on to rented rooftops so that they may look down into the temple, which non-Hindus may not enter. Every day, I passed a man who wheeled his wife in a roughly made wooden hand-cart to beg in the tourist areas around the cheap hotels. Her face and limbs damaged by leprosy, she holds out her poor arms in entreaty. The husband said the backpack Western tourists are more generous than Indian pilgrims. 'We frighten them.' He laughed, a cheerful rusty chuckle.

A culture of mendicancy grows in the shadow of both the holy city and the tourist city; it thrives on the piety of the devout and the guilt of the rich and healthy.

The seaside town of Puri stretches along the splendid beach of the Bay of Bengal, the green furls of its tides an endlessly opening leaf. The holiday-makers from Calcutta are followed in their strolls across the sand by cohorts of balloon- and toy-vendors, peanut-sellers, tea-kettle boys, sellers of shells, handicrafts, wood-carvings, paintings. Many of them are children, as indeed are many of the waiters and kitchen workers in the small hotels: 12-year-olds working for Rs50 (US$ 1.50) a month and their food, who send everything they earn to their family.

There are some 2,000 cycle-rickshaw drivers in Puri, many of them migrants from the hinterland whose land has been degraded. It is not surprising that many of them remain outside the Western hotels, offering the young foreigners those things they have learned are indispensable to Westerners' well-being: sex, drugs and shopping.

On the seashore, the fishing village remains: huts of sun-bleached palm-leaves, thatch and bamboo, densely built, so that they form a slum; rivulets of dirty grey water ripple the sand and are swallowed up in the ocean. The traditional boats are on the sand: two halves of bone-white wood tied together. These fish inshore with decreasing effectiveness in competition with the outboard motors, which can go far out into the Bay of Bengal. In mid-afternoon, the fishermen come in with their catch. A moment of great animation: women headloaders with their baskets come to buy, as the fish are sorted and graded according to size and price. There are always some surprises as the nets are spilled on to the dun-coloured sand – strange, shark-like creatures with razor-teeth; others with mother-of-pearl skin and a cavernous grinning mouth, long pale sea-worms, are discarded, and the children use them as playthings. Most of the fish is sold, sardines, dogfish, flatfish, and fish that spangle the polluted sand with their scales. Some women wait, silent, eyes on the horizon; the look of women who distrust the sea because they know that sometimes boats do not return.

What are the Western tourists who come to Orissa looking for? I spent some time in the Z Hotel, popular with Westerners, strongly – and deservedly – recommended by the *Lonely Planet Guide.** It is a slightly faded building, formerly the residence of a minor maharaja, arcaded and planted with gardens of hibiscus and calendula, with a small plantation of pines behind, which is open to the seashore; a place well suited to receiving minor maharajas from the West, with their fantasies of India.

These are discerning travellers rather than tourists, many of them in India for a fairly lengthy sojourn – six months or a year. They are driven by strange discontents to seek out something in India which they have not found at home; some scarcely seem to know what has impelled them here. A few have self-consciously abandoned Western materialism; others are merely taking a vacation from it. Some are driven by a deep revulsion against Western society, and are in flight, seeking a refuge from its market-driven compulsions. In a curious way, they, too, are asylum-seekers, although it is inconceivable to the West that anyone should want to leave it, when it sees its greatest problem as keeping out those migrants and 'economic refugees' clamouring to gain admission to its version of Elysium.

One woman who was a sales executive for an American computer company has abandoned her job in mid-career to spend some time in India. Her children are grown up, and they support their mother's right to lead her own life. She is a radical who has been marginalised by the way her own society has developed. This is true of many of the people staying here. Coming to India is both an escape and a gesture to their country of origin: a statement that they know that the Western way of life and the direction of its development are wrong, but that there is nothing to be done about it, except to run away. People in flight: this is what the decay of political, social and economic alternatives has led to in the West – personal escape, an individual way out of a society which you find intolerable. It is a sort of privatising of dissent: you cannot change the condition of society, but you can – at least temporarily – change your own. Many who came to India because they abhor the crude over-consumption, complacency and universalising pretensions of the West are horrified when they discover that India, too, is now embarked on that same developmental project.

People follow some strange pathways. One young woman is cycling round the world on her own. She had been badly injured in a

---

* India – a travel survival kit, Lonely Planet Publications, Hawthorn, Victoria, Australia, June 1990.

cycling accident in Britain. With the money she received in compensation for her injuries, she is cycling from Holland to Australia. She tried to get sponsorship but without success. Instead, she plans to write a book, and to give the proceeds to a charity dedicated to the rehabilitation of the victims of head injuries. So far, she has been on the road for seven months; the whole journey is to take two years. She travels alone, and has had a particularly tough time coming through Pakistan and India. It seems an extraordinarily complicated route for a charitable impulse to help others, that it should require to be directed through such an elaborate – and dangerous – adventure. The young woman, a nurse by profession, said she wanted to push herself to the limits of physical endurance, and she covers on average 100 kilometres a day.

A judge from Germany is spending a sabbatical year in India, visiting Buddhist, Jain and Hindu temples. He, too, is critical of the quasi-religious cults that have arisen in the West around consumption patterns. But his preoccupation with the life of the spirit had preserved him from any knowledge of even the existence of the BJP or the *RSS*, the growth of Hindu fundamentalism; a quest for purity in a social vacuum. Another woman, from the United States, announced that she had come to India to find herself, to discover who she really was. There are many such; but they are for the most part doomed to learn that identities disaggregated by consumerism cannot be reconstructed by an exotic form of tourism, which turns out to be merely another aspect of the same problem.

A number of young Britishers are visiting India in order to see the place where their parents or grandparents were born; grandchildren of the Raj, as it were, who have some emotional tug towards the country, although they have never seen it; some strange nostalgias, the verification of surrogate memories. A bank official has come to see his father's old school in Nainital, a middle-aged woman wants to trace her *ayah*, of whom she knows nothing more than that she was called Vijamma and lived in Bangalore. It is difficult not to wonder what she will say to her, and in what language, when and if they meet.

A young Swede has spent three months in Orissa, working on an MA thesis on the economy of a forest village. He has a word processor, a translator, a grant from the Swedish government development agency, and a questionnaire which he has issued to a representative sample of the people in the village. The sketchiness of his knowledge of India was surprising; less so was the conclusion of his thesis, namely that the poverty of the village is caused by population growth. He knew nothing of the Forest Laws introduced by the British, which had criminalised the original inhabitants of the forests, and was innocent of any awareness of the continuity in the forest policy between the time of the British and the government of free India. Doubtless, more evidence of the need for population control is what the agency wants to hear, and they will duly hear it. He will almost certainly then qualify for a well-rewarded post in some highly professional non-government organisation (NGO).

The *Lonely Planet Guide*, although well researched and useful, has, unfortunately, now signalled an alternative beaten track to visitors to India, one which minimises risks and discomfort to travellers who are less than intrepid; and many of the tales they exchange have a wearisome familiarity; how they survived epic train journeys of 48 hours, how their money-belt was slit in the night as they slept in the first class compartment and all their money taken, how they got the better of some cheating shop-keeper in Madras, a tout in Calcutta or some rip-off merchant in Benares; beneath it all, an unmistakable tinge of racism.

Some come for the drugs, remaining high for two days on the effects of a bhang lassi, while there are numberless vendors of *charas* and ganja, clusters of shadowy young men around the hotels. A few young Westerners who have become addicts lie sprawled on the beach, dirty and neglected, with matted hair and torn clothes; they have perhaps discovered the meaning of poverty in India, but scarcely in a way that will help either themselves or those millions of people in India for whom it was not an elective experience.

Meanwhile, the young men of Puri gather around the Western women on the beach; fascinated by the undress, the display of flesh; disturbed, too, by the perhaps too-studied nonchalance of the women. I had a heated discussion with a young German woman who said she was being harassed. She claimed it was her right to dress – or undress – as she chose on the beach, 'because it is my holiday and I have paid for it'. When I suggested that she had not paid for the right to disturb the cultural values and mores of the society in which she was a guest, she became very angry. The cultural consequences of her brief stay, the damaging influence of her presence on the lives of those in whom she had no interest, were, she maintained, no concern of hers.

On Saturday night, there is a 'beach party' at one of the res-taurants. It is also a festival night for Hindus. The temple music is easily drowned out by the throb of Western music, the ampli-fied voices of Sting, Madonna, Rod Stewart, as are the sound of the waves, the cry of the night-birds and the breath of the wind in the pines. At least next day, the tourists will depart, checking that they have all their purchases, their souvenirs and tribal paint-ings, the brass pots and handicrafts that will soon adorn their homes in Hamburg, London and New York. Silence will return; although whether the sea ever really effaces the prints they have made in the sand is much more doubtful.

Konark

About 33 kilometres down the coast from Puri is Konark, site of the splendid Sun Temple built in the thirteenth century in the form of a chariot for Surya, the Sun. The whole is drawn by seven gigantic horses, and the base of the temple consists of 24 wheels; the structure is covered with friezes, carvings, bas-reliefs and sculptures, many of them erotic. Indeed, the whole temple is alive with the carved dancing figures. God and myth, sex and religion, art and popular culture, all combine in an exuberant celebration of life. The weathered ironstone and sandstone contrast with the smooth blackstone of the rising, setting and noonday sun. The temple was probably never completed, and fell into ruin. Only when some of the sand and debris that had accumulated around the base were removed in the early years of this century was the true magnificence of the temple appreciated. Indeed, the most conspicuous plaque on the building commemorates, not the intricate skilled labours of local artisans, but the work of the Lieutenant-Governor of Bengal in 1903, which, with characteristic imperial condescension refers to 'this superb specimen of old Indian Architecture; to preserve which, the interior was filled in by order of the Honourable J.A. Bourdillon, A.D. 1903'.

Chittaranjan tells how 1,200 artists worked for sixteen years on the temple, without ever going home. *The chief artist had a son, whom he had never seen, because he was born after the father had departed to build the temple. After almost 16 years, they were in a hurry to finish. Shortly before completion, the artist's son came to the site, to assist the father he had never met. All that remained to be done was to complete the central tower. But each time they had almost finished the structure, it collapsed inwards. Four times this happened. The king for whom the temple was being built became very angry and said to them, 'If it is not completed by tomorrow, you will all be killed, all who have worked on the temple.'*

The artisans were desperate. The son of the chief artist said, 'If you follow my plan, it will be completed by morning.' By this time, they were ready to try anything. He guided them, and gave instructions, which they followed. Before the morning the tower had been finished and it did not collapse.

By this time, all 1,200 artists were very frightened. They said, 'If the

*king knows that the boy did what we could not do, he will punish us.
We will have to take credit for it. We have toiled for 16 years. Therefore
we must undermine the boy.' They held a meeting. Should the boy or the
community survive? The father said 'How can we kill him?' 'If he is not
killed, the king will know. Do you want your son to survive the twelve
hundred artists you have worked with for so many years?' The father
and son discussed the dilemma. He finally consented to let his son
perish. The boy jumped from the completed tower into the river and
died. It was more important for them that the community should survive, rather than the individual, however precious, however special. For
the community everything must be sacrificed, the individual, the family,
all other units are subordinate to it. The king duly came, and was
pleased. He distributed gifts to the 1,200 artists.*

*The story is a parable of the difference between Western and Indian
culture. For Westerners, the story is shocking. In the West, the boy
would have been the hero. He would have had to be saved, even if the
experienced artists and workers had all perished. India traditionally
subordinated the individual to the greater good.*

The temple was once on the shore, but since the time of construction, the sea has receded, and is now about 3 kilometres away.
On the seashore is a fishing village, a poor place, where most of the
people are deeply indebted. Chandrabhaga, an elderly man, says
that the earnings of fishing people here are between Rs20 and 30 a
day, averaged over the year. Some days in this, the best season, they
may get Rs500 or 600, but in the monsoon they cannot go out to
sea because of storms over the bay. Because they catch only seven
or eight months of the year, they must go to moneylenders in the
lean season. They have only traditional boats, and they travel out 6
or 7 kilometres into the sea. The people eat rice, some dal, no
vegetables. They drink because their lives are hard. V. Kelamiya has
six daughters. He says the women sell fish, they do not go out in
the boats. When fishing people have money, they spend it. They do
not save. He says 'We are like the sea – when the sea is bountiful,
we take what it offers, when it hoards its treasures we go without.'
There are subsidised alcohol shops in the village: the government
auctions liquor licences to contractors, and gives the licence to
those who promise the greatest revenue for the Excise Department.
The liquorshop owners have a vested interest in selling as much
liquor as they can. A road is being constructed along the beach,
towards the village from the main road: this is because an election is
due within a year, and the village is one of the government's vote-
banks.

The other wonder of Konark is the beach. Apart from the
foreshore at Puri, the rest of it has not been developed: kilo-

metres of soft undisturbed sand, and natural stands of *casuarina* trees. This is reserve forest; the narrow coastal road runs straight between the pine-like trees, bordered by pale red grass and clumps of succulents in the sandy soil; patches of the same rust-coloured grass shimmer in clearings between the trees; the sand then rises slightly into a dune, before sloping in a long silvery sweep to the unpolluted blue of the Bay of Bengal; a pearly mist over the bay, and a whey-coloured sky, where the tepid wind lightly ruffles the feathery leaves of the casuarinas. The area is sparsely peopled. The government leases the land on temporary contracts to the local people, so that the women may collect the dry pine-needles and brittle deadwood for sale. They use only the residue, and never touch the living trees. The small villages are fragrant with the breath of tulsi, exhalations of the earth itself, in which every living thing is a sacrament. On the red *mitti* walls, finger-paintings of plumes of white padi. Padi is not just food, it too is sacred. At this time of year – December – the harvest has just been completed. On bamboo mats in the village streets the boiled grain is spread in the sun to dry. At one place, a woman in a red saree is walking through a carpet of golden grain, kicking it to help it dry; an amber cascade over her feet, a flash of silver anklet, an unselfconscious grace, as she delights in the sensuous experience and, at the same time, celebrates the security for the family for the year to come.

This peaceful site has long been seen by the State government as a potential major earner of foreign exchange from tourism. The government has proposed a 9-kilometre-long beach resort complex. The State's Tourism Minister is himself a hotelier who had applied for land here in 1968. Clearance was given in 1989, only to be revoked in 1991 by the central government. In May 1993, the Union Minister of Civil Aviation and Tourism identified the Bhubaneshwar-Puri-Konark area as among 15 locations across the country suitable for 'intensive development'. This triggered no less than 74 applications by December 1993 from people seeking land in the area. The land would have to be dereserved before any 'development' can take place, and the Konarak-Balukhanda Wildlife Sanctuary would have to be denotified. Those who have expressed interest in tourist projects include Tatas, Birlas, Oberois, Ambanis – some of the biggest companies in India – as well as a number of multinationals.

A vigorous resistance movement to any such projects has grown up, led by Banka Behari Das, president of Orissa Krushak Mahasangh. Apart from the necessity of maintaining the integrity of the environment – removing the trees would simply lead to sand cover spreading far inland – and of preserving the livelihood of the local people, which depends on the cashew plantations as well as the casuarina forest, their greatest fear is the prospect that this wild and lovely coastline could be transformed into another Goa: Goa, which on the opposite side of the country, has been ravaged by tourism, construction, pollution and over-development.

3. Uttar Pradesh

In the Badlands of Banda

The coming to power of the BSP/SP (Bharatiya Samaj Party and the Samajwadi Party) coalition – an alliance of the poor, Muslims, Dalits and Other Backward Castes – in Uttar Pradesh (UP) in November 1993 came as a total surprise to many commentators, who had expected the Hindu communalist BJP to consolidate its hold upon the State. The BJP government had been summarily dismissed by the Centre after the demolition of the mosque at Ayodhya in December 1992. It seemed to many that, in spite the efforts of the parties resisting the BJP, with its upper-caste domination and Hindu supremacist views, there was little prospect of preventing it from coming back to power. In the event, the result was a virtually equal number of seats for the BJP and for BSP/SP coalition, with a rump of Congress and Janata Dal holding the balance.

Behind this electoral upset lay the revolt of the poorest of India's most populous state after centuries of oppression, violence and expropriation. It seemed that, at last, the poorest had come to realise both that their fate is not inevitable and that the only way it can be changed is by themselves. Indeed, since November 1993, India has been in what can best be described as a state of suppressed ferment, with the minorities demanding justice, and the upper castes, aided by the 'enrichissez-vous' atmosphere of the liberalisation of the economy, equally determined to maintain their monopoly of wealth and power. The state elections of 1995 have shown increasing polarisation between rich and poor: the BJP is now the dominant force in Maharashtra and Gujarat – the two most industrialised states in west India; while the left of centre Janata Dal gained Karnataka in the south and consolidated its hold in Bihar, India's poorest state.

Nowhere is the condition of the tribals more starkly revealed than in the Patha region of eastern Uttar Pradesh, a rocky, infertile area with inadequate water, and the physical as cruel as the social landscape. The early morning sun turns the jagged outcrops of rock a pale rose colour; patches of *bajra* and *jowar* grow in the fertile crevices between the barren slopes. Some stands of forest remain, especially around the pilgrimage area of Chitrakoot, where the forest people sheltered Lord Rama during his exile from Ayodhya; but the overall impression is of a mixture of Wuthering Heights and Arizona.

This 'remote' area contains all the horrors of rural India: bonded labour, seizure of land belonging to the tribal Kols by the rich landlord classes, the failure of all efforts at land reform and redistribution which successive UP governments have carried out on paper; insufficient resources, which the powerful have appropriated; corruption, armed bands of *dacoits* – bandits – terrorising the poor, often in the pay of politicians, and a police force demoralised, supine and corrupt.

And yet Manikpur, at the heart of the region, is a major railway junction. Each day trains from Delhi to Jabalpur pass through. The Bombay–Gauhati express stops here. Trains en route to Calcutta halt. Only, it seems, no one alights. No one of significance gets off. Few care to look into the depths of misery concealed in the folds of this strange barren landscape.

Gaya Prasad Gopal – a Gandhian – has been working here for 15 years with the Kol tribal people on a project in pursuit of social justice and education for the excluded. This has led to frequent collisions with the structures of rural power. (In fact, in UP the Kols are classified as Scheduled Castes; in neighbouring Madhya Pradesh they are Scheduled Tribes. Scheduled Castes and Tribes are supposed to be the beneficiaries of certain benign legislation to protect the most disadvantaged. For the people themselves, this distinction is academic, and the benefits remain in the realm of theory.)

A small bungalow beside the railway line, sparsely furnished, is office, home and centre for the activities of Akhil Bhartiya Samaj Sewa Sansthan (ABSSS), which works under constant threat from the landlords who have always dominated this part of UP and have no intention of relinquishing their privileges. The bungalow is the centre for the administration of a number of schools in the area where hundreds of Kol children receive an education which they would never know if they depended on the government, and is also seen as a refuge for Kol people abused, beaten, threatened, both by police and dacoits.

On my very first evening in Manikpur, I returned to the bungalow towards dusk, to see a large group of people huddled on the grass behind the building. They were standing close together, as though posing for a photograph. The men stood behind, with women crouching in front, holding their children, and on the grass before them, the flimsy bundles of their most valuable possessions – mostly cooking vessels, blankets, a few ornaments. But they were not smiling. Their proximity to one another was an expression of fear.

A whole village has come to ask for asylum here. Some are crying. The image is strangely familiar: these people are refugees, presenting the kind of TV picture you see of those displaced from their homes by earthquakes, floods or war.

War. It is war: the war of the dacoits of the Patha region and the police, their mirror-image and symbiotic dependants. The villagers are victims of both, in this local skirmish of what we must now regard as a wider war, the Third World War, the aggression of the rich against the poor.

Lal Bahadur, a 23-year-old, with deep, mobile eyes which themselves tell of the insecurity and unhappiness of his people, explains what happened. He shows a series of weals on his arm. Earlier that morning, a group of bandits had arrived, and forced the villagers to give them food. Terrified, the village people had no choice but to do the bidding of the dacoits: there have been too many examples of reprisals, beatings, rape and killings for them to refuse.

The police had come some time after the departure of the bandits. They had laid about the people indiscriminately, beating up men, women and children with lathis. Three men had been taken away by the police, including Lal Bahadur, an older man and Sukanandan, a 12-year-old goat boy. Lal Bahadur had been ill recently. He could not walk, and was released by the police. He came with the villagers to seek protection against what are supposed to be the forces of the law, a law that imposes nothing but disorder and violence in this place. This village is only about 5 kilometres from the town of Manikpur.

This is no new experience for the villagers. Ever since anyone can remember, the dacoits have come, beaten them, robbed them of food and belongings. In – not very zealous – pursuit of them, the police arrive and demand to be told where the *badmash*, or criminals, went. The people tell them as much as they know, which is actually very little, because the dacoits do not confide in them. The police return empty-handed, unable to find the dacoits. They then accuse the villagers of misleading them, of being in collusion with the bandits, and beat and abuse them. Then, when the police have gone, the dacoits return and accuse the villagers of betraying them to the police. There follow yet more beatings.

If and when the police and dacoits do meet, what do they say to each other, the villagers wonder. Who pays money to whom?

Or who is paying both sides? Are they all in the pay of the landlords?

The people met with Gaya Prasad Gopal and some of the members of the ABSSS, and discussed a strategy. It was decided to sit on a dharna at the police station in the biggest town in the region, about 40 kilometres away, to demand protection from senior police officers against their own men. In the meantime, they will sleep in sheds and in tents that have been erected for a school celebration that weekend. It is a cold night at the end of October. The people light fires and make food, huddle together for warmth under threadbare shawls and blankets.

The landlords of the area are numerically few, no more than 5 per cent of the population. They live in quite luxurious houses in and around the little town of Manikpur: structures with ornamental gates, shady terraces, two storeys high with ample courtyards, jeeps in the driveway. Theirs is a life of quite brazen luxury, which clearly expresses their lack of fear of those they have oppressed openly for generations. They have been able effortlessly to divert to their own use the resources intended by government for improvements in the life conditions of the poorest.

The Scheduled Castes and Tribes form the vast majority of the people, but there are also a number from higher castes who are impoverished. These, too, have been exploited by the rich feudal families. Life has worsened for the poor because of government corruption as well as drought, a consequence of diminishing forest cover. Because most officials are also dependent upon the dominant classes, many government initiatives remain as paper reforms.

Landlords own tracts of land of several hundred *bighas* (1 acre = 2.5 bighas), some of it usurped from the poor, some appropriated as a consequence of land reform schemes which were intended to provide land for the landless. Sometimes landlords have registered the land in the name of their labourers, without the 'beneficiaries' knowing anything about it. These continue to labour as they always have done. Some of the poor work as sharecroppers, which means they pay for half the inputs and receive half the produce of the land. Because the sharecroppers are so poor they often have to borrow from the landlord, and this must be repaid with interest when the harvest comes, perpetuating a cycle of impoverishment and subordination.

The majority work as day-labourers, receiving about 2 kilos of grain in payment. A permanent employee may get a small piece of land for his own cultivation, but the daily wage worker is vulnerable to unemployment. Bonded labourers are those who have become indebted and have been unable to pay back loans. They will never be free of the debt, since the labour they offer barely covers the interest, let alone the principal, even though this may be a trifling sum. In the event of sickness, the bonded labourer must send someone else in his place, his son or sometimes wife. Bondage can be inherited, and cases are known where it has come through two or three generations.

But this weekend, in October 1993, there is something to celebrate in Manikpur. For the ABSSS has organised a Baal Mela, a festival of children, at which ten children from each of the 40 schools it supports in Patha will be present. Government schools do not function here. Indeed, the institutions of the State reach the Kol people principally as punishment.

This is to be a festival of dance, music and singing. The children are accommodated in the biggest building in town – a hospital, unoccupied and unused. In the grounds of the hospital, the tumble-down leprosy eradication clinic is in ruins. But at least, for once, the empty building is serving some useful purpose. In every room, each group is preparing its presentation for the festival: a play, a tableau, some songs and poems, dances, storytelling. A high level of excitement: children whose lives have been shadowed by oppression, loss and violence, are to appear before their parents, friends, well-wishers, visitors; some human rights lawyers, academics and even a High Court judge from Allahabad will be present.

On the Sunday morning of the weekend's programme, a procession is organised through the streets of the town. Past the little shops, the vegetable vendors, the handful of rich houses, across the railway line and the rough land surrounding the station, 400 children, teachers, workers of the ABSSS, and the members of AWAZ, a radical street-theatre group who have come from Lucknow to perform for the children; behind them, some of the parents – labourers, *bigar* (corvee labourers) and bonded workers, landless agricultural and domestic servants – a spectacle of some of the most injured and humiliated people on earth, walking slowly through the rough, unmade streets; for one day escaping from their labour, so that they may share in the pleasure of their children's visible social advancement. The sense of raised pride is tangible, you can almost hear the dilation of hope in their hearts, see the look of cautious elation in their tired eyes, raised for the first time from the horizon of the earth they work so laboriously, the courage to hope that the long night of darkness and bondage may be nearing its end. Here, made manifest, are all the abstractions of oppression and subordination; here is the living flesh and blood, the worn faces and the hands, those scarred dexterous instruments of labour which, for once, are not serving others. As they walk through the streets, the words 'Sangasthan men Shakti hai', strength through unity, have a real resonance. At first, they speak the words out in unison, as though shyly. But as they walk through the autumn sunshine, some people stop to watch the ragged procession. Others find the courage to join them, and their voices become stronger. A moment of rare affirmation, an assertion of a humanity denied and injured. At the station, staff and tea-drinkers stand on the threshold, and look with respect on the procession.

The Kol tribals are people whose lives have been devastated, just as their forests have been laid waste. What is more, they have been criminalised by their exclusion from the forests, of which their life has always been an integral part. In theory, they are now forbidden to gather the fruits, the *amla* fruits, honey and nuts which used to supplement their diet, and the surplus of which they used to sell in the market. Only gathering dead wood and the controlled collecting of tendu leaves (broad leaves used in the manufacture of bidis, Indian cigarettes) are now open to them. Even then, the middlemen take most of the money given by government for the collection of tendu leaves.

Most Kols who have land have only the most rocky and barren places. Wherever improvements have been made or irrigation has come, the landlord seized the lands, by issuing false *pattas* (deeds) in the name of friends and relatives, in order to gain possession. Others have transferred useless land to the Kols. This is sometimes done at gunpoint, by what is euphemistically referred to as 'muscle power'.

Suvagarda village is about a 2-kilometre walk from Manikpur. The scene is one of complete tranquillity and rural beauty, characteristic of much of India: the cones of ripening jowar nod in the breeze on their long stalks, the cattle pass slowly through the fields, languidly eating straw or leaves. The air is full of the sweet smell of dry grass, *gobar* (cowdung) and wild flowers. Only the people in this landscape speak of the social desolation that lies beneath the deceptive appearance of calm: little girls of seven or eight are carrying broad shallow baskets of earth to mix with dung to renew the floors of houses; others follow the cattle, prodding them with rough sticks; one boy of about seven carries a cane in one hand and a baby of about one year in his arms. Women are bearing impossible headloads of fuelwood, their neck and back erect, knees bent, almost running, on their way to the station, where they will take the train to Karvi or even Allahabad, 80 kilometres away.

Suvagarda village. Ram Gopal sits beneath the veranda of his mitti and wood house. The red tiles on the roof he made and baked himself. His wife is pounding rice in a little cavity in the floor just in front of the house. The house is long and low, and it forms one side of a square, an informal compound. In the adjacent houses live other members of the family: two of Ram Gopal's brothers with their wives and children, and another brother whose leg has been withered by polio. One of Ram Gopal's three children, a girl of about eleven, also has had polio; one leg is perceptibly thinner than the other. There is no immunisation of children in this Kol village. There is no ration-shop – there isn't even one in Manikpur itself. There is water, but no electricity.

Yet the village does not present a spectacle of degradation. The enclosure is bordered by a fence, with the bright yellow trumpets of creepers, while the pumpkin vines climb vigorously over the rooftops, the great orange moons of their fruit ready for plucking. The floor of Ram Gopal's house is fragrant with a fresh application of gobar and mitti. Inside, the air is cool and fresh. It is not village life itself that is brutalising; only the social relationships, which cheat the poor of the fruits of their labour, and treat them as less than human, as objects for use by their social 'betters'; people who, ultimately, are more brutalised than the poor they despise, for they rape and abuse women as they see fit. Even those villagers successfully released from bonded labour must frequently do bigar labour, for which they are paid only the breakfast that will furnish them with the energy to complete the day's work. If anything, bigar is even worse than bondage, for at least the bonded labourer gets a *panchpav* of rice (about 1.2 kilos).

Ram Gopal has no land. He works as a sharecropper, but even that work is not guaranteed. Each year, when he hears of some land that is available for cultivation, he will go to the landlord and undertake the work of sowing and tending until harvest. His reward will be half the produce of the land, to which he and his family will have contributed all the labour. Ram Gopal's mother, a woman in her late fifties, also works to help the family income. She goes into the forest to collect wood. It will take her up to seven hours to make up a proper headload. She brings this home, then, next day, travels by train – without a ticket – to the market at Banda, to sell. She will make between Rs12 and 15 (40–50 cents) per headload, the reward for two days' labour. The headload weighs about 60 kilograms. She invites me to feel the weight of the bundle she collected yesterday. I cannot even raise it above my waist, let alone carry it on my head.

Ram Gopal invites us into his house. It is dark and cool. The walls are whitewashed. There are a few clothes on a bamboo pole stretched across the room, a clay chulha, or cooking stove, built into the floor itself. There are half a dozen vessels, a bicycle, one *charpoy* or string bed on a bamboo frame, and a big clay pot for holding rice. Nothing else. The wooden rafters are festooned with cobwebs in which flies and mosquitoes are caught.

Poverty is not inherent in this way of life: it is the violence that produces the poverty, the expropriation of the rewards of labour by the rich and powerful, by their monopoly of land. Dignity lies in the people reclaiming what is rightfully theirs, so that they may lead a life of secure sufficiency. They know what they want: it is an achievable and sustainable contentment, the most modest of human aspirations; yet, in this context, fiercely, violently contested by the vested interests of the possessing classes.

That this is their aim was made explicit by Semia, who lives in an adjoining compound, much larger than that of Ram Gopal; a more irregular space, with houses at less symmetrical angles; all one storey, of earth and wood, where very few objects in use – apart from a plastic bowl or two – could not have been in place two or even five hundred years ago.

The scene is a busy one; a girl of about 12 is reinforcing the mud base of the area under the veranda of her house. Some women are pounding rice, seated with their legs half-crossed around the hole in the earth where they work. They move with a quick deft rhythm. They raise the wooden pestle with one hand, and with the other scoop the rice back into the cavity in the earth where it is being dehusked. A hypnotic, regular movement, the movement of the *Adivasi* dances. Later, they will winnow the rice in a bamboo tray, throwing it into the air so that the husks are carried away on the wind, while a cascade of white grain falls back into the pan.

Semia's parents once owned 45 bighas of land (about 16 acres). Semia is one of five daughters. There were no boys in the family. When the daughters married, they went to the home of their husbands, as is the custom. Semia was the youngest. Her father and mother died within a few months of each other. When her father died, Semia went home to look after her mother.

For some time after the death of her parents, the land remained uncultivated. Then it was simply taken by a local *bania*, or businessman. This man is prominent in Manikpur; we saw him one day, calmly riding a bullock-cart on top of a load of rice straw. When Semia and her sisters saw that the land had been stolen, they, with the help of the ABSSS, filed a case in the High Court at Allahabad, and once again began to cultivate their land. The court found in favour of the rightful owners. When they went to harvest the produce, the bania had denounced the whole family to the police as notorious dacoits, and filed his case against them in Karvi, a town some 30 kilometres away. That was seven years ago. The case is still continuing.

When we went to harvest the crop, says Semia, *they came with guns. Even after we had filed the case, they came with anti-socials to chase us from our own land. At present, there is a stay order, and the land remains uncultivated. Despite this, the bania is still cultivating. Last year he took his crop of* sarsoon *(mustard), wheat and jowar.*

The Adivasis, the original inhabitants of India, are outlaws of the market economy. This is why they are criminalised. They represent, however vestigially, like the Kols whose habitat has been degraded and invaded since British times, a way of life that resists, and is a living critique of the imperatives of the market economy and its attendant money-driven culture; and that critique is lived in the most sensitive area of all: at the level of the material resource-base. The 'mainstream' blames the tribals, those who live on the produce of the forest, for degradation of the environment. The truth is that the use of the forests by those who depend upon it for survival has always been restrained and sustainable; quite unlike the violent predations of the market economy.

Kekaramar, a village some 8 kilometres from Manikpur, is almost completely inhabited by released bonded labourers. The terrain around the village is a high rocky plain, where small farmers are cutting their patches of rice which, this year, have been spoiled by drought. Some are cutting and winnowing the rice: there is almost no grain in the empty husks, which blow away in the wind. In the immediate vicinity of the village, the land is more fertile: sunflowers, jowar, tamarind trees, and palas trees, from the broad leaves of which children make plates which are used in the small snack- and tea-stalls.

The land falls gently towards a check dam, constructed by the Scandinavian charity Noraid, which has brought irrigation facilities to about a hundred Kol families. When land becomes fertile, land deeds are issued to the Kols in adjacent barren areas, while the rich landlords produce deeds claiming the irrigated land as their own.

Sardar, a man of about 40, was released from bondage four years ago. Until that time, he was forced to work at the whim of his master from six in the morning until eight at night. His wage was one panchpav of rice a day. The bondage had been inherited from his father, who had defaulted in his repayment of a small debt.

The labourers were organised with the help of ABSSS, and released, according to the law of India. There are, says Sardar, many still in bondage in the area, although not in this village. Most of them are doing bigar labour for nothing but one meal a day. The money which government gives as compensation and for the purpose of rehabilitating those released from bondage was, in some cases, taken by the police. The land they were allotted was mostly rough, difficult to plough. Sardar has about 12 bighas, but it is rocky and of poor quality, and does not produce enough for him, his wife and four children.

Chandan, who had been working for ABSSS, was taken into custody by the police during the agitation for the release of the labourers. He was tied head down from a tree and beaten up, in an effort to intimidate him. Defiantly, he says nothing will stop the fight for justice.

Kekaramar, if a little less poor, would be a good place to live. It is calm and peaceful, and the people have a degree of independence. The houses, self-built, are substantial, cool, created out of the environment, indeed are an emanation of the earth itself. Inside, the dark wooden ceilings are hung with silvery cobwebs; beyond is a small compound with a charpoy; some cones of bajra are lying in the sun to dry, the pale violet-grey of *urad* beans, giant yellow pumpkins on the roof of the veranda; orange- and lemon-coloured butterflies dart beneath the trees. In spite of release from bondage, the people of Kekaramar remain poor. Access to good land is denied them. Without structural change, without engaging with the wider social forces, these small islands of independence remain always threatened.

As we go back across the rough track – marked on maps as a tarred road, for which government money was given, but diverted into the pockets of the rich – we pass the house of the landlord whom the bonded labourers served. The little houses in the compound are now occupied by those doing bigar labour, which, says Chandan, is in many ways worse than bondage: everything still belongs to the landlord, and there is not even the guaranteee of a given quantity of rice at the end of each day.

Chunnu Ram is 24. He is the first Kol ever to enter university. His father is terminally sick with TB, and there are three younger children in the family. Yet he has been enabled to study with the help of the ABSSS, and serves as a role model to Kol children for the future. He says the Kols believe that they are descendants of the rishis and maharishis who attended the places of learning in the Patha region in the time even before Rama. But they lived in the jungles, and as the jungles were felled, or enclosed, or declared reserve forest, they were forced to become cultivators, even though they still yearn for the despoiled forests; their expulsion from the jungle is actually an eviction and remains, for them, exile.

Gopalbhai says that the people over 40 have been brutalised, but the younger people are now ready to resist. This is one of the functions of the schools run by the ABSSS: to ensure that the next generation will not tolerate the intolerable; and the purpose of this weekend's festival is to help restore the damaged self-esteem of the Kols.

It is an intensely moving experience. Parents, older brothers and sisters come and sit on the chairs under the huge shamiana, or tent of painted canvas, and listen to the songs, the poems, the speeches, entranced by the performance of their young relatives, some of whom show both extraordinary talent and growing self-confidence.

In India, those who work on behalf of the poor often find their lives are threatened. Recently, as Gopalbhai was driving back to Manikpur late at night, he found boulders had been placed in the road. The jeep stopped, and out of the shadows came five men with guns. He was ordered out of the car. When one of the assailants recognised him, he touched his feet; his child was at one of the schools. They had been paid to kill him, but not told who he was. Gopalbhai says, 'I have seen exploitation, but never so bad as it is here.'

One night, I stayed at the Forest Guest House in Manikpur. On the back of the *chitti* which gave authorisation to stay there was a list of regulations governing the behaviour of guests. It says, under a statute cited and dated 1902, 'All visitors shall conform to the European style of living.'

I met Gaya Prasad Gopal later, after the November elections which had resulted in the victory of the BSP/SP government in Uttar Pradesh. He said: *Any type of change that will not help the poor, those below the poverty line, those bonded and exploited by landlords and politicians, is no change at all. Although we should be thankful for small changes, in many ways the political situation is worse now, because the leaders of our country and their activities are all designed to benefit themselves and their friends. They are not bothered about society, the nation or humanity.*

Today's events in UP foreshadow what is to come: a more intensive caste war. Last month, I joined a public meeting in which a Minister of the new UP government was supposed to come and speak. The landlords and the upper castes occupied the platform. They captured and destroyed our banners, and the organisers ran away from that place. When I reached there with my friends, that organiser was waiting and he said, 'We have no platform. They have captured it.' I told him, 'Keep calm, and slowly we will march towards the platform, and with sweet language speak to the people occupying.' We captured it back. How? I said 'It is your village. We have come as guests. It is an insult to you if this meeting is not happening. We shall go.' Then they said, 'Oh no', and they permitted the meeting to go ahead. The State Minister came.

But these people will do everything to prevent political and social change. For so many years only they have been there. In my speech, I challenged them. I say to them, 'Baba, sit for a few years, let them work, they are your sons, observe what happens.' They imagine that those now in power will prove themselves incompetent. We can take advantage of that conviction.

When we come to know that the rich also have differences, I say that we, too, must learn to divide and rule, just as they have done. There are two powerful groups in our area, so we support one group. Every year, there are two or three murders on both sides; and while they fight for control of resources, we go about our work of awareness and solidarity among the poor. We have to form this kind of plan in every sector. Sometimes our friends think otherwise. When they see I am sitting with upper-caste people, they do not know what I'm doing, they do not see my plan. We have to get the support of some upper castes through our Brahmin friends. With the support of tribals, Scheduled Castes and Scheduled Tribes alone, we cannot win. We also need support from outside, we need our struggle to be observed by the media, by those who will monitor what happens.

They are very powerful, and we must win some of them to our side. In Indian struggles, Naxalite and others, we came to see that after a few years, they divide into factions and the struggle is nullified. We must avoid that fate. After learning from those experiences, we decided that if we have 20,000 people with us in a march, it is not our duty that shooting and firing should occur. I always avoid direct fights. Our group continues a peaceful struggle, even while in other parts of the country, in Andhra Pradesh and elsewhere, there are murders, fires, violence. We are for society, not our own personality, not any faction. In India, many work for their own image and personality, their desire to become leaders.

In Patha region, from Mughal and British times, the Brahmins were always advanced in education and power, and money and land and political power, all these go with them. Families of the Scheduled Castes and Tribes were always exploited by them. They had become just like a dead community: no reaction to any amount of indignity or injustice. They never expected to get political or social support; girls, wives and daughters were used by the upper castes for their pleasure only. And the Kols were relatively few in number. Now that the Scheduled Castes, Scheduled Tribes, Muslims and poor have come together for political change, this gives hope and courage to join in.

Because of Chitrakoot and the holy places, where kitchens and charities had been set up, this made the Kols feel they were beggars. This is not good for self-esteem; they think someone will provide for us; it leads to a culture of mendicancy and resignation.

We started to take lunch and dinner with the Kols in their huts. 'Baba', they would say, 'you provide. Malik, we have nothing, what can we do?' We said, 'We will take roti and curd, whatever you eat, we will take also.' Now they are happy. No one ever asked them before. If you accept their bread, that has a deep significance for them. We would sit in a group with them. At our baal mela, they provided all the food. They are proud. This has a profound psychological effect. While they sit and say, 'I am poor, how can I invite him, he is a big man, where will he sit, where will he eat?' nothing will be achieved. We have sought to get rid of these feelings of inferiority.

When the leadership is in political hands, this can lead only to violence. And violence is not useful for the lower castes in society. The upper castes want the Kanshi Ram-Mulayam Singh connection to be . destroyed. They will seek to create fights between the Other Backward Castes and Scheduled Castes and Scheduled Tribes. They will excite quarrels. How they will do it? My field has a good crop. If a buffalo belonging to a Backward Caste family enters the field of a Scheduled Caste, then by late evening, the Brahmin will call me and say, 'It is not going well. Your crop is spoiled.' 'What to do?' 'Go and lodge a f.i.r. (first instance report) against this fellow.' They are watching. They have newspapers, money, manpower. This type of change is good and useful, but we are not sure how many days, months or years it will survive.

All other parties, the BJP, but also Congress, all the upper-caste alliances are trying to separate and destroy. That is now our struggle, to build solidarity, non-violence and unity among the poor.

At first sight, Banda and Manikpur look like a feudal backwater, an archaic survival under the reign of the landlords and upper castes who have appropriated the resources, land and water, at the expense of the Kols and the poor. A network of collusion between landlords, police, dacoits and politicians creates a web of concealment and injustice. Worse still is the compulsory collusion between these powerful forces and the poor who are compelled to do forced or bonded labour for the price of clothing, shelter and food, while declaring to outsiders that they are free labourers.

But this struggle over resources is not simply a declining remnant of feudal conflict in the world. It is a reflection, a microcosm of the major global battle now engaged between rich and poor, the greatest war of all, the battle for survival of the poor pitted against the maintenance of privilege in a wasting, wanting world.

Indeed, there is more. The feudal elements in places like Banda join hands with the new liberalisation policy; for this places yet more pressure upon the resource-base and the people who depend on it. The imperatives to export the wealth of India in order to pay back the debt to the Western financial institutions and to underwrite the requirements of the privileged, mean that more and more people will experience the fate of the Kols, must expect to be evicted, marginalised, dispossessed. Atrocities against tribals and women, exploitation and oppression receive a new impetus and become the unspoken allies of new forms of extraction, plunder and violence – the imposition upon India of what is essentially a colonial economy and model of development.

This is the background against which the stirrings of new people's movements must be understood – a wide range of movements, by no means all successful in their struggle: Narmada, Chattisgarh, the Fishermen's Forum, Tehri, the continuing struggle for justice at Bhopal, and thousands of other, smaller efforts across India, of which the ABSSS is only one brave example.

The Uttarkhand Struggle

Late in 1994, the demand for a separate state by the people of the Himalayan foothills reached its climax. The Uttarkhand movement shares some features with other struggles for separate statehood – Jharkand and Chattisgarh, for instance; and it has been embittered by violence by the State government of Uttar Pradesh (of which the foothills now form part) and by years of indifference on the part of the central government.

The lower reaches of the Himalayas are a quite distinctive region, and the hill people have a separate identity and sensibility. The hills have been badly damaged by deforestation and over-exploitation, and the absence of work compels a majority of the men of Uttarkhand to migrate and to live outside. As early as 1938, Nehru stated that the hill districts should constitute a separate state, and the issue has remained more or less simmering since 1947.

Here, Rajputs are the dominant caste; Kshatriyas, fighters and warriors who came to what were then inaccessible forests from Rajasthan and other parts of North India as early as the time of Aurangzeb, to avoid Moghul rule. Their warrior caste tradition remained; and they formed a significant part of the army in British, and later, independent, India. More recently, the young have migrated to Delhi and Lucknow, where many have found employment in the service and tourist industries. The honesty and integrity of the hill people make them good servants. Many remain in and around Delhi, unemployed.

The foothills were also the place where the Chipko movement

was born, the struggle, led by the women who do not emigrate, to retain control over the forests which had been devastated. The most recent affront to the people has been the Tehri dam, 265 metres high in the hills, the electricity from which will go to the factories and sugar-cane refineries of the plains.

The area has been exploited by a colonial and extractive economy. With a population of some six million, there may be almost as many again outside; no one actually knows. Survival now depends upon the remittances of migrants. They are hills inhabited solely by women now that so many men have gone.

So why should the movement for Uttarkhand have reached a critical point only now, in 1994? It may be seen as part of the reaction by the periphery to the new liberalisation policy of the government of Narasimha Rao; but the draining of human and material resources from the hills is scarcely new. What is new is that in November 1993, the government of Uttar Pradesh passed narrowly into the hands of an alliance representing the poorest in India, the Untouchables, the Other Backward Castes and Muslims, in the administration led by Mulayam Singh Yadav. This government displaced the ruling Bharatiya Janata Party (BJP), the communalist Hindu party which had played such a significant part in the destruction of the mosque at Ayodhya in December 1992. The BJP has sought to take advantage of anger among the hill people against the 27 per cent reservation policy (that is, the reservation of government jobs) for the poor. The Rajputs are angered by the application of this to their area, while so many of the local people have had to migrate in order to find work, as waiters, domestic servants and clerks, often living in cramped miserable conditions for less than 2,000 rupees (US$65) a month; separated from their families, desperately depriving themselves so that those they love can survive in the hills. 'To redress one injustice by creating another is to solve nothing', says A. Rawat, lawyer and convenor of the Uttarkhand Andolan Sanchalan Samiti, the movement for separate statehood.

The leaders vigorously repudiate any alliance with the BJP, who they see as trying to hijack their movement for alien political purposes. As recently as 1988, the BJP had declared itself opposed to a separate state; only when it lost power in 1993 did it see a possible source of renewal among the higher castes of Uttarkhand.

This makes it difficult to extricate the complex social forces that make up the movement. Surendra Singh Bisht, a former naval officer, says that the hill people are themselves victims. Many Rajputs are poor; their land is insufficient and degraded. Indignation at long-term exploitation has now reached a level never previously seen. The Mulayam Singh Yadav government over-reacted: demonstrations against the application of the reservations system were violently suppressed in an area where poverty and out-migration have seriously undermined the culture of these hills which lie in the shadow of the huge icy pyramids of the Greater Himalaya. The whole question of 'reservations' for government jobs in the present context is heavy with social divisiveness and potential conflict. With 'liberalisation', government spending and employment will certainly decline. This will lead to higher unemployment, particularly among the educated, and to even fiercer competition for secure employment. The attempt by the V.P. Singh government in 1991 to implement the findings of the Mandal Commission (which had languished unimplemented for a decade) stirred up a violent reaction on the part of the higher castes; a number of young people committed suicide by setting fire to themselves in protest.

In August 1994, the police lathi-charged a demonstration against reservations in Pouri-Garhwal, in the heart of Uttarkhand; and a month later at Khatima in Nainital the first death occurred. On 2 October, as many thousands of people from Uttarkhand were making their way to Delhi, the police fired on them, and a number were killed – official figures admit to five, but eye-witnesses speak of many more than this. In fact, the absence of clear information only fed rumours of truckloads of bodies being buried unceremoniously in mass graves.

After the October killings, the movement set up a permanent vigil in central Delhi, not far from the Parliament building. Under canvas in the biting cold Delhi night, the leaders and their sympathisers try to keep warm. I met them on several days during December 1994. There is a constant stream of supporters. Rawat, who was previously with the Leftist movement, insists that what the people want is autonomy. *The hills are rich in resources, but none of the benefits come to the local people. We utterly reject all political manipulation. The Communists came and declared their support. We want no affiliation to any political party; all of them are corrupt. Even the Uttarkhand Kranti Dal, the political liberation movement, which wants complete freedom for Uttarkhand, has no vision. We have clear objectives for the development of our Uttarkhand. We shall not permit outsiders to come and buy land and build palaces, bringing the corrupt culture of the metropolitan cities. We shall preserve our own water resources, construct small-scale dams for electricity for our own people. The air is pure and dust-free, ideal for electronics assembly industry. The tea-gardens which have fallen into ruin can be revived. In the valleys we will cultivate apples, citrus fruits, walnuts, mangoes. We have uranium, gypsum, limestone, copper – all these things at present benefit others. We will also ban liquor which has ruined many families. In our region, there is no technical institution, no engineering college, no medical college. There are 15,000 students now in Delhi.* Rawat comes from Almora; his father was a freedom fighter, and Rawat was his posthumous son. He says, *I had to struggle for my education. Whatever the wrongs to the Untouchables, this will not be redressed by worsening the life-chances of the hill people.*

Rajendra Shah, who gave up his job with the Life Insurance Company of India to commit himself to the struggle, sits permanently on the dharna near Parliament. *For us, local autonomy means that everything except revenue, external affairs, defence and communications should be decided by us. We are not looking to the break-up of India. Everything leaves the hills, the resin from the chir trees used for industrial purposes, khilmora and other medicinal substances from the forests, basmati rice from Dehra Dun.*

But the real drain from the hills is not the diverted waters or stolen timber; it is the people, the permanent exile of the young men, and the anxiety of the women who must remain and wait for the money that may or may not come. A young man in the Border Security Force expressed it poignantly, when he said whenever he goes home, several days pass before his little girl will come to him spontaneously. *When our children see their fathers as strangers, how do you count the pain against the money that has to make up for the separations of the heart?*

The Uttarkhand movement exemplifies a complex moral dilemma for India; a sense of ancient grievance of impoverished Rajputs, caught up in a militant Hindu response to the new assertiveness of the Untouchables and the oppressed. Free India in general, and the Congress Party in particular, have taken for granted the loyalty and commitment of the people of this beautiful, impoverished region. Indeed, many of the exiles from Uttarkhand in Delhi bear witness to the fact that among the poor of India are many upper-caste people. I have to admit to a personal interest in this issue: my dearest friend in India is from Uttarkhand. He is a Rajput and fully supports separate status for Uttarkhand, a region made up of nine districts. He is an athlete in the Border Security Force, and desperately wants to return home. He would like to work as a sports coach in a school in Nainital, where his wife, daughter, mother and sister live, but he has been unable to find work in any government school. His mother, who raised him and his sister alone, living in a cowshed on a landowner's estate, says bitterly that she did not work an 18-hour day on other people's land for her son to end his days defending a distant border far from his home.

Now that people have died in the struggle, attitudes have hardened. It is a struggle unto death, says Rawat. He dismisses the BJP success in the hills (it holds all but one parliamentary seat). *The hill people are simple, religious people; it is easy to exploit their faith. But those who want to make our children bear the burden of traditionalism and obscurantism send their own children abroad to study. If we want to compete in the modern world, we do not need fundamentalism. Nor have the ecologists helped: even after the killings at Muzzaffarnagar in October, they still talk only of forests and water. This is not an adequate response, when we are fighting street battles against a corrupt government. The misdeeds of Congress led directly to the BJP success, but this doesn't justify either of them.*

The Uttarkhand struggle cuts across many of the current conflicts in India; it poses the question of whether caste is a stronger force than the movement for social justice, and how far victims can be mobilised against victims. What the Uttarkhandis seek to be liberated from is clear; what they and many other movements for regional autonomy in India will be liberated into if they are successful is another, perhaps even more interesting, question.

Uttarkhand is characteristic of responses all over the globe to the process of centralisation, of concentrations of wealth and power within a single world system; indeed, whole countries, let alone mere regions, are being marginalised in the global market economy – sub-Saharan Africa, Haiti, Guyana, Bangladesh; and the reactions of the people in those places are bound to be strong. The Uttarkhandis insist that their struggle is peaceful and non-violent; but they remain adamant that they will not tolerate further impoverishment and loss.

There is no point in trying to compare relative injustice among, say, the people of Uttarkhand and the Kol tribals; the subjective experience determines the reactions of the people; and where the feelings of local identity have been wounded, the response is likely to be even fiercer than in those places where centuries of inferiorisation have encouraged people to accept their low position and status.

4. Delhi, Rich and Poor

Patparganj

If there has been much favourable comment in the West on the emergence, during the 1980s and 1990s, of a new high-consuming middle class in India, this is not because those people are guarantors of social peace and civic responsibility; it is because they represent a highly lucrative market coveted by the West. In fact, the lives of this group of people, according to some estimates as many as 200–250 million, are increasingly articulated, not to India, but to the global market, and they have considerable purchasing power. This gives their luxury requirements priority over the necessities of the poor. The market in this way institutionalises inequalities, with the result that the whims of the well-to-do take precedence over adequate nutrition and health care for the poor. Whole new suburbs have arisen in the cities to service them. One of these in Delhi is Patparganj.

'Patparganj?' people said to me incredulously, when I spoke to them of the area where I was living. Why would anyone in his right mind want stay in a place like that? To many in the soft southern suburbs of Delhi, it seems both perverse and unnatural to go to such a remote spot on the eastern periphery of the city. It is, they assured me, a place of crime and high insecurity, where dacoits are a menace, where autorickshaw drivers will not go, and where the buses, when they deign to run, are intolerably overcrowded and full of pickpockets.

Patparganj is a raw new settlement. A lonely causeway, bordered by the fetid waters of a glassy black canal, leads to the bus depot. There, you stumble into (literally: the roads are pot-holed and ill-defined) a long vista of apartment blocks, in guarded compounds: a charmless landscape without infrastructure or amenity. The thoroughfares are rugged and unmade, with drifts of fine dust on the margins, which every passing vehicle stirs into an ochre fog. Bones are jolted and shaken as you ride over the uneven surfaces; ankles twisted in the builders' rubble. There are few traces of any growing things in the concrete wastes; such nature as had survived in the desolation of this part of Delhi was easily suppressed. The intermittent flicker of street-lamps, faint drooping flowers that scarcely penetrate the winter mist, throws an eerie light on the series of compounds where security guards from Bihar maintain their 12-hour vigils for Rs600 a month ($20), many of them without a single day's holiday in the year.

Yet the flats are being snapped up, as the real estate dealers in this surreal estate affirm. This place is coming up, this is where prices will skyrocket from the mere four or five lakh rupees now ($15,000), never mind what the snobs say.

Here, then, the new middle class of India is defining itself, emerging into the clear light of the late twentieth century. Here we see the formation of that market which offers such a vast outlet for Western goods. Here, the consumer society springs into palpable and voracious life. Spacious apartments with symmetrical rooms which cry out for the douceurs of Western consumerism: curtains and blinds to shield you from neighbours' eyes and the Delhi sun and dust; comfortable chairs and cushions so that when you return from your heroic bus journey from the office you can rest your weary body and tired mind with a glass of imported liquor and the latest reach-me-down entertainment from Star-TV, faded prints of *Santa Barbara* and *The Bold and the Beautiful*. You need every labour-saving device you can get to make up for the energy expended in earning the money to buy labour-saving devices.

In this place – as in thousands of similar developments in the cities and urban areas of India – the traditional sensibility is being broken and reassembled in the image of the market economy. It is a process as violent as it is unsustainable, the triumphal embodiment of tawdry privilege, that sets the middle class apart from the poverty of the mass of the people of India. This, it seems, is the only option for those who have recently found their way out of the ranks of the faceless, numberless poor. They are refugees, stranded in the no man's land of the buy-in culture; a place of only provisional sojourn, from which, nevertheless, it is unlikely they will ever move on.

Although there is a virtually total lack of public amenities, private enterprise has swiftly moved into the vacuum to service the needs of this new population, this newly created culture. There may be frequent power-cuts, which fill the windows with flickering candles like some shared religious observance, the public transport may be deficient, but there are at least five beauty parlours to choose from, and many stores which serve as outlets for Western cosmetics – Imperial Leather, Lux, shampoos, gels and aftershaves, talcum powder and all the lotions and perfumes which are now indispensable to human dignity. There are many conduits for the dumping of transnational pharmaceuticals: chemists and drugstores where you can buy substances to stimulate or to pacify, to calm or to awaken, to put you to sleep or otherwise to deaden the unbearable pain of being; many of them, moreover, banned in the West.

There is a brisk trade in convenience foods, noodles to which busy people must merely add water to create a nourishing meal, soups, packets of dust which can be miraculously transformed into thick flavoursome goodness, sachets of spices and herbs to keep women from the endless chore of grinding, fizzy drinks to quench thirst far more safely than a doubtful public water supply. There are, significantly, many shops selling things for children, from toys to fashionable clothes, sweets and chocolate from such noted childcare specialists as Cadbury and Nestle. There are chips and biscuits, wafers and ice-cream and all the other consolations of childhood long familiar in the West: consolations for privilege. What a paradox it is that the children of the well-to-do should need so much to compensate them for the advantages they already enjoy over the children of the slums! There are also one or two smart jewellery stores for the serious business of weddings, and many merchants of unreal estate, for the benefits of those aspirants to the community, those anxious to gain a foothold in this gilded enclave. In short, everything is here that is needed for the leading of a full and interesting life.

This is a place for the erasure of cultural memory. It is the site of obliteration of the past. This is where humanity is being redirected from the lost and overgrown pathways of self-reliance and frugality into the brightly lit broad avenues of mobility that lead to the mysterious satisfactions of waste, extravagance and excess, to dependency for basic needs on vast transnational entities whose humanitarian tenderness is well known. In fact, it isn't like Delhi at all, not even like India. It resembles all such (socially) high-rise places, from Moscow to Turin, from Manila to São Paolo, with its bleak public spaces, its decor of nowhere, in which the only response is to turn inwards to a world of private consumption, as a consolation for decayed community, an absence of public services, the dereliction without.

And social evils follow hard on the heels of the economic goods. It is no accident that the kind of social problems emerging here faithfully echo those that plague the West, although as yet they are only in their very early stages in Patparganj. But here, the nuclear family is being prised free from its extended predecessor. Of course, the family remains a powerful force, even among these economically emancipated people, since the welfare services of the State are negligible. But there are many stories of young people stealing to keep up with their fast-living, quick-spending

peers. Family relations are strained, relationships tested to breaking point. 'They have never done anything for me, why should I
care about them?' said one young woman, a medical student who
had studied in the USA, and clearly had learned there something
far beyond mere academic instruction.

In Patparganj, there is a widespread fear of crime. 'Do not
walk along the main highway after nine o'clock in the night', I
was solemnly warned. 'Do not use the buses. They are full of
pickpockets, people who use razor-blades to slit your pockets, so
they can run off with your wallet.' There are the beginnings of
that fear-psychosis that grips the West, as people retreat to the
fortified inner fastness of their homes, leaving the streets and the
public spaces at last to the army of thieves, muggers, robbers,
vandals, rapists, maniacs and addicts, who then do indeed become
free to work their mischief on the innocent passerby.

Also appearing is the incipient loneliness of women whose husbands not only disappear for long hours at the office, but also
prolong the day in the company of their friends and a bottle of
beer, rather than return to their empty exurban fortress. So their
wives fret and seek to find some way of passing the hours other
than in domestic chores which, in any case, are swiftly dispatched
within a couple of hours, or passed over to some ill-paid maid-
servant from Bihar or Madhya Pradesh.

Of course, the new Indian middle class is not quite the homo-
geneous mass seen by Western consumer industries, nor is it
monolithically a Trojan horse for Western interests, as some
Indian sociologists have suggested. There is also another middle
class, alive and well in Patparganj, less showy, more thoughtful, a
middle class that does not dream of foreign bank accounts and
luxury travel, whose children's future is not assured in some
foreign suburb of transnational privilege. For in parallel with a
raging consumerism, another middle class is growing, people in
places of higher education, in the media, in the arts, in NGOs
and the service sector, who have a clear analysis of what is happening, and who are well aware of the trap into which their
country has been lured by its Western mentors, and which is
replicated at the level of individuals. They know only too well the
likely consequences of the atomisation, the spread of a narrow
individualism, the conflict between the generations, the breaking
of rootedness and the wider social support systems; and many of
them are leaders of the resistance, as it were, in their efforts to
preserve all that is of value in the Indian tradition, now under
such sustained assault from the new, market-driven junk culture.

But these remain a minority. The high-consuming middle class has another, altogether deeper and more sinister purpose. For the dependency of the new rich upon their addiction to marketed commodities of the buy-in culture means they will stop at nothing to sustain and to further it. In the process, they will not care who suffers, who pays, who is disadvantaged. They will cling to what they have, and become indifferent to the fate of those who do not enter the market which serves them so well; they will become less sensitive to the suffering of others, prepared to accept any severity that may be required to keep the poor in their place, in order that their privilege will not be called into question or undergo any diminution. If the human rights of the poor must be abused, if they must be further impoverished, if they must sacrifice both livelihood and life, well so be it. That is the way of the world, this is the consequence of 'modernisation', the upgrading of callousness and greed into high principle, and the driving motor of wealth creation.

If there was one incident which illustrated to me the real nature of Patparganj, it was this. I was travelling in a cycle-rickshaw, carrying some of the basic essentials for setting up the flat I had rented. The driver was a young man from Patna, and he was pedalling hard over the rough terrain. The sweat was pouring down his face in the afternoon sun, and he was straining every muscle to move the vehicle forward. We were stopped by a man, perhaps in his late fifties, who advised me pleasantly, 'Do not give him more than 2 rupees.' I looked at him in surprise. 'It is people like you', he said severely, 'who come here and ruin the market by paying these people too much'.

I looked at the skinny, wasted body of the migrant from Patna. This is the real meaning of the new India: to hell with the body and spirit of the people, but whatever you do, do not spoil the market, that holy of holies, the sacred, the true deliverer of humankind.

Brutalising the Rich

Everyone knows what poverty does to people: it degrades and dehumanises. The urgency of survival makes even the most honourable cheat and lie. In extremis, there is nothing people will not do to procure for themselves the necessities for survival. All of us realise that we, too, might be tearing at our neighbour's throat to get on the last train or the final flight out of a besieged city. We might also be reduced to buying rats for food, like the people on the streets of Cuito in Angola, or bartering our last pitiful possessions for fuel like the citizens of Sarajevo. We would certainly be capable of such strategies as the elective anorexia of young women on the streets of Manila, who starve themselves so as to pass as children, to satisfy the exotic tastes of Western sex tourists. Poverty numbs the moral sense, absorbs all energies, puts to sleep scruples, takes human beings to depths of cunning and desperation impossible to imagine under normal circumstances.

But does wealth ennoble? Do riches uplift? Are the privileged significantly more honest, hard-working and moral than the poor? Scarcely – in spite of the efforts of privilege to project itself as the model of virtue and integrity, to proclaim the justness of the extravagant rewards it enjoys. Indeed, wealth creation has become sacralised, and its agents are now objects of global public reverence. With what indulgent tenderness the media dwell upon their showy lifestyle and intemperance, the vital importance of their contribution to society, the selfless dedication of their quasi-monastic commitment to money. At the same time, the rich spare no pains to dissociate themselves from the venal, destructive and criminal behaviour of the poor, who, nevertheless, are their own creation and mirror-image.

Everywhere in the world, the rich are retreating deeper into their compounds of privilege. Sometimes, this means whole countries, even continents, as when the European Community firmly closes its doors against what it calls 'economic migrants', those who must be excluded. More often than not, it means sequestered and well-guarded suburbs. In Manila, for instance, the upmarket residential areas are demarcated by means of fortified border-posts: security forces occupy watchtowers and elecronically controlled, yellow-and-black painted barriers block the way to all traffic. You half expect to be asked if you have anything to declare. For here, perhaps, lies the most significant frontier of all in the modern world, a frontier that has less and less to do with natural or national boundaries. This is the increasingly policed and impermeable barrier between global rich and poor.

With 'modernisation', this polarisation is increasingly evident in India. Traditionally, even the most cruel inequalities and social injustices were at least integrated into a belief system that was deeper and more subtle than the stark antagonisms that appear between haves and have-nots. This more naked confrontation leads to a growing fear among the possessing classes who, accordingly, become more insensitive, more clamorous in defence of their fragile security, and more censorious of those excluded from it. As the world outside their gilded refuges turns increasingly into a wasteland, the resources enclosed and appropriated by the market economy, the commons used up, so the efforts of the poor to survive will become more desperate, and their strategies for doing so more crude.

Indeed, this is already happening, as may be gauged from the drawing-rooms of Delhi. At any social gathering of the elite, there will be a competitive exchange of horror stories about the crime wave, the menace on the streets, the growing disregard for life and property. An old woman was killed for the sake of a little gold jewellery. Chains are snatched with impunity in the streets. A house was invaded at gunpoint in broad daylight, with the connivance of the *chowkidar*. Elsewhere, all the servants decamped with their mistress's valuables.

What an irony, that these sorry tales should actually be an index of the 'success' of the new economic policies which, in every other respect, the rich applaud so noisily. For this is the meaning of wealth creation, modern-style: it is a zero-sum game, whereby some can be enriched only at the expense of others. And these others have no recourse but to recover some of the stolen energies, the confiscated labour, the destroyed self-reliance, the filched time, the broken spirit; and the only way open to them in the market economy is by a form of private enterprise called crime. This is also a caricature of the virtues of wealth creation which the well-to-do preach tirelessly, when they are not busy making killings on the Stock Exchange, scams and shady dealings, filtering their wealth into safe havens abroad, or flaunting their black money.

In other words, rich and poor live in a dynamic symbiosis; a double degradation which damages everyone; but a degradation of which the poor are not the initiators.

In Delhi last year, I spent a couple of weeks in an exclusive part of the city, a place which some friends lent me while they were out of town. In the leafy, salubrious retreat, where no one walks on the streets, and where there were more trees than people, did I find security or peace of mind? Not really. If I was permitted for a brief time to wander through the empty rooms of privilege, to live the spacious dreams of the rich, I also dreamed their worst nightmare. Are the bolts of the doors secure against intruders, will the metal grilles, the guard dogs, the automatic sensors that turn on the lights – will all this be enough to preserve me from attack?

It was impossible not to wonder whether the rich ever speculate on what might be happening beyond the secluded gates of their compound. When the car purrs to a halt at their marble doorstep, in order to whisk them away to some meeting of bankers, some bash of industrialists, some official political celebration, as they waft through the ample rooms whose doors are opened by unseen hands, do they not occasionally pause and ask themselves what would happen if all the people took at face-value the promise that has been made to them under the present regime, that everybody can achieve the same levels of amenity and comfort as the rich take for granted?

A deep resonant silence hangs over the sheltered habitations of the rich; broken only by the faint swish of the sweeper at 6.30 in the morning, the worn hands scooping up the fallen petals of bougainvillaea, the soundless movement of the cloth over marble floors, the faint trickle of water as it seeps through the terracotta flowerpots on the terrace. Disembodied hands put everything in its proper place, beds make themselves, objets d'art remain miraculously free of dust, laundry appears, freshly ironed, in the morning, meals arrive punctually at the table – are they laced with poison? Not, of course, the poison of arsenic or mercury, but the toxins of resentment and rancour of those who are doomed daily to contrast their own impoverishment with such excess.

Although no whisper of it reaches the ears of those who employ them, it is not difficult to learn of the discontent of the chowkidar who sits wrapped in a blanket against the freezing smoky dawn for Rs1,200 a month, the gardener who never has a day off in the year, the security personnel who have not seen their native Bihar for three years, the hunger of the children of domestic servants, the fatigue of the driver compelled to make a journey of 400 kilometres without a break, the sadness of the exiles from Kumaon and Garhwal, who see their loved ones for only 15 days a year, and who send two or three hundred rupees a month in compensation for their perpetual absence, their separation from cherished flesh and blood.

Yet these people are the lucky ones: any breath of dissatisfaction, and ten more people are waiting to fill their place, at even lower wages, with even longer hours of work, prepared to act out even greater displays of servility: the emaciated bodies around the ashes of last night's fire on the pavement will see to that.

Instead of becoming more sensitive to their plight, the rich build up a defensive mythology that dehumanises those impoverished in their service. They are thieves and drinkers, they beat their wives and have more children than they can feed. They have come to the city to prey on us; they are idle and improvident. Some even mutilate their own children, so that they will become more accomplished beggars.

The rich are now defending the indefensible. The present economic policies are designed to exacerbate, not close, the gulf between rich and poor. Those who have so energetically embraced liberalisation, modernisation, the Western way, should know that in

Britain, the distribution of wealth in the 1980s was as unequal as it had been in the heyday of Victorian squalor, the 1880s. So much for those who claim that 'ultimately' the market economy makes everyone rich. Ultimately is a long time. The poor cannot wait so long; ultimately, they will be dead, and their children also.

With the apparent demise of Communism, the privileged have assumed that conflict between rich and poor has abated, has even been laid to rest. They could not be more wrong. It may be that one form of political struggle has been vanquished, but new forms are already appearing in the alliances between the poor, Scheduled Castes and Tribes, and Muslims and Other Backward Castes. In any event, growing social injustice does not necessarily mean class war: crime, violence, criminal networks and mafias, assaults upon strangers for gain – these ornaments of Western civilisation are likely to become much more part and parcel of a streamlined modernised India.

One last glimpse of the privileged in Delhi: I was going to the airport by taxi in December 1994. In front of us, a vehicle with a VIP numberplate, a beige Mercedes, was holding the middle of the road, to prevent my driver from overtaking. Its occupants were two young men, clearly the sons of the owner, who, according to the numberplate, is someone of importance. It seemed they were drunk; at least, they were obviously taking great pleasure in weaving to and fro, so that each time the taxi tried to overtake, it came within millimetres of touching the car. At a roundabout, the taxi took a wide curve to avoid the vehicle. Enraged, the driver of the Mercedes crashed into the back of it. The taxi driver, a middle-aged Sikh, leapt out of his Ambassador car, and ran towards the Mercedes. He was furious, and prepared to pull the driver out and thrash him. The Mercedes backed rapidly – into an oncoming Honda scooter whose rider was thrown into the air. He landed on the road. We ran towards him. Both his legs were broken. The Mercedes had driven off at high speed. We later reported the incident to the police. When we told them the number of the car, DAD6, the police were obsequious and thanked us excessively for reporting the incident. The fullness of their thanks was the clearest indication that no action would follow.

Living on the Streets: The Cycle-Rickshaw Drivers in Winter

Nobody seems to know quite how many cycle-rickshaw drivers there are on the streets of Delhi; certainly the elderly rickshaw driver who insisted there are 'five lakhs' was exaggerating. But that there are many tens of thousands is beyond dispute. Many lead a strange double life between the reality of Delhi and the dream of home, and many travel frequently to and fro, going to the village in Bihar or eastern UP for a wedding, to help with the harvest, to avoid the rainy season in the city, returning whenever the earnings have been used up.

On winter nights, when the rickshaws are parked along the streets, in the Delhi shroud that is a mixture of fog, smoke and dust, they stretch into the distance, a tangle of wheels and handlebars, aligned in single file, with the drivers lying, head under the hood, torso along the crossbar and feet on the handlebars, swathed in dun-coloured blankets, like rows of bodies laid out after some terrible calamity. They demonstrate in what discomfort human beings can find sleep – a sleep so total that comes from a using up of energy, an expenditure of effort which scarcely replaces itself each day, so that to the natural process of ageing and loss is added another wear and tear, a net daily deficit of energy which the death-like sleep in the fragile vehicle can never restore.

Delhi only appears to be a flat city, a city of the plains: to the rickshaw driver, every small incline and declivity is known. He knows where he must get off and push, where he can freewheel for a kilometre, which journey will strain every nerve and sinew, which will drain the body of all liquid, so that he needs to drink and drink even in this, the coldest season.

Some share a room, five or six together in *jhuggi-jopris,* slum hutments, paying a rent of Rs300 or 400 a month between them; at least there they have the smoky warmth of a fire and one another's body. There is just such a settlement beneath the Barakhamba flyover, less than half a kilometre from Connaught Place; a series of mean huts, draped with black polythene and sacking, an invisible settlement nestling beneath the road designed as a monument to modernisation and speed; a place that stinks of piss, in permanent semi-darkness, dank and fetid in winter, intolerably airless in summer, heated by the furnace of the sun on the concrete above.

At least those who live communally can make their own food more cheaply than those who live without shelter. What these save on rent, they must spend on food. For Rs15 or 20 a day they can eat three times. Some men both live outside and prepare their own food: little improvised fires on the pavement, where rice and roti and a little vegetable can be bought for Rs 10 a day. This is how they manage to send money home – some as little as Rs100 a month, some 200: by living at the lowest level of subsistence.

And home means all over India, but especially Bihar; 'Patna se age', beyond Patna, they say. No, they have no land, the only work is seasonal, on the land of others. Many say they scarcely receive wages there, but work for food; bondage in all but name.

Mohammed Rashid is 65. He came to Delhi over 30 years ago. Delhi is his stepmother, he says mysteriously, perhaps meaning that here at least he survives; Delhi gives him enough to eat, whereas at home he must give everything to his five children.

Only when we get a government that is run by the poor, says Ramesh, a younger man, also from Bihar, with three children and no land, will we be free. Ramesh says his wife is a stranger and his children scarcely know him when he goes home. Articulate, radical, not the image of the patient long-suffering poor of India. He says we have been patient long enough. The day we get our freedom, that will be Independence Day in India. It must come. We are many, we are 80 per cent of the people. They are only a small minority, how can they stop us from taking the government, from giving justice to the poor?

But there are others who turn up their palms and their eyes and say Kya karna? What is to be done? They endure the cold in winter and the rains in summer. In the heat of Delhi, in May and June when most people find it too hot even to walk, they must still work; with a cloth or scarf around their head, their bare feet are splayed by pressing too hard against the pedals, the muscles in the thighs and calves are overdeveloped, the rippling muscles in the buttocks and back, after a few years of such work, grow stringy and spare. The oldest man I met was Khaled, originally from Lahore, who came to Delhi at the time of Partition, and has been a cycle-rickshaw driver there ever since. He said he was 76, and looked it. The youngest was a boy who said he was 12; driving on the dangerous road alongside the canal at Patparganj, he said he is the only earner in the family since his father died.

Why do they come to Delhi? The simple question elicits some strange responses. One boy of 15 had a quarrel with his father, and he left because he had beaten him. The family has 15 bighas of land, so it was not poverty, but wounded pride, that drove him the 200 kilometres to live independently in Delhi. Another boy told how he had been abused by a man in the room he shared; a man who had offered to look after him and protect him, but who used him as a sexual object; he tolerated it for three years because, he said, he had had no experience of Delhi, and imagined that this was a common practice in the city. A young man from Kanpur, a thin sad-faced 19-year-old, said that some people do not even pay the fare. 'Sometimes, they will throw 2 rupees at me, even for a long journey, and occasionally, nothing at all. What can I do? If I fetch a policeman he will beat me or ask for money. Most passengers do not talk to the drivers, and scarcely even notice their existence. They merely state the destination or dispute the fare.' And indeed, many do quarrel with the modest 5- or 10-rupee price which is the standard fare for a journey of a few hundred metres; as though to be swindled by the sweating, exhausted humanity that saves them the short walk is a humiliation not to be endured.

Is it demeaning work? Is it dehumanising for people to sit on the shabby red plastic upholstery while the vehicle judders and bumps over the speedbreakers and the pot-holes, while it is scratched and threatened by motor cycles, menaced by oncoming cars, sometimes overturned by speeding buses? It provides an income – average net profit is between Rs50 and 100 a day, but much depends upon luck, long hours of work, the vigour and strength of the driver. They must pay between Rs15 and 25 a day to the owners, according to the condition of the vehicle. Who are the owners? *Bara paisewalas,* but the driver has to pay for repairs if there is any damage. Kalu, a man in his forties, says that if it earns him an honest income, it is not degrading. 'How can it be, if it provides food for my wife and children? I am not ashamed. I can sleep at night, which those who cheat and steal from others cannot.' 'Of course,' says Shantiram, 'if there was other work, we would not choose to do this'.

The work is dangerous and unhealthy. The smoke from exhaust pipes swirls around them, the grit and carbon monoxide that simmer in the airless city streets, trapped by winter fogs, give rise to respiratory diseases, TB, constant coughs. They spit the red-coloured juice of betel in long crimson jets, as though disdainfully spitting out their lifeblood. If some of them drink – frightful decoctions reinforced with industrial alcohol or battery fluid – who can blame them for seeking some consolation for a life of eternal separation, loneliness and endless labour?

It is a sad thought, that only the bodies of these men, many emaciated, prematurely used up, lined, sweating, shabby, in soiled lungis and ragged vests, stand between absolute destitution and those they love; each one must support perhaps five or ten people in Bihar, eastern Uttar Pradesh or Orissa. The survival of vast swathes of rural India is dependent upon this migrant, casual and despised labour. What a cycle of waste, that the villages should become unable to support their people, without these debilitating migrations, in order that the village families should survive.

The work is degrading: it degrades them physically, even though this does not impair the dignity, even nobility, of the men whose life is continuous sacrifice for those they love. I spoke with one man who had had a long bout of fever, and who could scarcely work. He said, 'I have stopped sending money home. I spent what I had on medicine.' He raised a wasted arm. 'But it has not cured me. I cannot go and tell them that I am no longer fit to earn. I prefer to stay silent, and to die alone in Delhi.'

One story I heard two or three times, although nobody could identify the individual concerned. A man from Bihar has come to Delhi to work as a cycle-rickshaw driver. He is involved in an accident with a bus; his limbs broken, he is unable to work. At home, he has five daughters, the oldest 19. This young woman cuts off her hair, comes to Delhi and works as a man, driving the cycle rickshaw, and sending money home to the family. She lives on the streets, her sex undetected, grimy, strong, resolute. She has worked like this for seven years. Folklore? Perhaps, but not uncharacteristic of the extremes of sacrifice and love which many poor people, both women and men, continue to endure each day in India.

5. Uttar Kannada

After Appiko

There are three well-defined ecological zones in Uttar Kannada, the region covering the western Ghats in the north-west of Karnataka: the coastal belt, where most of the population is concentrated; then the central forested slopes of the Ghats, occupied mostly by prosperous farmers, including the owners of the *areca* gardens; and the eastern plain, where there are two crops a year, padi and a dry-season crop like *mungphali* (peanuts). In the coastal area, traditional varieties of padi have not been displaced by homogenised high-yielding varieties, because the traditional rice is resistant to sea-water.

Biodiversity in the hills is highly visible: the variety and density of tree cover in the areas of reserve forest are among the richest remaining in India: over 80 species of tree that were traditionally used for medicine, fodder, fuel, fruit, construction. Even encroachers who have, in places, invaded the secondary forest have not destroyed the trees: Shantaram built himself a house close to Sirsi using sun-baked bricks of mud gathered from the forest floor, areca-palm wood for the roof and bamboo for the frame of his house. Only the roof-tiles were purchased. Shantaram had a shop in Sirsi, but it failed and he had to sell; this is his response to failure. He has to walk a few metres down the rock, across the crisp brown furls of dead leaves that crack like shells beneath the feet, to fetch water from a perpetual spring. In his small enclosure, there is a hedge of tulsi, a plantain, a bush of white *nityapushpa* or everlasting flower (which is used as a medicine against cancer in the West), and some *ayurvedic* medicinal plants.

In the forests around Sirsi, the Appiko movement was born: the response in south India, inspired by the Chipko movement in the Himalayan foothills, to deforestation and the commercialisation of the forests. Conservation of the forests on which the people's livelihood and life itself depend is part of the very fabric of their lives.

The Appiko movement began in the villages of Salkani and Gubbegadde. The forest near Salkani is known as "the goddess forest", and it is traditional to worship the forest deity there', says Pandurang Hegde, who was born in Karnataka, and is a passionate voluntary activist in the movement to save the forests. By April 1983, after the Forestry Department had allowed a local plywood factory to fell trees there, what had once been thick forest was transformed into a barren site. The villagers had also observed that the streams on which their smallholdings depended were drying up. They decided to organise a movement of protest against the Forestry Department.

At the same time, the youth club in the neighbouring village of Gubbegadde, hearing of plans to clear 40 hectares of natural forest, took responsibility for organising village meetings of protest. Gubbegadde is about 6 kilometres off the main Sirsi–Kumta road, down a sandy red track, rocky and almost impassable for vehicles other than motor bikes. Older people here, like the father of areca-nut farmer Mahabaleshwar Hegde, say that fifty years ago, as soon as you stepped outside your house, you were in the jungle – it reached the front door. Now you have to walk 2 or 3 kilometres before you find natural forest. When he was a boy, there were tigers which used to come to the cattlehouse in search of food. It was not uncommon for herds of elephants to destroy the areca plantations. There was even a man who used to come and kill the wild elephants, a man known as Anebatta, the Elephant Man.

The areca-nut farmers are mostly Brahmins, and well-to-do, long-established landowners. Areca-nut cultivation is an ancient practice, and the houses of the farmers are substantial and beautifully constructed. Mahabaleshwar Hegde's is characteristic. The original house is over 100 years old: an earth-covered structure of wood, with a broad veranda and, in front, a shelter which is renewed annually for the storing and processing of areca nuts. The entrance to the house is through an elaborately carved door of solid rosewood and jackfruit wood, with motifs of elephants and flowers in the panels, and set in a yellow and blue painted frame. At one time, the entire extended family lived in this house, a series of dark rooms without windows: only the daylight from the front and from the back courtyard throws a cool thin light into the heart of the house, where the *puja* room with its shrine is illuminated by a dim red bulb; the offerings, hibiscus flowers and silvery slices of coconut, themselves seem to be the source of the strange muted radiance that lights the room. Behind is the dining room, where the whole family eat from banana leaves, sitting in two long lines against the wall; and beyond, the garden, where roses, chillis, hibiscus and *brinjals* (aubergines) grow.

This structure has now been expanded or, rather, four more

rooms have been constructed adjacent to it, three at right angles, so that they form a square where the areca processing takes place. A ladder leads from this central area to the red-tiled roof where, in January, the freshly harvested nuts are put to dry: orange and grey spheres detached from their clusters, laid out on bamboo mats in the sunlight. And the sunlight here, in this upland area, has a purity and density that you can almost touch; it throws shadows sharp as etchings into the dry earth.

Underneath, the women – migrant labourers together with family members – open up the tender green nuts: they sit on a wooden board with a sharp knife, curved like the crescent moon pointing upwards; with the point of this they impale the nut, and remove the shell, throwing the pale, flat kernel into a basket. The juice from the skin covers their hands, and creates a pervasive, bitter, resinous smell throughout the compound. Among the women working in the house of Mahabaleshwar Hegde is Bangara, a woman of 70. She wears a lilac-coloured blouse and grey saree. She works deftly, even though her hands are not as quick as they once were. Bangara is landless. Her family migrated here when she was a child, she does not know from where. She lives with her two adult grandsons, as she calls them, although in fact they are her sister's grandchildren. They all make a living in other people's fields, planting padi or harvesting areca nuts. She earns Rs15–20 a day; her grandsons get Rs25. She says, 'We can eat, we are not begging.' She considers it harder work to tear open the areca nut than to transplant padi, because the shell of the nut is tough and it requires considerable strength to prise it open. She works seven hours a day. In addition to her wage, she will have breakfast here – vegetable and roti – as well as lunch, which is generally masala dosa.

When her paid work is finished, she goes home to her domestic labour – collecting fuel, water and fodder for the cattle, and preparing the evening meal. Her boys are good, they will bring water and fuel. Fodder for the cattle must be bought, because they have nowhere to grow their own. Sometimes she will also cut fodder from the forest on her way home. Fuel she gathers in the natural forest, taking dead branches only. As she works, Bangara chews areca with tobacco; she spits a blood-coloured jet of liquid on to the earth. Here, says Bangara, we live happily. During the course of one day she will open about 3,000 nuts. In the villages, she says, there is no retirement. Livelihood finishes only with life itself.

There are about 120 families in Gubbegadde. Of these, 20–25 are padi farmers, cultivating rice on the valley floor; a similar number are owners of areca gardens. The rest have small pieces of land, varying in quality and productiveness, and there are about 25 landless families, who work as day-labourers on the land of others. They are more fortunate than the landless in many other places, because this is rich, fertile country, and there are rarely periods of the year when they cannot find employment. Furthermore, the areca farmers are for the most part enlightened; they pay their workers well, and do not oppress them.

The day-labourers are Scheduled Caste families, and they live – illegally – on what is minor forest land. They have migrated from Kumta, from the village of Hegde, about 50 kilometres away. In their home-place, they have a little land, which other members of the family cultivate. They migrated because the land they own cannot support them all. They work in Gubbegadde in the areca gardens and in the padi-fields, performing any seasonal labour the landowner requires, transplanting padi in the rainy season, harvesting padi in December, then harvesting the areca nuts, or grass-cutting in winter. In summer, they collect dry leaves from the forest for the areca gardens, fetch soil to nourish the trees, or take manure from the cattlehouse to the areca trees. Men earn Rs20 a day, the women Rs15. That is not enough for a livelihood, but when several members of the family are working it is sufficient. I asked why the women earn less than the men, when the work they do is apparently the same. They considered the question, and then said it was because women cannot carry as much as men, and women cannot climb trees to bring down the areca nuts. Maru Gouda, a man in his sixties, organises the migrant families to work in the landowner's fields. In his family, five or six members work in this way. He is both organiser and contractor, and for this receives some commission.

Because they have not migrated a long distance, they return home frequently. Maru Gouda had visited his native place only one week earlier. The people work seven hours a day in the fields, and when they return, they have their own work to do. Most have one or two cows; they buy fodder at the rate of Rs10 per head of cattle. Fuel they take from the natural forest. There are six in Maru Gouda's family. The women say it costs Rs90 per day to eat adequately – that is the total combined daily wage of four women. Everything has to be bought in the market – rice, coconut, vegetables, *togri* or *hessera* dal, even chillis. The people are traditional agriculturists of the Mukri caste, but as the families have grown, their own land has become insufficient to support all their members; hence the necessity for migration. Yet it is not such a brutal and sad migration as that of people who must travel vast distances to the city to work as construction labour. A sense of dignity and rootedness remains.

The houses of the migrants are self-built, decent structures which are pale imitations of the far grander houses of the land-owners: a veranda, under which are stored the tools of their work, the scythe and axe, and the board with the blade which is used for opening the areca nuts. Because they belong to Scheduled Castes, they get some help from the government, for instance 500 roof-tiles for the house. Apart from that, the house costs nothing but the labour of constructing the bamboo frame with its coating of earth. The people eat non-vegetarian when they can; some chickens are searching for food around the small compound. They catch fish in the *nalla* (stream) with a net, sometimes using the powdered bark of a tree to stun them and so take them more easily. There is one electricity point, also given by the govern-ment. A well stands just beyond the house, but this dries up in summer. There is no health-post in the scattered village, and the nearest doctor is 10 kilometres away, at Sirsi. No bus passes within 5 kilometres, where the main road begins. They have cycles and a radio, but no TV and no motor cycle.

They discuss what is rich and poor. They are indeed poor, says Maru Gouda, 'but poverty is not eating us up. We work, and that gives us self-respect, and people with self-respect are not poor.'

The compound provides them with a small garden. The well is deep – about 40 feet – with mud walls, and is covered by a wooden roof thatched with coconut husks. The water is sweet and pure. There is a big tamarind tree, brown pods of the fruits ripening. Its shade covers the whole compound. They have no legal title to be here, but no objection is made because they are in the service of well-to-do people, and they have no alternative source of livelihood.

But it is partly the presence of migrants in the village, says Mahabaleshwar Hegde, that is responsible for the pressure on forests. The other, more intensive, pressure has come from illegal loggers, timber merchants and contractors, many of whom have powerful political backers. It is too easy to blame the poor, who are taking only enough for their daily needs, but who are highly visible, when the loggers and contractors do their work surrepti-tiously, and cover a wider area. The cultivators take only dead branches, working for subsistence, but the large-scale fellers work from greed.

I walk with Mahabaleshwar Hegde around the *betta lands*, which serve his 2 acres of areca nut. The betta lands are essential to areca-garden owners, to serve their needs for manure, fuel and fodder. Like the minor forest areas, the betta lands have also been over-exploited. On the edge, the pink blossoms of glycidia, the leaves of which are used for manure: pale pink blossoms on bare grey branches. The betta lands create a strange landscape: trees may not be cut down, but they have been lopped in such a way that they look like the ruined pillars of some great architectural structure fallen into decay; and in a way that is what they are, because once they were dense forest.

The trees on the betta lands are lopped every three or four years to cover the roots of the areca palms. This year there has been a lopping: the side-branches and dead leaves are piled up on the ground, leaves of *mutti, honala, kavla.* Even in the degraded betta lands, there are some 50 species of tree, although in the natural forests, ten times as many may be found. Hegde points out *kassaka,* which is used as a pesticide, while *amlaka* is useful for cleaning teeth.

The poor depend upon the natural forest for many things that make the difference in their lives between a cramped poverty and a reasonably comfortable sufficiency. The poor need the forest for medicines, fruits, fodder and fuel. Most will not go to the doctor with attacks of fever or dysentery, but will go to the forest, because they know where to find effective remedies. People know which fruits come in season, winter fruits now, like the amla, which is a kind of tough gooseberry, but rich in vitamin C and also effective against some kinds of dysentery; in the summer, a different crop of fruits will come, and again in the rainy season. The poor will sometimes catch and eat hares or even wild boars. Geru nuts are now in season, and also the soap-berries which are drying outside some of the houses: crushed, these will make a lather for washing clothes as effective as anything produced by the multinationals.

We sit on the enclosed veranda, which is a kind of antechamber to the house: a wooden settle and big wooden bed, where Hegde's father sleeps now. Some folding tin chairs, clocks, graduation certificates and family photographs on the wall. A staircase of stained rosewood, and an upper balcony of the same wood. The floor is stained a dark red. There are bars at the windows, and birds wheel in and out of the open door, perch cheekily on the photographs of deceased family members. Outside, the rasp of the areca-nut cutters, the occasional trill of birds. Thin slivers of rich orange sunlight penetrate the cool shady interior; a place of peace and calm, of which these prosperous Brahmin families are the custodians and guarantors.

In this village, Appiko was born. *All members of society depend upon the forests in one way or another,* says Hegde, *so it was easy to get people to unite over the issue. Everybody had seen the decline of the forest. Between 1950 and 1990, forest cover was reduced in Karnataka from 85 per cent to around 25 per cent. For 30 years, there had been clear-felling of natural forest, first of all for monocultures of teak, then of eucalyptus, and then more recently of acacia. People were shocked to see the forest disappearing closer and closer to their own land. Then some 100 acres had been marked for clear-felling, 100 acres of natural forest. The people in the villages around could not believe it. But they felt helpless because the forest officials were there, representatives of government, marking the trees for felling.*

We discussed it among ourselves, What could we do to halt the destruction? This had not happened suddenly, not in one day. For a long time, we had been seeing the ruin of the forest environment. But the helplessness was there. We had made applications to the Minister, to officials, to the Forest Department; but nothing happened.

The village youth club, my brother among them, were discussing what to do. By chance, Sunderlal Bahaguna, of the Chipko movement, was coming to Sirsi taluka to make a speech. Somebody told us we should go to Sirsi to meet with him and take suggestions as to what to do. We were despairing, so we went to Bahaguna. We discussed with him, and brought him to the forest where the trees had been marked for felling. We called a meeting in the school. It was the rainy season, and he had to come by jeep. That night he made a one-hour speech in our village, telling us about Chipko and what they had achieved. More than 200 people came to the meeting. It was an inspiration. He filled us with such a powerful sense of what we could do. The youth club and others knew then what was needed; and we didn't feel helpless any more. The seeds of Appiko were sown at that meeting.

The work started. People began to watch the forest, to look out for officials or contractors who would come to cut. This is called the Bilekal Forest. People went to live among the trees, staying in groups, day and night. When the axemen did come, they requested them not to damage the trees, but to go away. The axemen belonged to the same community, their families also depend upon the forest. The contractor then came, and we tried to convince him of the importance of the forest. He came back with officials, and said he was going to bring the police. Bahaguna had said to us that there should be no violence. There was none, in spite of their attempts to provoke the people.

They cut ten trees by night. From that moment, the forest was guarded constantly. But in some other forests, in nine or ten places, trees had also been marked for clear-felling. The movement spread to the other villages around. Pandurang Hegde came and he translated Bahaguna's speech into Kannada; he helped us to spread news of the struggle.

The Forest Minister of Karnataka came and met the people. He was convinced by the devastation that had already occurred and was continuing. He gave orders on the spot that there should be no more clear-felling. Then the Forest Department made some efforts to fell in a more selective way. But even that we opposed. People were saying, 'This is natural forest, it should not be touched.' The movement spread. For two or three years, our people covered three talukas with a padayatri, telling the message. People can take the dead trees, the old leaves from the forest, but nothing else. No living tree shall be touched. People cannot come from the city just like that, and take away that which sustains our life.

After that, the message changed from 'Save the Trees' to 'Plant the Trees'; from being a negative resistance, it became a positive fostering and nurturing of the forest, a protest against monoculture.

Appiko began in September 1983, over ten years ago. There were many seminars and discussions. People came from outside, to understand the movement, to hold discussions. The press came, people from abroad. We made songs and constructed dances and music about our trees. I myself wrote many lyrics for the songs. Appiko is the Kannada equivalent of Chipko: in Kannada it means the same thing. Hug the trees.

In 1984, it became State policy that the natural forest should remain untouched, no green felling. That remains the policy.

People use the natural forest without looting it, because the forest forms the basis of their lives. They will not degrade the natural forest. But contractors and smugglers do not see it that way. Smuggling continues, of course. There are corrupt forest officials who will connive at the irregular and destructive felling. People still watch out for smugglers; people come and go in the forest at all hours of day and night. If I want a medicinal plant, I'll go to the forest. If a tree has been cut, I'll come and tell the people, and they will be vigilant in that place.

The minor forest is different. That is common land for the farmers' use, for grazing and so on. That has been degraded by over-grazing and over-cutting. In the minor forest areas, they are now planting acacia, which the Forest Department takes to its timber yards to sell. People are against acacia plantations, as they would be against any other monoculture, even if it is mutti or honala or any local species. So we say 40 per cent of the acacia plantations must also be natural forest. But at least, now they are not cutting in order to plant acacias: they are leaving the existing trees and planting around them, in the gaps between.

The damage done is already considerable. The spices which the British came for originally are also vanishing: the pepper creepers are dying *from some virus. Nobody knows how to treat it. The bananas have also died in the area, another fungal problem. The Agriculture Department doesn't know anything. Some say it's the effect of deforestation, mono-cultures, climate change, untimely rains, soil erosion – there is no short-age of reasons. The village people notice even minute changes in the patterns of natural phenomena that govern their lives.*

The traditional way of maintaining the betta lands must be kept up, or they will be irretrievably lost also. That means cutting the trees only once every three or four years, and bringing the leaves and branches to the plantation. Other years, simply collect the dry leaves and any fallen branches. The betta lands have become degraded, because people are not following the traditional way – the land can-not support the pressure placed on it. People have come here from outside the area, because their land is unproductive, and they can find a livelihood here, they can find labour. Some migrate seasonally, others have settled here. One quarter of the people in Gubbegadde come from elsewhere. If the population is now 1,000, then 300 will have come from outside, and that may be enough to make the differ-ence between what the land can carry and what it cannot. People who have migrated to our village have come, either from the coastal area, or from the rainshadow maidan – plain – to the east. Most are Mukris, Scheduled Caste people.

We return to the house. Mahabaleshwar's son, a boy of about nine, walks half an hour to and from school each day. He pauses in the forest with his friends to enjoy the fruits, nuts and edible berries of the forest. 'In our gardens we all grow tulsi, not only because it is sacred, but also because it is useful for certain complaints, like mouth ulcers. When we want medicines urgently we do not run to the pharmacy. There is none, anyway. We have a forest pharmacy at hand. There is the long leaf of a parasite that grows on one species of tree, which is good for ear infections: simply put the leaf on the fire, take one or two drops and the pain will disappear. *Kahigirige* is a small plant used for fever. It is very bitter: just boil it in water, mix with milk and sugar, and it brings down the fever. In our garden we have nityapushpa, which is used for diabetes. Amla will be effective against dysentery, and is rich in vitamins. In fact, we recognise different kinds of dysentery and the various remedies for it. The bark of the *atta* tree will cure another form: boil it in water, mix with *gur* or sugar; green bananas also will cure yet another kind of diarrhoea. The leaf of the *shunti* plant is good for bad digestion or overeating. The people don't have to be taught all these things. Every family knows the uses of everything in the forest.

The government seeks to destroy self-reliance. Modernisation means the end of self-sufficiency, and development means violence against the self-reliant way of life. The people here will be happy if they are permitted simply to continue to be self-dependent. To us here, development is a war-like thing, a declaration of war against people who just want to be left alone to live. We did not initiate this violence: it was begun by contractors, forest officials, government workers and business people who want to turn our peaceful life into dependency.

Mahabaleshwar's father says: *The suffering of the common man is the same as it was in the British time. It lives on through our system of government. When 'development' comes, there might be more facilities, but as far as peace of mind goes, it is simply not there. People are restless. They do not know the satisfactions of working with the forest. For us, forest means natural forest, or it isn't forest. If it does not fulfil the farmer's need, it is not forest.*

Mahabaleshwar shows me through the complex series of houses where his extended family lives: a long vista of dim, fragrant rooms, with the light falling on hard, earthen floors. There is an upper storey, a long guest room, with blankets and mattresses in a corner. In the middle, fluted rosewood pillars of a girth which you never see in contemporary rosewood, more than a foot in diameter. The wood is hard as iron. The furniture – rambling *almirahs* and cupboards of teak, rosewood or jackfruit. The house is an apparently random congeries of structures, but cool and airy, with the warm wind passing through the slatted windows. At the back, a garden enclosed by a crumbling mitti wall, tulsi in painted earthen pots, starry jasmine scenting the air, the smell of sweet dry grass, gobar and buffaloes. The betta land behind is strewn with dead leaves in this, the winter season, huge leaves, some wasted to the threadbare skeleton of the leaf.

Everything in use in the house and its dependencies is recyclable: mitti and wood and gobar; as though these human settlements had come up with the earth itself; and although of some antiquity, they can readily be reabsorbed, without pollutants, with no residue of poison or contaminant. A hive of wild bees which Mahabaleshwar found in the forest, built into an old piece of wood, hangs from the veranda; the bees form their complicated skeins of movement in the air, filling it with their musical vibrations; honey is taken once a year, for its medicinal use.

The dazzling afternoon sunshine from a clear unpolluted sky at 600 metres above sea level sends dense shafts of sunlight through the air, lighting up the dust, chaff and the tiny shimmering insects. On either side of the rough track out of the village, the red dust has discoloured the foliage, so that it looks like rusty metal ornaments rather than living things. As the road passes through stands of natural forest, the air cools perceptibly, and the fresh breath of the forest is a relief after the harsh sunlight. Here, the rich are not extravagant, the poor not wretched; people are united in their dependency upon and defence of the forests.

The Farmers' Movement in North Karnataka

The farmers of northern Karnataka have been leading the resistance against the government of India acceding to the GATT negotiations which were formally signed in Morocco in April 1994. Opposition grew throughout 1992 and 1993 to the implications for India of the setting up of the World Trade Organisation, which came into being in January 1995, and which is to 'police' the arrangements contained in the GATT agreement. These will have significant repercussions on India, and indeed are seen by many as an assault on the country's independence: its patent laws will have to be amended, and it must recognise intellectual property regimes which will give yet more power to multinational corporations, notably to those in one of the most sensitive areas for Indian self-reliance – control and manipulation of the seeds from which the country's food crops are grown.

The GATT talks were taking place at the time when the Indian government was negotiating with the International Monetary Fund and World Bank for significant loans which have increased the foreign debt to around $90 billion. This precluded any resistance – which, it has to be admitted, the Indian government showed little desire to show – to the provisions of GATT, however disadvantageous these might turn out to be to the people of India.

There are two fundamental issues. One is the hold which the parastatal companies will have over Third World farmers, if they become dependent on their seeds. The farmers will have to buy afresh each year, and will not even be permitted to keep seed from their own crop, as they have traditionally done. Secondly, these seeds 'owned' by the parastatals come from germ-plasm given freely by Third World farmers, having been bred over centuries as being best guaranteed to survive in the climate and the ecological niche where they were developed. The genetic manipulation by the seed companies – often only a minor modification of the originals to produce high-yielding varieties – then gives them proprietorship over seeds whose evolution has actually been a long and painful process in situ. This, say the farmers of India, is piracy, a theft of intellectual property rights on a grand scale; compared to this, the copying or counterfeiting of the artefacts of a Western junk culture, which is one of the chief concerns of intellectual property regimes, is an insignificant offence.

But the most important consequence of this enclosure and patenting of the heritage of humanity, the seed, is that it will spread monocultures, and will make the world dangerously dependent upon a narrowing genetic base for its food. Genetically engineered strains may produce high yields, but they can wipe out diversity over a vast area in just one season, as indeed has already occurred in many parts of the world. Dependency on a single strain of one crop may lead to widespread losses if the crop is attacked by a single pest against which no remedy exists. The most spectacular example of this in the modern world was the Irish potato famine in the 1840s: a single variety of potato, introduced from South America, was completely destroyed by a blight which it could not resist in the place to which it had been transferred, with the consequences for Ireland that are well known. Similar occurrences are inevitable, as the diversity of strains of major crops shrinks. At issue is the biodiversity of the planet – the range and richness not merely of food crops, but also of medicinal plants, many of them still untested in the threatened forests, the survival of myriad species of plants, animals, insects and birds which are of incalculable value.

The priority for the Indian government under its burden of loans is to earn foreign exchange so as to service the debt. This means a shift from self-reliance, which has been at the heart of Indian rhetoric (and, to a lesser extent, Indian reality) since Independence. And a movement away from self-reliance is a shift from food security. When non-food crops or, indeed, luxury foods are exported, there follows a reduction in the land available for food crops to be consumed locally. This leads to dependency on imports of food, further draining resources and deepening subordination to creditor countries.

It has been seen by the farmers of north Karnataka as an issue of freedom versus servitude. This is why, on 2 October 1992, the Seed *Satyagraha* was launched in Bangalore. One year later, at a gathering of almost half a million farmers on Gandhi's birth anniversary, Quit India notices were issued to the Cargill company, whose high-yielding sunflower seeds had been used by many farmers in north Karnataka, particularly around Raichur. The promised yield of 15 quintals per hectare had been far from realised; few had harvested 5 quintals.

The movement is seen by many in India as a new freedom struggle, a rejection of what has been described as the colonisation of the seed. The only thing that stands between the farmer and famine is his own seed; and if that seed has been patented by a transnational company, its use would become outlawed under the new intellectual property regime.

To deal with these novel forms of subordination, representative democracy is inadequate. Direct action becomes necessary. The Constitution of India must be retrieved, taken back into our own hands from those who are defiling it – the representatives of the people, says Professor Nanjundaswamy, who speaks for the farmers. *The biotechnology industry is leading to the patenting of life forms, to control over life itself. The Green Revolution, which had depended upon expensive inputs, chemical fertiliser and pesticides controlled by the parastatals, also led to a loss of diversity. Gene-banks controlled by the West now hold the diversity of the farmers' fields; and these are patented as their property.*

The law of the market is now superseding all others. On Independence Day, 15 August 1993, we declared independence and collective property rights. We insist on a free exchange of seed and knowledge across the globe, boycotting and bypassing the enclosers, the landlords, the controllers of a biodiversity, which belongs to the people. The movement, based on resistance, is now becoming a more positive assertion of popular rights; a new meaning of the word 'freedom' is being defined.

Everywhere I went in India in 1993, I found farmers and cultivators concerned about GATT, the World Trade Organisation and its likely implications for India. It has become a major popular issue, in Orissa, Andhra Pradesh and Uttar Pradesh as well as Karnataka.

Vandana Shiva, now an adviser to the FAO, since her study of the effects of the Green Revolution in the 1970s, has devoted herself to spreading understanding of what the erosion of biodiversity means. For a long time, she says, it remained a puzzle to her: how to make visible something so abstract, an unseen malign process. In the end, she says, it was done for us, by Dunkel and the GATT issue and the pressure from the United States on India to alter its patent laws.

GATT and Dunkel were the embodiment of an intellectual property regime and of the violence this would do to us. Resistance came at first from the indigenous pharmaceutical industry and health workers. This is because the Indian patent laws have a process patent but not a product patent: broadly, this means that Indian manufacturers can make vital, life-saving drugs more cheaply by a different process from those controlled by the multinationals. This has made many essential drugs available to the people of India, which otherwise would have had to be bought from the transnationals. This freedom would be swept away under the new intellectual property regime, and the cost of drugs would soar, as indigenous manufacturers were forced to give way to transnational monopolists.

While this rather difficult struggle was going on, the farmers had already seen clearly that the seed, the symbol of life itself, was the next object of colonisation.

Our second unlikely ally in making visible the biodiversity crusade was the structural adjustment programme. Liberalisation had opened up the seed sector for the first time in 1992. That was the first year Cargill began marketing seed. Previously there had been no multinational interest in that area. Cargill's publicity had promised a yield of up to 15 quintals per acre for its sunflower seeds. Many farmers in northern Karnataka who had bought the new hybrids discovered that the yield was nowhere near this. They knew from experience that they had been cheated. Given that background, their frustration and anger enabled them to see the significance of the new global political economy of biodiversity. That is how the struggle for seed freedom, the Seed Satyagraha, came into existence.

The farmers' response was on a scale we could not have anticipated. It began on 2 October 1992, and by March 1993 it had drawn half a million people. And scientists and social activists from all over the world have linked themselves to the farmers' struggle. The farmers did a remarkable thing. They collected pots full of coins, 50-paise, 25-paise, and presented it as seed money for the setting up of an international institution for sustainable agriculture. Land is being acquired, and there will be a centre for the exchange of knowledge, information, training and research. The farmers will do it, in partnership with scientists and others who recognise the urgency of the task.

The Cargill struggle is only a small part of the new Quit India Movement. The idea is eventually to cease using all multinational inputs. But it is so inspiring to see a spontaneous popular movement come into existence. The Congress(I) has tried to keep the issue as a matter for experts, as though it were too important to be left to the people. This is what happens in the West, where people's knowledge has been so profoundly invalidated that almost everyone is ready to surrender to experts and professionals. It has not happened here. In fact, GATT turned into a major electoral battleground. One of the encouraging things is that there has also been support for us in Europe and the United States, where demonstrations were held outside Cargill offices. International solidarity will increase, because there are two globalisations at work – global popular mobilisation has begun against the globalising tendencies of the transnational corporations.

There could be no more profound or resonant metaphor than the colonisation of the seed. The link with women needs no explanation. Women's concern is with the conservation and enhancement of life.

They know instinctively that patenting and private ownership of life-forms run counter to this.

I have drawn much strength from the women in Chipko and similar struggles. In Staying Alive,* *I wrote about the women who had been beaten up after protesting against mining in the Doon Valley. They were attacked by goondas with chains and rods. I went up there, expecting to see them all bandaged up and incapacitated. They were in bandages, but they were all back on the site. I was overwhelmed. I asked them where they found their strength. One old woman said, 'We grow our own food, we milk our own cows, what can they take away from us? We are like the grass that grows: when it is trampled, it springs back. We are like the trees we lop for fodder: each year new growth comes. We have that same power to spring back.'*

Loss of freedom begins with the loss of control over food production. You can have other freedoms, but these will always be superficial, limited and dependent. Once you have lost that basic freedom, you have no grounds on which to reclaim it. This is something most people in the West, except those on the fringes, do not understand. In India, this is one of the basic freedoms the farmers have and are fighting to retain.

Lutzenberger, the Brazilian ecologist, came to our meeting in Bangalore. He said that in today's world 'No one is free but those who produce their own food. But because you are free, you are the biggest threat to the system, and they will try to get rid of you. They will introduce unproductive technologies in the name of progress, destructive mechanisms to eliminate you and call it advanced technology. Technology is used as an instrument, not of liberation, but of enslavement.'

In a few months, we have moved from a negative struggle against the patenting of life forms to a collective assertion of the maintenance and protection of life. In farming, women and men are together in partnership with the soil. What is being violated is the collective heritage of Third World countries. When neem *is patented by a Western company, this is not recognised in Western jurisprudence as theft. Only individuals can steal. The great irony is that collective intellectual property piracy is taking place, precisely by those claiming intellectual property rights. At our rally on 2 October the farmers declared that the characteristics of seeds cannot be created. Nature and farmers together form a creative process. This is co-creation, co-production, coming from those who participate in it, in their daily lives.*

---

* Vandana Shiva, *Staying Alive*, London, Zed Books, 1989

Vandana Shiva offers another dramatic example of the dispute over the patenting of products derived from plants on the basis of indigenous knowledge: the patenting of neem. For centuries, the Western world ignored the neem tree and its properties, even though neem has always been used as a biological pesticide, and neem twigs are still used by people all over India to clean teeth – a far more effective preservative and cleansing agent than anything sold by the transnationals.

The practices of Indian peasants and doctors were not deemed worthy of attention by the majority of colonists. However, in the last few years, growing opposition to chemical products in the West, in particular to pesticides, has led to a sudden enthusiasm for the pharmaceutical properties of neem. Since 1985, over a dozen US patents have been taken out by US and Japanese firms on formulae for stable neem-based solutions and even for a neem-based toothpaste. At least four of these are owned by W.R. Grace of the US. Having garnered their patents, Grace have set about manufacturing and commercialising their product by establishing a base in India. The company approached several Indian manufacturers with proposals to buy up their technology or to convince them to stop producing value-added products, and instead supply the company with raw material. Grace is likely to be followed by other patent-holding companies. 'Squeezing bucks out of the neem ought to be relatively easy', observed Science *magazine.*

W.R. Grace's justification for patents hinges on the claim that these modernised extraction processes constitute a genuine innovation. However, the novelty consists mainly in the context of the ignorance of the West. Over the 2,000 years that neem-based biopesticides and medicines have been used in India, many complex processes were developed to make them available for specific use, though the active ingredients were not given Latinised names.

Vandana Shiva believes that the Karnataka farmers' movement would not have become such a focus for resistance without the pressures from the macro-economic 'reform' package. Without this, she believes that India might have been subjected to a slow erosion of biodiversity, which would have made it more difficult to organise public feeling against the process. Without Dunkel and Manmohan Singh, the Finance Minister, there would have been no Seed Satyagraha. The 'shock therapy' of economic restructuring creates its own response. If it had happened slowly, that response might not have come.

The farmers used the same tactics as the mainstream. Opposition came as a mirror of the process. They dismantled the Cargill plant in Bangalore. They did it in half an hour. At six it was standing; by

6.30 *it had been demolished. The farmers have been able to maintain solidarity because even the police have rural roots, and they recognise that the farmers' struggle does not run against the interests of themselves and their own families.*

The biggest threat to the world will be if the present burst of colonialism succeeds in making the ownership of life possible, in making life-forms private property. To achieve this, violent, coercive structures have to be set up. In reaction to it, a second violent response occurs, not always against the perpetrators, but against other victims – in the guise of communalism, caste and ethnic violence.

The farmers' struggle inspires hope, because it creates a block to the spread of the communal virus. Because people have something positive to strive for, their constructive agenda overrides all the destructive forces in the country.

The farmers' efforts have made the successful transition from a reactive struggle into an endeavour towards sustainability and justice, a reaffirmation both of popular action and social hope.

Nanjundaswamy says that the farmers of north Karnataka were victims of propaganda. Cargill had promised high yields for sunflower, and is now making the same promise for its strains of maize. *The propaganda and promises worked for two years, but the experience of the farmers ran counter to their claims. Now Cargill have stopped talking about sunflowers and are promoting maize instead. Maize will not be used for consumption, but will become part of the value-added products of Cargill for consumption in other countries. Indians will not consume what they grow here.*

We have made the seed the symbol of the Second Freedom Movement; where Gandhi used the spinning wheel, we are using the seed. For us, there is no schism between environment and social justice; it is one and the same thing. In Europe it may appear differently, because the majority of people do not depend directly upon the land for their sustenance, or if they do, there are so many processes interposed between them and their dependency on the earth that they do not perceive it.

The struggle is not new. It began in 1980, as a fight back against the effects of the Green Revolution. Not only in Karnataka, but in Punjab, Tamil Nadu, Maharashtra. It was widely felt by 1980 that the Green Revolution enslaved farmers to the multinationals: crops as diverse as sugar cane, rice, wheat, oilseeds, cotton, silk, all of which had been promoted as miracle seeds, began to show declining yields, even as doses of fertiliser and pesticides increased, became excessive, and soil fertility declined; increasing pests accompanied by increasing debts. Many farmers became landless. A declining number of people worked as farmers and cultivators.

The second factor in the enslavement of the farmers was the intellectual property rights regime which simply makes their dependency more total. The government says we have no choice over the protecting of seeds, plants and living organisms. We say we do have a choice. To have no choice is to be unfree. We say that choice is self-reliance. Under the rules of GATT there will be no government of India, but a governance of multinationals. Government is reduced and bypassed, will become a spectator of the fate of India.

The government knows what it is doing. It operates out of self-interest. To pass the destiny of our country over to the West is treachery. There is no pride and no patriotism left in it. What does the West intend for us? What do they want? Control, the better to exterminate. They have for 500 years plundered the earth and eliminated those peoples who were an inconvenience to them, whether Aboriginals, natives of North America, the inhabitants of the Inca and Maya civilisations. Now what is inconvenient to them is the poor. What they call population. Well, that means our people. Extermination has never been far from their project of conquest, and nor is it now. Famine, hunger, death from starvation, this is their weaponry in what they call economic adjustment, but is actually their war on the poor. What has occurred in sub-Saharan Africa can occur in the entire Third World. And it will not matter to them.

The farmers realise that their freedom is jeopardised. They are having second thoughts about cash crops. There will be a shift towards sustainable agriculture. Not subsistence; surplus farming is possible with sustainable agriculture. But the increase in cash-crop areas makes them vulnerable and dependent upon imported food.

I deny the government's claim that we are self-reliant. We achieve it by keeping half the population half-starved. We have to reduce cash-crop areas and shift to food production. There are many distortions in our agricultural production. There is a shortage of pulses because of areas that have turned to cotton or silk-growing. Pulses are the food of the poor. They fetch a low price, and that is government policy. Cash crops are more attractive than growing pulses because of a defective agricultural policy.

The modernisation process, whether Congress Westernising and liberalising, or BJP, also liberalising, will serve the interests of only the topmost castes and classes, that is about 6 per cent of Indian society, 4 per cent Brahmins and 2 per cent Vaishyas, traders. The so-called fundamentalists accept GATT, they want to link India's fortunes to external forces for their own benefit. This does not mean that the traditional Indian upper-caste sensibility is weakened. On the contrary, it is a reinforcement of it, through this new linkage with global capital. It is an externally buttressed version of the internal caste system. Indeed, this is India's gift to the world, a global caste system in which the poor are destined to remain for ever excluded. GATT and the World Trade Organisation represent that process. The elections in UP in November 1993 [bringing to power the Mulayam Singh Yadav government, a coalition of *Dalits*, Other Backward Castes and Muslims] *show the reaction coming from the backward classes to this cultural and monetary imperialism. But whatever confrontations may occur, these have not been sought or initiated by the poor. The war that has been declared is the war of the rich waged against the global poor.*

The Farmers' Movement contested the State elections in Karnataka in October 1974. Not only did it fail to gain more seats, but Nanjundaswamy, who had been elected to the State Assembly four years earlier, lost his seat. Many now feel that electoral politics undermines the moral force of popular movements.

6. Calcutta

In a small park near the Esplanade in Calcutta there is a statue of Marx and Engels, standing together. The statue is enclosed by protective metal railings, a monument to heroic socialist unrealism. Their eyes are fixed upon a distant horizon, far beyond the limits of Calcutta.

On the opposite corner of the park, rats swarm out of holes in the ground. People, fascinated, feed them bread and *channa;* a grey seething mass on the grey earth which is honeycombed with passages, and has subsided here and there, leaving their nests exposed to the light.

On the grass in the park lie some of the poorest of Calcutta, an exhausted wreckage of humanity, people whose lives have been eaten away by poverty, sickness, alcohol, despair or drugs. Some of them are sprawled in attitudes of utter abandonment, others curled foetally against the world. Many are almost naked apart from a ragged lungi or a vest that is a lattice of holes.

Above this scene soar the imperial structures of the Raj, many of them now ruinous, with broken Corinthian pillars, eroded capitals, crumbling balustrades, great stone doorways befitting the ceremonial comings and goings of servants of the empire. On collapsed roofs and decayed brickwork an eruption of foliage and flowers.

In the shadow of these dilapidations, a population of hawkers and hucksters, selling – mostly imitation – Western luxury goods, perfumes like urine samples, labelled Estee Lauder or Givenchy, false Hechter shirts, bogus Nike sportswear, fake Gucci bags, a vast pirating of intellectual property rights of what, even in its original form, is high-class junk. And then a host of petty vendors of watches, razors, calculators, sunglasses, novelties and toys, cars operated by remote-control, yo-yos that light up as you throw them. Finally, the sellers of the degraded artefacts of former rural artisans.

In the tourist areas around Sudder Street, the warm Bengal night is peopled with whispering shadows, nice Chinese girl, clean and cheap, you want some hash, you like *brown sugar,* change money, Indian boy 200 rupees suck, 400 rupees fuck.

Calcutta, site of multiple overlapping imperialisms and ideologies that have done nothing for the people of this ruined, energetic, pitiless city. In Calcutta, there is no bottom line, no level below which a human being will not be allowed to fall.

The authorities have not even effaced the racist engravings from the public statuary of the Raj. Lord Bentinck, Governor-General of India, looks benignly upon the prostitutes who emerge out of the dusk, a pale, brief dance of colour in the gloom, before they pair off with the loitering men, and merge into the roots of the flame-of-the-forest trees. On the plinth where Bentinck stands, a scroll states that although he was

> placed at the head of a Great Empire, he never laid aside the simplicity and moderation of a private citizen, who infused into Oriental Despotism the spirit of British freedom, who never forgot that the end of government is the welfare of the governed, and who abolished cruel rites ...

Not, however, the cruel rite of colonial domination, which once more makes its triumphal reappearance in a deindustrialising socialist West Bengal, where the shining imagery of the global market economy rushes into the vacuum created by the surrender of ideologies of social and economic justice.

What used to be called the contradictions of capitalism have not disappeared from the world simply because one version of socialism was unable to resolve them. On the contrary, they have simply been exported to some of the poorest places on earth, where the most wretched people must come to terms with them as best they can.

In 1992, the government of Germany gave a substantial contribution to the International Labour Organisation (ILO) for 'the progressive elimination of child labour'. In India forty-two projects received grants, of which seven are in Calcutta.

At the same time as this act of international solidarity took place, the Western financial institutions, which have pressed upon India a debt of some $90 billion, were attaching conditionalities to their munificence; among them was more rapid 'liberalisation' of the Indian economy. In simple terms, this meant, among other things, a reduction in social spending, including food subsidies, health, welfare and education, and the removal of protection from workers. Despite recent gestures to the poor, notably in the 1995 budget – a concession not unconnected with national elections due in 1996 – fundamental policy has not changed.

In Calcutta this has the pleasing effect of driving the poorest to the edge of subsistence, so that they have no choice but to use their children to supplement the wages of hunger. The abolition of child labour in such a context amounts to the abolition of the children themselves: malnutrition and disease will see to that. So while Western leaders praise the Indian government for its 'bold and courageous reforms', as it faithfully carries out the prescriptions upon which they insist, the children of India are pressed into the service of a 'competitiveness', that will continue to stunt their bodies, undermine their health and abridge their lives.

As to the question of whether humanitarian sentiment or economic necessity takes precedence in the single global economy, the wasted, emaciated bodies of the pepople give their own mute answer: the child, less than one year old, who has learned to mime hunger with its tiny hand, the old man asleep on the sidewalk, bolt upright, his hand stiff as in rigor mortis, held out in a gesture of perpetual supplication.

Narkeldanga, in the heart of the city: even the name seems to evoke the sluggish canal, with its dark viscous water, and the fragile, closely built huts of bamboo, dry palm leaves and polythene clinging perilously to the slopes which lead to the canal; buffaloes half-submerged in the inky water with crows perched on their heads; a slimy trail of waste water like an incontinence dripping from the flimsy huts in crooked streams that join the discoloured liquid lapping at the bank. The roofs of these wretched dwellings are of plastic and sacking, covered with monochrome grey dust in this dry season, and held in place against the wind by stones, old tyres, pieces of rusty metal.

Here live the squatters; those whose homes have been neither regularised nor approved. They have no rights, no security, no ration card, no vote. They do not exist as citizens of Calcutta. The huts overflow with recycled materials – paper, cardboard, plastic, metal, glass bottles, scrap iron, fabric of all kinds – apparently the most thrifty place on earth, if it were not for the reckless squandering of the precious human energies expended on this labour of reclamation. Beside the bridge that crosses the canal, the most imposing building is the police station, a structure that would not look out of place in Liverpool 8 or Handsworth in Birmingham. On the corner of the canalside, there is an Ambassador car with a megaphone, advertising patent medicines for stomach ailments. The road along the canal is broad, rough and flinty, strewn with straw in places, for there is an important goat market here. Opposite the hutments, more solid buildings, small shops selling paan, sweets, medicines, and a tea-stall with an outsize kettle on a fire kindled with dried coconut husks.

Many of the long-established *bustees* (slum areas) in Calcutta have long been legalised and provided with basic amenities. In fact, people who have lived for two or three generations in such places have improved their dwellings over time, with the result that many of these are now brick structures, with tiled roofs. The vista of some of these streets and courtyards is reminiscent of working-class areas in Britain in the mid-nineteenth century: lines of washing, people on the doorstep, small workshops, children playing in the gutter – another haunting image of Calcutta that throws back to the West strange reflections and fleeting recollections of its own effaced past.

The achievement of a certain measure of security for many in Calcutta has unfortunate consequences for the poorest. First of all, within the authorised bustees, many owners have sold their houses to developers, who have constructed four- or five-storey buildings on the small pieces of land. Some of these illegal structures have collapsed, with loss of life to neighbours. Both owners and developers have already disappeared. Much of the construction was made possible through a network of corrupt officials, police, employees of Calcutta city authorities.

The second unhappy result has been that those who have no such security must squat either on the pavements or on land belonging to the railway, the municipality or private owners. And this is why the canalside inhabitants of Narkeldanga live in constant apprehension of the attentions of police, political goondas or criminals. The bustee people are the vote-bank of the Communist Party of India (Marxist), in power in West Bengal for over 15 years; the squatters owe no such allegiance, except under duress. When people from the squatter settlements go to fetch water from the public taps, they are frequently chased away or beaten by the bustee-dwellers. Their daughters are often molested by police or political cadres, their homes raided, their small livelihoods damaged by the predations of officials and anti-socials (often, it sometimes seems, the same people).

Those living in the unauthorised slums are the poorest of the poor: Mehrun Nisa, an elderly woman whose husband sells potatoes to earn Rs5 a day (15 cents), while her sister picks rags. The men work as cart- or rickshaw-pullers, running with the shafts of the vehicle in their hands like beasts of draught, or sell some trifling knick-knack on the pavements of the city. Asmi Khatoon shows the cheap bevelled mirror which her husband sells to provide her family with its livelihood, if that is not an exaggeration of the Rs10 a day he earns. Other women work as domestic servants, at Rs150 a month ($5). In one small hut, a miserable place constructed out of *kachera*, junk, rusty cans, bricks, rubble and plastic, a child is lying on a mat. He is sick with measles. His mother cannot afford the medicine he needs. Because of the low level of nutrition, he may or may not survive.

The income of the people here is so low that without their children's labour they would not eat, they would not find the strength to replenish their energy for the next day.

In this context, it is impossible to imagine what the Western agencies and financial institutions are proposing in their virtuous efforts to abolish child labour, for this is all that stands between perishing and survival. Do the governments of the West and the International Monetary Fund and World Bank envisage strictly enforceable living wages for all who work? While they continue to preach the supreme desirability of becoming competitive in the world, there will always be those ready to reduce costs by paying less than subsistence to people on the edge of extinction. The devotion of the West to 'free labour' conceals a truth in its own treacherous lexicon: it is precisely that – virtually free to those who abuse it.

Opposite the canal, behind the *pakka* buildings, there is a labyrinth of small streets, workshops and factories where many of the squatters' children labour. A cardboard box factory is open to the street. All the workers are under 16. Six or eight boys sit cross-legged around a low table, folding boxes that have been cut by machine. Beside them, two smaller boys, aged eight and ten, are pasting rectangles of cardboard to reinforce the ends of the boxes; a round dish of paste, a stack of pieces of cardboard. These they pass on to boys who paste the finished boxes at either end to make them stronger. Another boy further strengthens them by binding them with white adhesive tape. These boxes will then be used for toys or sweets, none of which the children labouring here will ever enjoy.

The children work in the stifling room in deft silence apart from the sound of the cardboard as it strikes against the trestle. Yet another child bends the lids into shape, and then the ready boxes are piled up on the pavement outside the workshop. The boys earn Rs20–30 a week (66 cents – $1). At least for them working conditions are relatively safe, with no toxic materials or heavy machinery. Nasim Hussein is 10; after his six hours of work, he goes to the school in the slum run by FOCUS, one of the NGOs in Calcutta that has received a grant from the ILO. There, he can retrieve a little of the education he has been denied, reclaim perhaps a fraction of his confiscated childhood.

Tinnu is a rag-picker. He trails behind him a large jute sack, darned many times with coarse thread. He works 12 hours most days for Rs10 a day. Foraging among the wastes of Calcutta, he is liable to respiratory infections; his skin is covered with cuts and grazes that have festered, his eyes are often swollen and discoloured, damaged by chemical-impregnated rags and papers.

On the edge of the industrial area, on the dusty pavement, Ruksana is making chains; a young woman, sitting cross-legged beside a pile of iron pieces about 3 inches long. She places each one on a metal plate, and pulls a lever that bends it to an angle of 90 degrees; then she inserts the hook thus formed into the chain she is making, and pulls the lever again, so the link is closed. She gets 10 paise (one-third of one cent) per foot of chain. Each day she will earn between Rs5 and 10, according to how long she sits. She has three children who are, as yet, too young to earn. Nearby is her husband's vegetable basket: a few red carrots, some sweet potato and slices of white coconut.

In one of the small brick-built units, little more than dark windowless rooms, perhaps 3 metres by 4, a man sits at a machine which shaves the soles of shoes ready for the heel; the process gives off a continuous blizzard of white plastic dust; this completely blanches his knees, abdomen, face and hair. On the other side of the narrow thoroughfare, a young man is straightening iron rods, ready for chain-making; to his right, another is welding the joined links in a flash of blue light and cascade of sparks. In the third unit, between these two rooms, sits a child of nine, who is cutting the iron rods into pieces that will form the links of the chain. He sits on a wooden board, holding the rods with his left foot as they feed into the machine, and operating a lever with his right hand, so that the pieces of iron, of equal size, fall beside the machine. The off-cuts of each rod are thrown aside for scrap: a solitary figure in a gloomy brick shed, doing solitary work. Engels's evocations of the Black Country in Britain in the 1840s spring to life again.

Karim, 12, is mending bicycles in a repair shop beside the canal; the shop is a wooden structure, with a metal flap, under which the child works, providing some shade against the sun. The oldest of four children, Karim has been working for two years. His father washes long-distance trucks for a living. Karim sits in front of the dismantled frame of an old cycle, one pedal missing, handlebars bent. He will put it together again, replace the wheels, insert new spokes. He may reassemble two or three cycles a day; and earns Rs10–15 (33–50 cents).

Calcutta is full of these sad wraiths, ghosts of children. Many of them work, not in large-scale industry – that is reserved for adults – but in small industrial units, workshops, manufacturing units and repair garages. On the pavement, sitting inside the shell of a derelict Ambassador car, a ten-year-old is working away with sandpaper to remove the rust from it: a thin child in a blue shirt and shorts, looking out of the empty window of the car, a sorrowful tiny face covered with rust.

A girl of 12, whose mother has ambitiously called her Shahjehan: she has long thin legs, and the slightly swollen joints of the malnourished. She wears a dingy once-white frock with tiny red flowers, and over it, a ragged striped football jersey, fastened with a safety pin where the buttons once were. On her feet, a pair of plastic *chappals*. Shahjehan earns a livelihood by collecting cowdung from stables and from the roadside in the wake of wandering cows. She mixes it with a little water and perhaps some coal-dust, and makes it into flat fuel-cakes, which she lays out to dry beside the railway track. There, they dry within two or three days, and she sells them to neighbours for Rs3 a hundred (10 cents). There are deep dark shadows beneath her eyes, and her face is pinched. Only when she smiles is there a radiant transformation from which you gain a glimpse of the child imprisoned in the prematurely used-up body.

Bhuno Bibi looks little more than a child herself: a delicate round face, head shrouded in a street-stained saree, she has two children. Her husband, a rag-picker, deserted her and left her completely destitute. She makes a living as best she can in the neighbourhood, washing utensils, looking after other people's children, cleaning houses. Sometimes she is given food by the neighbours. She lives in a derelict house in the bustee, for which she pays the landlord Rs80 a month.

Educate the parents, say the middle class, so that they will not exploit their children. Alas, the parents have already been only too well educated in the harsh existential school of Calcutta. Zafia Khatoon, what is she to do, her husband blinded by a works accident? Galvanising metal, the flame leapt up and burned his eyes. Or Buli, whose husband is also infirm and cannot work? Buli is a domestic servant, from six till ten in the morning, and then from three till five in the afternoon. Paid Rs150 a month, that is Rs5 a day (15 cents) or less than 3 cents an hour, she is the lowest-paid worker I met in Calcutta; the going rate, what the market will bear, but not enough to feed a single human being, let alone a family.

They would certainly be better off begging for a living. Miraculously, the destitute of Calcutta still manage to touch depths of compassion which one might have thought long ago exhausted in this impoverished, hungry city of mendicants. Samad, a dignified old man, carries a bamboo cane. His wife is handicapped and his son crippled by polio. When I met him, it was in the last days of Ramazan, just before Eid: he says at festival times people are more generous, more charitable towards the misfortune of others. This means he can get Rs25–30 a day; at other times of the year,

Rs15–20 is the best he can hope for. His polio-affected son also begs, and can make Rs20 a day.

The myths about beggars are mostly invented by the well-to-do, in order to justify their unwillingness to contemplate their own relationship to poverty: the beggars are syndicated, they are controlled by gangs, parents mutilate their own children at birth in order to make them more effective beggars – as though the bequest of the dignified Samad to his son was the 'gift' of polio, in order to provide him with a livelihood.

Subratan sells damaged fruits in the Tiljala slum, mostly to schoolchildren who have a few paise to spend. She buys the rotting fruit from the wholesale market in the early morning, blackened bananas, mildewed oranges, spoiled guavas, and cuts from them the edible portions. In the second half of the day she cooks and sells sweet potato on the road. She was abandoned by her husband when she was three months pregnant. With two small children to feed, Subratan says she needs between Rs40 and 50 a day to provide them adequate nourishment. She rarely earns half as much. When her children are older, as soon as they can earn, they will have to contribute to the household income. Their future is predetermined. Not the German government, not the Indian government, not the ILO, and certainly no humanitarian sentiment is going to provide her with the income her family needs.

Zarina Bibi wears a bright green saree, and green stones in her earrings; a set of lime-green bangles on her right hand, a set of lilac ones on her left that clatter as she moves her hands; a proud, unsmiling woman in her thirties. She lives in a squatter settlement in a narrow space between the branching of two railway lines: a precarious life in a dangerous place without security. She comes from South Bengal, and has been in Calcutta for 12 years. She works as a domestic in a 'residence', that is a middle-class household, for Rs70 a month (just over $2). She has two children. Her six-year-old is already rag-picking. When she goes to work, she has to leave her other child in the hut, under the eye of a neighbour. She knows she is taking a risk but has no choice: she cannot permit a six-year-old boy to be the only breadwinner in the household. She heard recently that the railway authorities are going to demolish the squatter settlement. 'Where shall we go? We have no other place. My husband is a rickshaw puller in Canning where we come from, but he lives on the road, can provide no shelter. Sometimes he sends money, sometimes not.' Zarina says when the children are ill, the hospital refuses to accept them when they find out they live in the squatter settlement because, they say, squatter people 'have no address'. Doctors will not even issue death certificates because they fear trouble in case it was murder. 'People look through us', says Zarina Bibi, 'as though we do not exist. What are we, ghosts before we have even died?'

Mariami Bibi is 70; a sweet, faded face beneath a mustard-coloured saree. I ask her how she lives. 'Mangti hun', I beg, she answers simply. Her husband died long ago; one son is sick, the other no longer lives at home. She begs at different places within 2 or 3 square miles of where she lives. Rs15–20 a day is an average 'earning' for those people who are afflicted or elderly.

As we walk along the railway track, a woman stops us. I say something in Hindi, but she says with dignity, 'It's all right, I speak English. We are Anglo-Indians. Come and see my home.' Between the bamboo and polythene huts there is barely room to walk; when people meet, one has to shelter inside the low doorways to allow the other to pass. In her hut there is nothing but a large wooden bed, a crucifix, a tin trunk and a few utensils, and some ashes in the chulha from last night's meal. On the bed lies her son, sick with fever. Ruth Martin looks after other people's children for Rs150 a month. Her son lives and works outside Calcutta; he has come home because he is sick. They have a hospital prescription but cannot afford the medicine. She looks at me accusingly. What to do? We are Christian people. She seems to be saying, 'This is the reward we get for having served the British, for having been used by them, as labour, as sexual relief for the imperial exiles'; a fierce long look of unforgiving resentment. The words that my own family were working in factories very like those here in Tiljala, making shoes at that time, freeze on my lips. There is nothing to say.

The security gained by the bustee dwellers certainly gives them advantages unknown to the squatters; and this scarcely promotes feelings of solidarity with them. But even in the longest-established bustees, people remain poor, prey to the kind of social evils that blighted the manufacturing districts of Britain in the nineteenth century. At the same time, the neighbourhoods produce their own activists and defenders, people like Sudhana Singh, who has remained to teach in the bustee of Panchanantala, a long straggling settlement beside the railway track, where she was born 28 years ago.

The government says schooling is free, but the schools always take money for fees, for building and maintenance, for electricity. The poorest children do not attend, and if they do, they drop out because of the need to work, or because of the hostility, incompetence or neglect of the government teachers.

We have 280 children, of whom about 250 actually attend each day. Some of the girls do domestic work before they come to school, for Rs70 or 80 a month; many of them have to fetch water and do household chores as well, look after the smaller children, because their mothers are also domestic servants, earning no more than Rs200 a month. The boys stop school to work in tea-stalls, garages, clothes shops. Many of the men are construction workers, skilled artisans, carpenters and masons, but they are employed under contractors, people who take a contract from the builders, and then employ the workers. They are very experienced, they can tell whether the soil is suitable for high-rise or not, and their knowledge is used without being rewarded.

But everyone is insecure. Although the men earn a living wage, they spend on themselves; alcohol, regular beer or chullu, or drugs; so the women have to work, and the families remain poor. Some of the young people take brown sugar. Some take it because of sorrow or poverty, but the young people take it lightly, casually, and then they are addicted. In one house near where I stay there are four addicts, parents of children I teach.

Amenities are still lacking, especially sanitation. One latrine is used by a minimum of 15 families, more often 30. There are two tubewells. Most people use kerosene stoves for cooking, or they make gul, coal-dust with water, for fuel.

There are levels of misery in people's lives which are not adequately conveyed by the word 'poverty'. People may have to spend virtually all their earnings on food. It costs Rs1200 a month to feed a family of six. If both parents work, they'll earn enough. There is a regular supply of chullu coming into the neighbourhood from outside. It is carried by women in plastic jars or bladders, they sell it in the illicit liquor shop. It's made of palm sap mixed with fermented rice, and spirits are sometimes added, and jaggery.

When I was younger, this place was notorious. People used to snatch and loot, they would stop and raid the trains; but over the years, the community has become more settled, most people work hard for a living.

My father was a worker in a steel company. There were no girls going to school when I started. I had to fight hard in the family to get an education. Because my father had a good job, I was not under pressure to work as a child. There was more of a problem with the neighbours, who thought it odd and unnecessary that a girl should go to school and take it so seriously. I have two brothers; one drives a taxi and the other is a driver for an industrial company. Now all the children go to school, although many drop out. But at least girls now see that it can be done, that girls from the slums can go to college, become teachers.

Sudhana is unmarried. One of the problems is that she is too clever: it is hard to find a suitable husband for her within the neighbourhood. She remains committed to the people. She speaks of the neighbourliness and mutuality, the co-operation and solidarity at times of sickness and death. People do support each other, hold on to one another, when there is suffering. *People have seen so much suffering, they don't wait to be asked. They just come. The love of people for one another is one of the most valuable things we have here.*

Layers of irony ... You can see the meaning of a sub-political solidarity here, a sense of existential communal understanding of a common predicament – precisely what animated the best of the working-class communities in Britain. Of course there is social injustice, there is oppression of women, there is drunkenness and irresponsibility. But there is equally a sense of knowing that the destiny of all in the slum is a common one, that all need one another; and the power of the networks of women, especially, to humanise and make a life of exploitation and injustice tolerable remains one of the enduring characteristics of the slums, for all the ambiguities and the enduring oppression.

It's a rooted life. Everyone knows their neighbours. There are no secrets, there is no privacy. There is a bustee committee, elected by the people. This side of the railway track is regularised, the other side is not.

When Sudhana goes out of the slum, to college or meetings with other teachers, they might think she is of higher caste; but when they come into the slum and see where she lives, they no longer want to know her. They are mainly Scheduled Castes here, although in West Bengal, caste has less importance than in some other parts of India. Love marriages are permitted, although few marry outside their caste.

The road meanders along the railway line, women scouring vessels at the tap, houses colour-washed pale blue, very crowded narrow thoroughfares with crooked alleys at right angles to the main street. Most people here go outside the slum to work; a machine-tool factory worker earns Rs1200 a month, a carpenter about 900. But there is nothing for the young to do, especially the young men. Ravi has a tea-stall: a sketchy place, a canvas shelter, a kettle, a bench, and a cluster of unemployed young men. He earns Rs50 a day, enough, he says for himself, his wife and baby. A boy with a 'City of Joy' T-shirt says he does nothing. His friend says he was sacked from his last job for stealing. The boy laughs and says his friend drinks too much chullu. He gets money by thieving and begging. A friendly scuffle follows.

Some of the people here have become quite well off, but they cannot move out because there is no affordable housing. There are 1,200 families here, at least 6,000 people. A train comes to a halt beside the vegetable market which is close to the track. 'Highly Inflammable' reads the message in English on the brown cylinders of the wagons. This might well serve as a designation for the slum itself, with its growing numbers of young workless, with their unused energies and wasted abilities. Here, says Sudhana, the promise of schooling – that it guarantees better jobs than the menial occupations of the parents – can be seen to be an illusion. Faith in the possibility of a better life through education is being undermined here, and when that happens on a large scale, it threatens new and dangerous forms of destabilisation for India. Does the government of India understand what empty promises and hunger for power actually mean for the country it claims to love? Such questions are being framed, not so much in the universities and places of higher education, but in the slums and settlements where education is coming to mean instruction in social and political realities from which the middle classes are increasingly estranged.

7. Indian Summer

Udaipur/Jaipur

All but the most tenacious visitors have deserted the plains of India by early May; the scorching wind they call *loo* has set in, a violent desiccating gale that sends whirlwinds of dust across the countryside and into the city slums, where people shelter under sacking and cardboard from the parching heat of the pre-monsoon period.

But this is the time to see India, to feel its intensity. The hot nights are filled with the scent of jasmine and frangipani. The *gulmohar* trees, kindled by the sun, burst into flame, the bells of hibiscus send forth the sensual exploratory tongues of their stamens, while the bougainvillaea continues its endless spillage of cerise and purple, like a conjuror producing coloured fabric from an empty hat. In the villages, they have finished harvesting the rabi, the dry-season crop. In Rajasthan the wheat has been threshed, and the baked thoroughfares are full of scintillas of wheat chaff, so that the dust storms sparkle as they pass through the little streets.

Udaipur. Tourists in the palaces-cum-hotels look through the railings towards the portion of the palace occupied by the present Maharana: a figure in a cane chair behind an ornamental fountain, dreaming, perhaps, of the time when the rich used to send their laundry to London for a correct, crisp wash; or of when over a hundred guests sat down to lunch, all holding a cloth before their mouths, so as not to breathe the same air as the highness into whose presence they had been admitted.

Sunbirds, iridescent blue-black in the sunshine, swoop from the trees, *bulbuls* and finches set up an explosion of colour as they fly from their perches, startled by the splash of a diver in the hotel pool. Only the hunched shoulders of a vulture on a bare bony branch suggest another world beyond the sequestered enclosure of the hotel.

In the City Palace, the Maharana has given space to traditional painters from Delwara, a village about 50 kilometres from Udaipur, where royal artists trained people nearly three centuries ago in what subsequently became a hereditary craft. They use the minerals in the rocks around Udaipur for colour – malachite for green, coral for red, lapis lazuli for blue, sulphur for yellow, crushing the rock and mixing it with water and gum arabic. Dipak, like hundreds of thousands of craft-workers in India, says that for him, painting is like walking – he can no longer remember a time when he did not do it. The artists work on silk, marble, wood; ivory now being forbidden. No artificial chemical colours are used. The work they do consists entirely of replicas of miniatures that already exist: a stream of Krishnas and gopis, intertwined lovers on silk cushions, marble enclosures by moonlight. The art has become frozen, because visitors want to possess examples of the works that hang in the palaces.

The rulers of Udaipur were courted by the British, as part of their strategy for the control of India. On an ornamental scroll in the palace there is an extract from a poem called 'The Lay of the Empress', written by Edward B. Eastwick in 1882, purple praise to indigenous rulers the British had either conquered or intended to divest of their wealth and power. At the head of the poem, it says 'Canto IV, Vol. Two':

Chief among chiefs is he of Rama's line
Whence heroes sprang when earth itself was new,
The Mewar Rana claims a stem divine;
The poet's homage first to him is due.
As stars in radiant sunlight fade from view
So in his presence other crowns look dim
And princes somewhat of the purple hue
Of majesty forgo; then first to him
Let bards the goblet of their praise fill to the brim.

The nineteenth-century paintings in the palace are overwhelmingly of hunting scenes: the now-denuded hills are depicted as tree-covered and full of tigers: hunters on elephants blast their guns in all directions in a burst of stylised orange flame. Sometimes white men are present. Now the hills around the city are empty and degraded, sometimes little more than bare rock.

In Udaipur, there are many tourist-oriented handicraft and painting workshops. Children are employed to wheedle visitors into them, knowing youngsters who befriend tourists and tell them they are students of painting, and offer to show them their work. These appealing children are paid by the workshop owners according to their ability to inveigle people into buying the products.

But the real contemporary creativity around Udaipur, as in all the towns and villages of India, is to be found in the busy, practical workplaces. Men are hammering metal into vessels, creating delicate bird-cages out of thin rods of silver, making ornamental grilles over an open flame, remaking the bodywork of a broken-down auto-rickshaw, riveting zinc buckets and trunks. The hollow carcases of an old Ambassador car is being renewed. Broken fans, radios, watches, wrecked vehicles, oily engines, ancient carburettors are being restored: a tremendous capacity of dexterous fingers to make do and to mend, to improvise and to invent. Half a dozen young men pore over an old engine, a clapped-out machine, a smashed chassis, deeply absorbed in their work of restoration; the air full of the metallic music of tapping and hammering; a labour-intensive, resource-saving wonder of human energy use and minimal abuse of scarce materials.

All the experts coming from the West with the intention of in-structing India in the mysterious arts of wealth creation should come here, to these unprepossessing places, to pay homage and humbly ask lessons in conservation. Instead, they preach the impor-tance of replacing this precious resource-husbandry with gimcrack mass-produced goods that will disemploy millions of Indians. The 'upgrading of technology' acccompanies a degradation of human creativity and resourcefulness.

Here, then, is the heart of the Indian alternative way of devel-opment. It exists already. It is embodied in a daily living struggle against the throwaway disregard for resources and humanity alike, which underlies the Western model, under whose tutelage India has now passed.

Yet it is so commonplace and unspectacular a sight that nobody pauses in the oily, stifling workplaces, where such an expenditure of effort and inventiveness goes unsung. The young men, covered in oil and grease, wearing shorts and vests that are simply a network of holes, look up from their work: a smile of complicity through grimy oil-marked faces; dazzling teeth, intelligent eyes – here, you are in the presence of the most precious of India's raw material, the brains and hands of millions of people; what the leaders of India now regard as 'population', a problem to be solved, rather than a skilful-ness and sensitivity to be applied, celebrated and held up to the rest of the countries of the South as a way out of the trap of capital-intensive waste, value-added junk and permanent debt-bondage to the West.

In the heat of May, to move around comfortably, people are up by five o'clock. As you travel through Rajasthan, the sun looks pale and coppery as it rises over the dusty hills, innocent of the ferocity with which it will burn before midday.

Jaipur was set out by Maharaja Jai Singh in the early eighteenth-century: rich earth-coloured buildings in broad avenues. The narrow

alleys that intersect the main thoroughfares were originally constructed so as to receive just enough sunlight to warm them in
winter and keep them cool in summer. Each lane is devoted to a
single trade or skill within the division of labour of the city: one
filled with the sparks and arc-lamps of welding shops; another with
furnaces for the making of glass. One is the site of gem-polishing
and cutting, another the place where metal goods are made; two
centuries of continuous artisanal pride, not yet displaced.

Hand-printing and dyeing were traditional low-capital occupations, in which the family formed the unit of production. Dyes came
from native plants gathered locally, indigo, madder, pomegranate,
turmeric. Work from each district could be recognised by the particular colours of the locality as well as by the distinctive motifs of
the individual workers.

Formerly all the villages around Jaipur did block-printing. The
carving of the intricate wood-block patterns is an ancient art. The
British began the destruction of the local traditions. They took
the wood-blocks to Britain, copied them for screen-printing and
then sold the cloth back to India. They did much to eliminate
community-based crafts, breaking up the village organisation
which had ensured continuous production for the artisans.

The industrial market has now displaced most of the block-
printers. Demand for material from beyond the self-reliant radius
of the village has radically changed the structure of the craft. The
export market is large but unreliable, and changes in fashion at
distant points of consumption can abruptly throw large numbers
of people out of work. In any case, most foreign consumers
cannot discern the difference between screen-printed and block-
printed material.

Similarly, the *bhandej* (tie-dye) work is also rapidly being displaced. Traditionally, women did the tying, men the dyeing; but
now the work has been industrialised, heavily concentrated in
certain areas of Jaipur, so that the drains in Lal Ghar Nalla are
stained crimson, indigo and ochre. The work of tying the patches
was very arduous, but it was a collective and convivial activity, in
which the children could also participate, while the youngest
could be looked after at the same time. Women had control over
the times at which they worked. When the work is substituted by
screen-printing, it becomes more industrial: fewer people are employed, and many of the bhandej workers lose their livelihood.

Raj Kumar is chief designer for the Rajasthan Handicrafts Centre
near the City Palace in Jaipur. The old dhabus, or vegetable dyes,
were used with a mixture of lime, gum and wheat-flour to make the
background colour fast, but now it is done in industrial units with

chemicals. As a result, men have taken over the dyeing, because women cannot work in industrial units. Originally, it was not an industry at all – each house did a certain amount, and sold a little in the market. It supplemented an agricultural livelihood. That is the point about the handicrafts of Rajasthan. Because of the dry climate, there was only the rainfed crop, and people developed skills to survive at other times, making things that they sold in the local Saturday markets.

Some of the more intricate bhandej would take 15 days to make. To make it worthwhile, people would have to ask Rs120, whereas screen-printed sarees can be sold for Rs30 or 40. In ten years' time, it will be gone completely, unless it is kept alive as an art rather than a craft. Bhandej could have been maintained as a labour-intensive domestic occupation. But we see all these things being industrialised, employing fewer people, leaving more and more without employment or livelihood.

People used to drive their sheep or camels to weekly markets, and take with them their handicrafts at the same time. It was a way of living, an integrated life, where there was one crop in the monsoon, and the rest of the year each district had its own tradition, making something it could exchange with its neighbours. Now they have to capitalise, concentrate in the towns, which pollutes the water there, and meanwhile the village disintegrates, the sense of wholeness goes. Vegetable dyeing also involved many diverse and complicated processes, which gave work to more people. In some places, even the underground water has become polluted by chemical dyes, so dyeing has been banned there.

A similar process is at work with almost every other artefact. The blue pottery of Rajasthan, for instance: the quartz powder, which is the principal ingredient, was traditionally made by hand by women; the colouring from cobalt, chromium oxide and manganese oxide. As each object was made – plates, vessels, jugs – they were dipped in a flour-based finish and then painted, glazed and fired. The bhattis, or furnaces, were wood-fired, and the potters knew by looking at the flame how to judge the temperature at which their pots should be fired. The technique came from Persia 250 years ago, when Jai Singh brought artists from all over the then known world to Jaipur. The gem-cutting industry of Rajasthan is another aspect of Jai Singh's legacy; brass engraving, too, which also originated in Persia.

Until now, the crafts of Jaipur have not been too intensively industrialised. Its domestically based labour makes it small-scale, more peaceable; small homes with gem-cutting machines keep the work manageable. The presence of women, the absence of large-scale industrial concentration, means it is less polluting, less violent.

Rajinder Kumar is colour-master in the Rajasthan Crafts Organisation. He says that when a block-printed shirt is marketed, a Western department store will ask for 3,000 pieces. It can't be done by block-printing, so it must be done by screen instead. The designer makes a pattern for the screen-printing, because the store wants delivery in a hurry. For the foreign buyer, the blockworkers take too long to execute the designs. Some of these involve the most intricate and delicate carvings. But if block-printing had been encouraged, this would have employed far more people.

Mechanised printing requires 22 times the capital of hand-printing. Many skilled printers, formerly self-employed, are now wage-earners, unorganised, and without access to the capital that would be required for them to work on their own account. In any case, regular employment is denied them, because much of domestic demand is met by synthetic textiles and mill-printed fabrics. The government, in spite of its intensive promotion of Indian arts and crafts, has provided no safeguard for ancient crafts that have been practised and transmitted in India for thousands of years.

The questions asked by the workers in the cellars and workshops of Jaipur are direct and simple. *Why should we not continue with our traditional craft? My father and grandfather did it,* says Iqbal, a hand-printer. *I learned to do it as a child; no, I wasn't taught it, I acquired it, it developed. It is a skill, like language or walking, you absorb it by imitation and example. My child would expect to do the same thing. Must I strike from his hands the skills that his fingers ache to acquire? What kind of a future is that?*

The appropriation of skills by technology is a source of great anger to many – mostly powerless – people. The model of development which the country is now following is one that breaks valuable systems of cultural transmission and substitutes alien technologies. At what point does the division of labour become injurious to people? This question is posed in India by craftspeople who see themselves as the last practitioners of ancient skills. It is a question rarely asked in the West where the constant deskilling and disemployment of people maintains them in a state of chronic insecurity, infinitely malleable, ready to adapt to the latest whims of the market. The division of labour has gone so far in the West, that many have little comprehension of the overall purpose of their own labour, let alone that of their neighbour.

The dispensability of people is the repeated message of the Western system. To import such an ideology into a country whose principal advantage is the skill and knowing of the people is a terrible act of violence against them, and against the earth itself, for everyone admits that the people of India will never reach the 'standards' of living of the West. To revalidate and to restore ought to be the purpose of economic endeavour, self-reliance and sufficiency its goal.

Instead, a country that jettisons sufficiency in favour of more, while half the people are abandoned to perpetual want, is embarked upon a road whose end it cannot see. But the society that emerges from this alien transplant is unlikely to be either pleasant or peaceful. The apostles of change count upon the eternal resilience of India; but even that fund of endurance is not infinite, especially when taunted by the spectacle of an abundance which the majority can never attain.

Many Western homes now contain artefacts, handicrafts, objects from India, the trophies and souvenirs of holidays, trekking, 'exploring' in India, or perhaps simply purchases imported into the West by shrewd Indian entrepreneurs, aware of the market for all that is ethnic, picturesque, traditional. It is common to see dhurries and blankets, shawls and silks, brass pots, silver filigree, pottery, sarees, khadi, paintings on leaves or ivory, bamboo and wicker products.

The presence of these things tells a poignant story: for the hand-wrought objects which excite such admiration in the West are also memorials to skills, abilities and cultural practices that have decayed there as organic emanations of a culture. In other words, the richness and variety of hand-made things is an ironic comment on the high-tech, mass-produced, buy-in culture of the West. What they are buying in from India and other countries of the South is not just the caprice of market-dictated fashion, but also a reminder of what they have themselves forfeited. For what the West makes now is, principally, money; and far from providing the absolute freedoms and independence which money is supposed to bestow upon its possessors, it reminds them of how little they can do or make or create or produce for themselves and each other.

In Jaipur, rich Westerners crowd into the emporia and shops, gather at the doors of workshops and potteries, fascinated by the crafts on display. To them, making things in this way is a source of great wonderment. It is a poignant paradox, a confrontation between the resourceful and the resourceless, between the money-rich and the skills-rich, between impoverishment on the one hand and a kind of gilded depowerment on the other. This strange equation is, perhaps, the key to the fascination which the rich exercise over the poor, and the strange compulsions that drive the rich to seek out those who have not yet been driven down the paths of the curiously dispossessing plenty which nevertheless leaves so many basic needs unfulfilled.

The Handloom Weavers

Perhaps no other group in India has been so badly affected by these processes as the handloom weavers. Their plight has uncanny echoes of the degradation of the handloom weavers in Britain in the early industrial era. Between the 1820s and the 1840s, the handloom weavers in Britain suffered more than any other group of workers. Their labour was superseded by the powerloom, and the organisation of cloth production in the factory. But their worsening condition in that period was caused equally by the great influx into their ranks of others who had been deprived of livelihood – former agricultural labourers and refugees from the famine in Ireland among them. The surplus labour worked at ever lower rates of pay, and actually delayed by a decade or more the introduction of machine-made goods.

What had been the supreme advantage of the handloom weavers – their independence, their ability to work when they chose and to perform their labour in conjunction with other activities, like tending a small piece of land, rearing chickens and a pig – eventually became the source of the most terrible exploitation, which was made all the worse by being apparently self-inflicted. Without protection, fiercely competitive, they were reduced to working 14, 16 hours a day, and were still unable to provide themselves with the necessities for subsistence.

The continuing story of dispossession of the handloom weavers in India has a different origin, having been originally inflicted by the British, determined to sell their inferior factory-made goods in India.

The most recent twist in their fate has come directly from the 'liberalisation' policy of the Indian government, under the expert tutelage of the Western financial institutions. According to Michel Chossudovsky, Economics Professor at the University of Ottawa:

A study on starvation deaths among handloom weavers in a relatively prosperous rural community in Andhra Pradesh which occurred in the months following the implementation of the new economic policy enables us to pinpoint the transmission mechanism underlying the IMF programme. With devaluation of the rupee and the lifting of controls on cotton yarn exported, the jump in the domestic price of cotton yarn led to a collapse in the pacham (24 metres) rate paid to the weaver by the middlemen (through the putting out system). Radhakrishnamurthy and his wife were able to weave between 3 and 4 pachams a month, bringing home the meagre income of Rs300–400 for a family of six. After the Union budget of July 1991, the price of cotton yarn jumped, and the burden was passed on to the weaver. Radhakrishnamurthy's income declined to Rs240–320 a month. Radhakrishnamurthy of Gollapalli Village in Guntur district died of starvation on September 4, 1991. Between August 30 and November 10, at least 73 starvation deaths were reported in only two districts of Andhra Pradesh. The IMF/World Bank programme, rather than eliminating poverty, as claimed by the WB President, Lewis Preston, actually eliminates the poor.

In Sawan Park in the north-east of Delhi, there are about 5,000 silent looms, belonging to 147 extinct co-operative societies. Most of the people here migrated in the 1960s from the area around Farukhabad in Uttar Pradesh. The livelihood which had become precarious in the villages at least found markets in Delhi, even though they were exploited by middlemen. They have now learned that the surplus of weavers in the city – there are over 35,000 – has only depressed wages even further. Those who can earn now labour day and night for a few rupees; others have found casual work on building sites; some sell channa and balloons on the streets.

E.P. Thompson,* writing of Britain in the 1830s, said:

> The degradation of the weavers was very similar to that of the other workers in the artisan trades. Each time their wages were beaten down, their position became more defenceless. The weaver had now to work longer into the night to earn less; in working longer, he increased another's chances of unemployment. There was a pool of surplus labour, semi-employed, defenceless, and undercutting each other's wages.

This sounds like a description of Sawan Park. Inside the weaving sheds, the looms stand idle. The shuttles hang in clusters from a rusty nail, covered with dust. The looms were made by traditional carpenters, who have also been impoverished by the decline of the craft which they served. The only fabric on the loom is cobwebs, which hang in dusty loops, shining iridescent in the sum-

---

* E. P. Thompson, *The Making of the English Working Class*, Harmondsworth, Penguin, 1960.

mer sun; the spiders mocking the craft of the weavers, who sit on an ancient trestle shiny with use, and play cards with fingers capable of weaving the finest and sheerest cloth. The price of thread, they confirm, has gone up. It is simply not available. It has been pre-empted by powerlooms. Even so, the people have not lost their dignity; nor, because of the skills they possess, have they lost their hope; even though they will now earn only one or two rupees for making a *chadar*. Some have done no work for two or three years. They say there is little point in teaching what they know to their children; even so, they say with pride, the children grow up knowing anyway, from watching their parents, and from generations of tradition.

The handloom weaver [E.P. Thompson continues] opposed the introduction of the factory system. Weaving had offered freedoms denied to those coerced by the harsh rhythms of the factory.

> Weaving had offered employment to the whole family, the young children winding bobbins, older children watching for faults, picking over the cloth, or helping to throw the shuttle in the broad-loom; the wife taking a turn at the weaving in among her domestic employments. The family could sit down together, and however poor meals were, at least they could sit down at chosen times.

These words echo those of the people of Sawan Park. 'Six looms', they say 'give work to 65 people; with winding the spindles, weaving, sizing and dyeing – why would it be in our country's interests to replace the handloom? We should not even think of such a thing until work is assured for those who are thrown out of work. Machines increase production at the cost of a dignified, honourable employment of millions of people.'

The weaving sheds at Sawan Park are close to a garbage dump, where some women and children sift through the offal, coconut husks, rinds, shells, bones and rags, in search of something to sell. Babu Lal says, 'Is this the best we can expect for our children?'

Dharampal Singh gets Rs2 per metre for the bedsheet he is making. This will earn him about Rs35 a day. More complicated work may earn Rs3 or 4 a metre, but this proceeds more slowly. It requires 40 strokes to make one inch of material. Many of the workers develop respiratory diseases – asthma, bronchitis, TB are common. Anara Devi, a woman in her sixties, sits winding yarn on to bobbins. For one kilo of yarn she will be paid Rs5, and this will take much of the day; every time the thread snaps, she must mend it with her fingers.

The handloom census of 1987, which does not take into consideration the displaced weavers, claims that there are 437,600 weavers in the country. The same census states that of these, 143,200 earn Rs501 and above per month; 133,400 earn between Rs201 and 500, and 204,000 earn Rs200 or less, which means less than one rupee available per head per day, or less than one-eighth of a bottle of Bisleri water.

Even the starvation deaths had their counterpart in Britain, as shown in the evidence given to the Parliamentary Select Committee in 1827 (quoted by E. P. Thompson in *The Making of the English Working Class*):

Mrs Hulton and myself, in visiting the poor, were asked by a person almost starving to go into a house. We found there on one side of the fire a very old man, apparently dying, on the other side a young man of about eighteen with a child on his knee, whose mother had just died and been buried. We were going away from that house, when the woman said 'Sir, you have not seen all.' We went up stairs, and, under some rags, we found another young man, the widower; and on turning down the rags, which he was unable to remove himself, we found another man who was dying, and who did die during the course of that day. I have no doubt that the family were actually starving at the time.

Balraj Kumar, economist, says:

With 38 million people officially unemployed in India, and possibly 50 million not registered, but effectively without livelihood, not to mention the millions underemployed, it is clear that liberation from weaving skills can lead only to a state of even greater dereliction. The more capital input that goes into the market, the more jobs are lost. 'If wages increase', we are told, 'inflation occurs.' Yet we have inflation while the wages of the weavers fall. This means that the poorest people in India are subsidising the rich. One factor of production is not free to negotiate a living wage, so how can the market be free?

India, Britain; late twentieth century, early nineteenth century. These are the continuing human costs of 'technological progress', of 'keeping down labour costs', of 'becoming competitive in the world'. This is the price of 'structural adjustment', 'market reforms', and all the other jargon phrases that cause to disappear the flesh and blood on which these abstractions must work themselves out.

In India, however, the process of 'liberalisation' has led to much protest and debate, and vigorous efforts to formulate other possibilities. Uzramma of Dastakar, an organisation working for the retention and enhancement of traditional crafts and skills, in Andhra Pradesh, close to where the recent starvation deaths of handloom weavers occurred, declared at the Congress of Traditional Sciences and Technologies of India in Bombay late in 1993:

We have been debating questions like 'Are handlooms viable' on too narrow a plane. However crucial viability is at the level of the particular, it becomes irrelevant in the sphere where societal choices have to be made. We do not demand narrow economic viability from, say, the defence of our national borders. We do not abandon general elections on the grounds of affordability. Similarly, but much more importantly, a technology choice has to be made that leads every one of us to a life of peace, dignity and harmony.

It is in this context that artisanal production, in this case, of textiles, needs to be looked at as a whole activity of household production of cloth, an activity linked into a self-sustaining rural economy, a way of life into which cloth-making is integrated.

Uzramma tells of a weaver who was delighted to have made it to a 'regular' job, no longer yoked to the uncertainties of his traditional trade. He was a highly skilled weaver of Adilabad district in Andhra Pradesh, 30 years old, celebrating his new-found status as an un-skilled worker at the Mineral Exploration Corporation Limited. Others like him had been fortunate enough to become *peons*, office boys, and domestic servants in places as far away as Jamshedpur. To others, salvation had come in the form of powerlooms in Surat or Bhiwande, where they now inhabit the slums. They are happy, not for themselves but for their children, who they are determined will not fall into traditional labour, but will be 'educated' for a government job.

A traditional skill like weaving has been an article of faith, a matter of pride and indeed the very identity of the community for generations. Why is it now facing such a widespread threat of erosion and extinction? What trauma has the process of modernisation inflicted, that a people who were relaxed, graceful and artistic by temperament, now at best end up with the crumbs of salaried jobs? What psychological damage has weakened the weaver's spirit to such a degree that he does not wear his own product, but prefers that of the mill?

The functions of a society and its evolution depend on the strength of its social fabric. And the strength of a fabric depends not on its stronger strands, but on the strength of its weakest threads, and the way they are interwoven. The few who find jobs and the many who don't are the weak threads, and through our neglect of them, the society threatens to tear itself apart. But the threat is avoidable. It is the vast, unstructured and unsupervised rural economy that has the potential to strengthen the weak threads and to mend the fabric.

The textile industry of the future has to be seen in a complete, whole way, with its associated agricultural practices, its tool makers, its dyers and printers, its spinners, ginners and carders, a veritable dynamo for rural prosperity. There is no pollution and no waste. It will be a people's technology with access for all to the skills, the materials and the markets.

Uzramma and her colleagues in Dastakar have been working with some of the weavers in Andhra Pradesh. *We had followed the fate of a family from Kanoor, who were of a caste with many weavers in it. They went from Kanoor in Andhra to Sholapur in Maharashtra to work in the textile mills. Then those mills closed, so they went on to Bombay, where he is now an unskilled labourer and she is a domestic worker. You can trace the decay of people's skills and status; that is repeated in millions of households throughout India.*

Uzramma knows, too, the ambiguities of the weavers with whom they have worked. *In several villages around Anantapur, the sarees are polyester, where they used to be cotton. The quality is bad, but there is a market for it. The weavers know how the market works. They realize that it deskills them. I say to them if you weave a better saree, I'll help you sell. The weaver knows also that he can make money out of the traditional skill; but he can't be bothered, he exploits the existing market.*

On the other hand, they get pleasure from making good sarees. They say 'I'll make polyester and get as much money as I can.' Then they see their neighbours also selling poor quality, so they do it for some time, then they want to make a good saree again.

They have seen another way; we've struggled for three years to get them to make a good-quality saree. Now they'll do it. They didn't believe they were doing good-quality work; they have to put in more skill and more capital, and it still looks about the same as the polyester. 'Why did I put in 10 days' work and Rs4,000 which will give me the same return as the inferior one?' But with the traditional saree, he can get someone to value the good work, and sees people willing to buy, because they like it, not out of pity. Many want good-quality sarees. That gives them pleasure. Then after about 10 sarees, he has doubts and says, 'I'm working so hard', and he'll run away and go back to the inferior work.

It has been a silk-weaving area for 100 years. It used to have a good reputation for silk sarees. Our work was a success and a failure. We pulled out because they treated us as though we were part of the commercial system, they didn't see us as a different way of doing things. Now, out of 20 weavers we worked with, some of them ask us to come back.

The value of the business is large, controlled by three or four master-weavers, who are traders for the weaving community. They give working capital for the saree to be woven, then buy the saree at the price they value it at. They pay him the cost of material and a little extra for him. He makes a saree worth Rs2000, and he gets Rs200 for a week's work; the master gives the design, colours, everything. Even when the weaver does it independently, with a lot of skill and money, he gets little extra.

They have to buy the raw material at changing levels of interest. The master-weaver says, 'I'll give a week's credit, then after that, interest at Rs5 per hundred if you don't give back what you owe.' If he weaves the saree within a week he pays no interest, but he must sell it to the same fellow. He must pay interest if he gives it to someone else. It's a cartel, no one else will take it. Then he gives the saree and gets paid little, because the price is the same everywhere.

To break through the commercial pressure is not easy. Every point in the chain has to be broken. Not only financing, but marketing and raw materials. At every stage you need to intervene. Moreover, they get protection from the master-weavers against outsiders. They say to us, 'Tomorrow you won't be here.' If there is a problem between two weavers they will go to the master. We are not there. You can't take up the issues when you don't stay where he has to stay. The system is there for him always. If we are not there, he'll go to the master weaver, take a loan of Rs2000 and pay Rs5 per 100 per month. If he has a bad record, he'll be charged more.

We know what our vision is; it's simply that the present system militates against a fair return for good work; it isn't that the weavers don't want to do their best work. To revalue the skills and make sure they are adequately rewarded, this is the challenge to those who wish to disengage from the existing system.

Textile-making activity makes it clear that technology is not merely the aggregate of tools, techniques and skills. Technology comes into existence and derives sustenance from several supporting structures, complex social relationships and value-systems. Traditional technologies were not created in cloisters by experts seeking to hand down goodies to the ignorant masses. They were evolved by a synergy of artisans, crafts-men, farmers and others, each one involved creatively, without blindly accepting any single person or group as having a monopoly of expertise. Technological development was a collective pursuit rather than one where a large section of the population is led by the nose, as it were, by a minority pretending omniscience. That remains our objective, our work of restoration.

8. Bangalore

Rashid

'You'll love Bangalore', people said, often adding, 'it isn't like India at all'. Now there's a dubious recommendation if ever there was one.

I didn't love Bangalore, especially in the beginning. As I came in from Hyderabad, the whole of central Karnataka seemed to be swimming in milk: the remains of a fierce winter cyclone that had struck Tamil Nadu had spread westwards and flooded the fields, with a rose-coloured liquid that overspilled the boundaries of rivers and tanks. The sky was grey and swollen, the streets chill and humid.

Bangalore looked pretentious, Westernised, with too many pubs and discos, full of cynical, knowing young people wearing the livery of nowhere, the uniform of transnationalia. Perhaps being ill with a high fever had something to do with my perceptions.

The Lal Bagh gardens didn't even reconcile me. The Lal Bagh is one of the most impressive botanical gardens in India, full of strange monstrosities of vegetation; bombex cybeia, like a huge crumpled elephant, with a vast tangled canopy of green, neither animal nor vegetable; enormous ficus trees transplanted from Madagascar or Java, the soaring pagoda-shaped pines from Australia; and the red earth beneath, as though these strange growths were fed with blood.

At the top of Mahatma Gandhi Road, a bleached stone figure of Queen Victoria looks sideways at Gandhi. In her hand, she still carries orb and sceptre, symbols of imperial triumph. The spectral stone face has been weathered into a disdainful smile. See, she is saying to Gandhi, you outlived me, you gained your independence, but now who rules India?

Cubbon Park; 250 acres of woodland in the heart of the city; sheltering, in the daytime, a population of derelict humanity, addicts and the workless, lost migrants, the sick and untreated, sleeping, indifferent to sun and shadow.

Recovering from fever, I spent many hours beneath the trees in Cubbon Park; the jacaranda spathodia, the red bell-like blossoms scattered on the red earth; they are called *uchche kai* piss-pods by the children because the buds are full of water and they squirt them at each other. It was there I met Rashid.

Some of my most poignant meetings in India were chance encounters. One of the most disturbing was with Rashid, who sat beside me on the weathered bench in Cubbon Park one morning in January. Perhaps the meeting was less random than I imagined. It may be that Westerners are singled out by unhappy individuals, partly because, as transient foreigners, secrets are likely to be safe with them, and partly because they may be considered more sympathetic to those who are strange, offbeat or marginal in India. Rashid later admitted that he was taking a desperate decision that day, when he decided to talk to me, a stranger, and to share the confidences of his unhappy nineteen years.

Rashid is slim, with fair skin and intense dark eyes. After a few preliminary exchanges, during which it emerged he was studying science, he asked me abruptly, 'Do you find me womanish?'

I looked at him in surprise. What I saw before me was a rather androgynous young man, barely out of adolescence. Evidently, this was not the response he sought, and his face darkened.

Rashid is a woman trapped in a male body. Ever since he can remember, he feels that the gender attributed to him is false. His life has been ruined by the failure of others to recognise what he considers to be the core of his identity. Not only do they not acknowledge it, but he cannot even talk to anyone about it.

I listened to the urgent gravity of the disclosures that then came spilling out. I was the first person to whom he had spoken. No, he corrected himself, that is not quite true. He had mentioned it to a fellow-student last year, who had laughed, thinking his friend was joking. 'Yes', Rashid had confirmed, 'I was joking.'

Rashid has always identified himself with women. As a child, he avidly read magazines with pictures of fashion models and film stars. He says he does not wish to change his gender, but to have his true gender recognised. His slim body and good looks have attracted many gays, but he says, 'I don't like homosexuals. I want to be loved by a real man.' For the same reason, he is repelled by *hijaras*. 'There must be no ambiguity about my gender', he insists, 'I don't want to appear as a man masquerading as a woman.'

I told Rashid of a forum for transsexuals in Britain, and I promised to send him some of their literature. Apart from that, and assuring him of my sympathetic, non-judgemental understanding, I was not sure what else I could do. He said, 'You can treat me like a woman.' 'What does that mean?' I asked. 'Open the door to let me pass first, draw my chair out when we go into a restaurant, things like that.'

Rashid's notions of being a woman, it soon appeared, were of the most entrenched, sexist nature. I told him I did not treat any of my women friends in Britain like that, and it would be unnatural for me to treat anyone in such a stereotypical way.

But something more unsettling emerged. His images of women were highly glamorous, clichés of movie stars and show business, an iconography of archaic stereotypes. And they were all Western. What was more, the majority of them were dead. He said he was a great admirer of Marilyn Monroe, Marlene Dietrich, Madonna, Whitney Houston, Josephine Baker. His fantasies of sexual mutation involved a change of culture and, possibly, even of race.

The truth was, he had never viewed himself as an Indian woman at all. I told him that a man wishing to undergo a physical change of gender has to live for some time as a woman. I could not imagine how he was to survive as a Marilyn Monroe lookalike on the streets of Bangalore.

Rashid is a very intelligent young man, with considerable insight and humour, much of which has derived from his marginal position in society. He responded positively to the irony with which I spoke, and admitted that many of the ideas I was putting to him had never occurred to him before. He had not really considered the consequences of what he sees as an urgent need to become authentic, and to reveal himself as he feels he really is. He had projected himself into a future in which he would always be the centre of attraction. He was convinced that, as a woman, he would be desirable, beautiful, irresistible; it had never crossed his mind that he might be without the means to pursue such a life. The men who would be attracted to him would presumably take care of all that.

I suggested to him that if he were to follow the path prescribed for those crossing the mysterious and shifting frontier of gender-definition, he might not be at all glamorous after surgery and hormone treatment. Suppose you turn out to be plain, even ugly, as a woman? What will become of all the fantasies you have entertained of this phantom figure, culled from the pages of Western magazines, advertising and show business?

Furthermore, I went on, you are not going to lose your intelligence, your faculty for analysis, the insights which your position on the edge of society has granted you. If you were to be an unattractive but fiercely intelligent woman, what then? Such a prospect had not entered his calculations at all.

We met several times while I was convalescing in Bangalore. After the relief of unburdening himself, Rashid became an interesting and stimulating companion. He loved natural history, the countryside and landscape of Uttar Kannada. His English, which he had acquired partly through his study of literature, as well as the magazines, was excellent, even though it was his third language, after Urdu and Kannada. He had a quick sense of humour and an eye for the absurd. I learned more about him in the days that followed.

He came from an ordinary working family. His father was a security guard in an office-block in Bangalore and they lived in a small shelter constructed on its roof. His mother had returned to Hyderabad, where her own mother lives, taking with her Rashid's only sister. No, there had been no quarrel, but his parents lived apart, and met only on significant family occasions. I asked whether he felt his mother had deserted his father. 'Yes, I suppose so', he replied.

Rashid is deeply attached to his father, and is desperate for his approval. He has persistently indicated his sexual nature to him. But his father, a genial and conventional man, tells him to stop playing games and be a man. With him, Rashid behaves in a way that is both outrageous and seductive, telling him that he wants to be recognised and treated as the daughter he is.

Rashid is driven by guilt at his mother's departure, and, at one level, he desires to take her place in the household. The relationship with his father is complicated and intense, although these psychological complications make no difference to the underlying feeling of falsehood and pretence that he must live through each day. His emotional and sexual preoccupations prevent Rashid from achieving as well as he should in his education. He does not study much, but relies on his intelligence to carry him through examinations.

Later, I sent Rashid some literature on transsexuality, including an angry essay by a Frenchwoman whose thesis is that men only want to become women to prove that they can do everything better than women, including being a woman.

But nothing has changed Rashid's conviction, arrived at so early in life, that he must express to the world his true nature. He does not see what he can do in India, and dreams of going abroad so that he can explore what he feels is his true identity. I write to him regularly, and he tells me that I am the only person in the world who has the faintest understanding of the dilemmas and contradictions of his life. I tell him that whatever the resolution of the issue, it will have to be somehow within the context and constraints of the society in which he is destined – he uses the word condemned – to live. A sad story of the taboos and proscriptions that cramp human lives. The diversity of which India boasts, he says bitterly, does not

113

extend to acknowledging those outside the conventional norms of family and social propriety. We spoke about self-oppression and victimisation. In the end, he said, *Somebody has to fight for the rights of others like me. Among India's 900 million, there must be many who have a similar experience.* He said, *It's no good waiting for anything to be given to us. No marginalised or oppressed group has ever been granted freedom as a gift of governments. If we have to fight for the right to be recognised, we'll do it.*

From Slum to Community

Bangalore now has a population of about four million, and is one of India's fastest-growing cities. About one-fifth of the people live in slums, and these comprise the largest element of the urban poor. Because of its reputation as a 'garden city', the corporation has had frequent bouts of 'beautification' which, in most cases, means demolishing the homes of the poor and exiling them to remote places beyond the city boundaries.

Ruth Manorama started work with slum women in 1979, and the organisation Women's Voice now has over 15,000 members. In May 1993, almost 100,000 urban poor gathered for a rally in Cubbon Park. Over the years, Women's Voice has petitioned the High Court and Supreme Court for stay orders against demolitions; and indeed, the Slum Clearance Office has now adopted a policy of providing amenities for the poor rather than evicting them from their homes.

Lakshmipuram was a slum on marshy ground opposite the Muslim and Christian burial grounds on Ullsoor Road, originally an uninviting place where people squatted in the 1950s and 1960s on what was then worthless land, on the periphery of the city. There were 127 families in the slum, a population of 600 or 700. *Why did the people come here?* says Ruth Manorama. *The truth is all urban poor were once rural poor. They have fled drought, flood, deforestation, debt, development.*

The people of Lakshmipuram had been in the city for 30 years when, around 1980, the city authorities discovered that the land they were occupying was valuable. The slum dwellers had raised its value by reclaiming it from the marshes; their work and tenacity had transformed a swamp into a desirable piece of real estate, the more so since the city had expanded, and what once appeared a distant settlement was increasingly part of the central area. There was a plan to turn it into a commercial area, and to banish the occupants to a site some 30 kilometres away.

At that time the slum had no facilities, only one water tap. During the monsoon the huts were flooded, and all the vessels and belongings would float away on the water. The houses were kachcha, of rags, polythene, bamboo and palm leaves. *We had a meeting of the people to decide their priorities for development,* says Mrs Swarnamohan, who has worked in the community for the past 14 years. *The poor have every right to stay in the city; the rich depend upon the services they provide. The women and the youth approached the Bangalore City Corporation to ask them to provide street lighting and paving for the road.*

At that time, says Glory, health worker for Women's Voice, *infant mortality was very high. If a child had measles, for instance, the people thought that the disease was a god who was visiting them. Their way of making the measles go away was to neglect the child, not to feed it, to let the house get dirty. By doing this, they thought the god would cease to be drawn to the child, and would go away. The measles had come because of the love of the god for the child. That way, many children died from what appeared to be neglect; although there was an inner logic in the people's reaction.*

The slum was insanitary, unhealthy; its symbolic situation between the burial grounds showed how short was the journey from life to death. Most of the families are from Scheduled Castes; there are nine Christian families. The people's attempts at self-improvement were cut short when the Corporation announced in 1984 that the community was to be relocated in specially built Bangalore Corporation tenements outside the city.

Madevi, a domestic worker, says *They were dumping us there. We could not leave this place, because our work was here, as domestic labour, construction workers, coolies, labourers, vegetable vendors.* In fact, 75 per cent of the women were working as domestic labour; it was, therefore, the women who led the resistance to relocation to a site where there were no opportunities for work.

According to Mrs Swarnamohan, 127 families were staying on a long triangular-shaped site, only 1.08 acres. The community had become strong over time, and wanted to remain together. If new housing was to be provided, they wanted to remain in the same place, close to the source of their livelihood. The Corporation said it was impossible to accommodate so many people in pakka housing, concrete and tiles, in so congested a space. Mrs Swarnamohan, says *We approached the Ahmedabad Study Action group, to help us draw up plans that would keep everyone together. A number of plans were put forward, and the people chose the one they thought best. This was then submitted to the Corporation. The design was such that there would be a number of tenement dwellings facing the main road, 20 feet by 20 feet, while the row of houses alongside, and in the narrow streets behind, would be 10 by 15 feet, with a small upper room, 9 feet by 6, and a terrace fronting the road.*

Bangalore Corporation agreed to provide the materials for construction, while the people – most of the men were in the building industry – would supply the labour. The venture was to be financed by the Housing Development Finance Corporation (HUDCO). *But HUDCO had very strict rules. They demand minimum standards for width of roads and so on. That was impossible given the size of our site. Their norm is 30 feet for main roads, and 15 feet for side roads. We had to reduce these to 12 and 9 respectively. At the apex of the triangle, the road narrows to a mere 3 feet. The estimated cost of the housing was Rs16.13 lakh, about $50,000, for 127 houses (about $400 per house).*

The people knew they would have to live elsewhere during the period of construction. The Corporation refused to provide temporary accommodation: if they had done that, the site they gave would have become a permanent slum, with others coming to occupy it once the present inhabitants had moved into their new accommodation.

They told us to occupy Corporation land. There was some vacant space in the burial ground. We agreed to move there. But the residents of the area objected: they said the slum-dwellers would disturb the bodies of the dead. If the people moved there, they threatened to attack the slum with kerosene and fire.

So we had to make our own arrangements. Some domestic workers would be able to stay in the compound where their employers lived. Others could go back to their native place. Half the site would be evacuated, and then, when that was finished, the other half would be evacuated.

The people did as they had agreed. The houses were not demolished by municipal workers in a tangle of wood and metal, but were dismantled with dignity by the owners themselves, and the materials stored for when the new houses were completed.

Work began in 1988, a new form of community building. The construction workers here had also been unionised, and had done away with contractors, the exploitative *thikedars* and middle men. They were used to negotiating directly with builders for contracts. Carpenters, masons, labourers, formed themselves into the Lakshmipuram Housing Construction Association, and operated for the first time as contractor to the Corporation. The material was duly supplied, and the workers completed the first 38 houses within the space of a few weeks, as high as roof level.

It seemed too good to be true. Then work had to stop: the

status quo on the site must be maintained. A private person, falsely claiming the land was his, had filed a stay order.

Work stopped. It was hard for the people, because they were all scattered. They had to stand by and watch while the rain damaged the half-finished structures. Women's Voice approached an advocate: the dispute was, technically, between the Corporation and a private individual. But the people did not trust the Corporation to fight with any particular vigour on their behalf. For one and a half years the lawyer fought for the people. Some women from Lakshmipuram went into the courtroom every single day. The decision came in their favour early in 1991.

Work began again. On the same day, another legal stay order came, from the same person. This time, he was challenging the notification of the slum, a legal technicality. Once again, work had to be stopped. This time it lasted two years. *We became very frustrated. We began to think we would never see our houses built. It looked as though the powerful had everything in their favour. All we had was our solidarity. We stuck together.*

The case was again found in favour of the people. Work began in earnest once more, after a gap of three and a half years. It was finished very quickly. By the summer of 1993, the houses were ready for occupation.

The site has been transformed. Beause they knew they were building for their own community, the work was carried out with great care and attention to detail. The row of houses on the long edge of the triangle fronting the main road looks like a street from industrial Britain in the early nineteenth century, except that it is better paved and drained. Each house has a small bathroom and a toilet, and a front room on to the street.

Because the houses are of restricted size, many people sit on the doorstep to do their work. The atmosphere is convivial, open. Some women are sorting rice, picking out the bad grains and small stones; others are chopping vegetables. One man is stitching garments with a sewing machine on the threshold. Everywhere children are playing, with marbles, old cycle tyres, pieces of wood transformed in imagination into the chariot of Rama or a jet engine. Kanakamma, a woman in a grey saree, with silver stud in her nose, is a herbal medicine healer. She is removing the leaves from small twigs which, boiled, will serve as a cure for a neighbour's rheumatism. A creeper grows from a terracotta pot, and climbs the wall of her house. This is good for both blood pressure and diarrhoea, she says. She will not tell the name of her plants, because she fears they will lose their potency. Kanakamma learned what she knows from her mother. Her family came to

Bangalore from a small town about 100 kilometres away, where a gold mine had been closed. Both her father and her husband worked there.

Madevi is nursing her grandchild. She is a strong woman, a powerful figure who has been instrumental in keeping the community together during the period when it was scattered. She says it is tempting now for poor people to sell their property, to turn it into quick money to pay off debts, or to finance marriages or festivals. *This must not happen. The community has to stay together. We have been through so many hardships, we cannot fall apart now.* Madevi herself had five children; but her daughter will have only two, three at most. *It is like this. Now people feel that their children will live, they do not need such big families. When our children died, we had to have some who could replace them, or who would take care of us when we are old, who would work for us when we become infirm?*

Some of the houses have been decorated in bright colours, with patterns on the walls. There is a tulsi plant in a pot in front of some doors; a few chickens scratch among the roots. Most of the houses are colour-washed, yellow, blue, pale green. Clothes hang over the upper-storey balconies, drying in the mild winter sun. Some people are cooking outside the houses. Each house has a concrete window-frame forming diamond or lozenge patterns. There are strings of sea-shells at some doors, over others, a thread of chillis and a green lime to ward off the evil eye. Vendors walk with difficulty through the narrow thoroughfares, some with carts and cycles – a scrap metal man with some Palmolein and *vanaspati* cans tied to his cycle, and a perilous roll of rusty barbed wire; a vendor of beans at Rs6 a kilo, a seller of brushes with plumes of blond grass tied around a bamboo handle.

The problems of the community have not all been solved; but the issue of security has. There is much youth unemployment. Illiteracy is still high. The economic straitjacket remains. The Corporation subsequently tripled the estimated cost of the housing. People had agreed that they would pay for the cost of the materials at the rate of Rs105 a month ($3½). The Corporation has yet to fix the final rate. There will certainly be resistance to any rise in the original assessment. There is to be an official civic opening of the houses. Water has not yet come, but every house now has electricity.

We have been building the people as well as houses, says Mrs Swarnamohan. *Women used to think this is fate, whatever happened to them. Now they know things can be changed. And once you have a victory like this, it is wonderfully empowering. We have achieved a far*

118

greater equality between men and women than ever existed before. One young woman, not far from here, was kidnapped, raped and murdered. The police came here, pulling in all our youths, beating them and asking them who was the culprit. Of course they didn't know, they were not involved. We wanted the culprit to be punished as much as anyone, but we don't want our youth abused. We sat on a dharna in front of the Police Commissioner's office, demanding that all police station committees should have women members, bold women, women who know their rights.

In the pre-school class in the slum, there are now 35 children. Here, the women know through direct experience that when child mortality is high, families will have more children: what gives people the confidence to reduce the size of their family is the first glimmering of social security.

Self-help, self-reliance, self-restraint – this is the vision of India coming from the slums. Whether those obsessed with Western mirages of expansion, wealth and endless growth will have the wit to make use of the vast wisdom, the reservoir of human resources at hand in every such settlement in India, remains to be seen.

Sarojimma: A Woman from Lakshmipuram

A mature woman, with creases around the eyes, eyes that are deep amber, full of humour and pathos: her hair is scraped back into a still luxuriant bun, but is silver at the sides. In her nose, the silver daisy of a stud; her mouth breaks readily into a smile. She has large, work-worn hands. Sarojimma wears a vivid green saree that shows to advantage the colour of her still fine skin. A dignified, powerful presence.

It was not always like this.

Sarojimma was born in Lakshmipuram, youngest of four children. When she was a baby, her father deserted the family for a woman with whom he went to Bombay. To keep the family together, Sarojimma's mother went into domestic service. She worked 'not as a servant', Sarojimma insists, 'but as a domestic worker', in an Anglo-Indian household. The employer helped the children with their schooling, although Sarojimma's youngest brother died at this time. They lived in an outhouse in the employer's compound, and Sarojimma's mother was at the call of the employer at all times. Exhausted, she died at 35.

Sarojimma was then 15. She herself married soon afterwards, and went to live with her husband's family. He proved to be a drinker and gambler, and after three years he abandoned her, pregnant. She lived with her one remaining brother in Lakshmipuram. Within one month of giving birth to her daughter, Sarojimma, too, went into domestic service. She worked in the house of a Sindhi family, cleaning, swabbing, cutting vegetables. She was paid Rs25 a month. This was not enough to keep herself and her daughter. She went to work in a popcorn factory, where the wage was Rs120 a month. She lived in one room with her daughter, at a rent of Rs50 a month.

When her child was five, Sarojimma married again. From this marriage she has five children, of whom two are still at school. One of her boys has dropped out of studying. 'He ran away. He just comes back to eat and sleep.' Sarojimma says that unemployment and lack of earning power are the worst afflictions of young people in the community. They are constantly tempted to waste their time, playing cards, drinking, falling into bad company. Sarojimma is proud of her oldest daughter who has gone to Delhi to work as a domestic. She has a good employer and sends money home, although she is often lonely, unhappy at the separation from her family.

Recently, Sarojimma's second husband died. He was working in the Bangalore dairy. Also a drinker, one day he fell down at the bus stand on his way to work. He had a stroke, went into a coma, and died. If an employee dies on duty, another member of the family 'inherits' the job; and Sarojimma's second daughter is now working in her father's place.

This sad outline of Sarojimma's story gives little clue to the achievement of her life. For Sarojimma is now president of an ambitious effort to organise domestic workers in a trade union in the Indiranagar area of Bangalore.

In 1984, when the slum was scheduled for demolition, Sarojimma was living in a hut, 6 metres by 5, on the road. This hut belonged to a woman prominent in the Congress(I) Party, to whom Sarojimma paid rent. When Bangalore City Corporation wanted to demolish the slum, the owner demanded possession of her hut, so she would be entitled to compensation. When Sarojimma refused to move, the owner denounced her as a prostitute, and gave the police money to evict her. The women of Women's Voice supported Sarojimma and urged her not to move. She was very frightened. Her friends took her to the police station and confronted the Police Inspector. 'How can you support the right of a woman who lives in a big house against a poor woman living in a hut?' The Police Inspector was convinced by the women's insistence that those who occupied the huts should have the same rights to rehousing as those who owned them.

Sarojimma's landlady brought men with knives and clubs to

evict her at midnight. The people of the community came out to
support Sarojimma. They drove off the assailants; and the right to
rehousing of those renting properties was established.

During the period while the slum dwellers were waiting for
their houses to be rebuilt in Lakshmipuram, Women's Voice supported Sarojimma in her effort to organise the women workers.

They still work as domestic labour. Their consciousness has
certainly risen, but not their economic status, according to Ruth
Manorama. Sarojimma is committed to seeing an end to the exploitation which destroyed her own mother, and which remains
the curse of women workers who are believed to be beyond the
scope or reach of trade unionism.

In many families in Lakshmipuram, children also do domestic
work, both before and after school. Sarojimma says that to feed a
family of seven people, Rs50 ($1.60) per day will just about en-
sure survival, but for good nourishment Rs100 is required (about
$3.30). In the morning, most families eat only rice or chappati; at
midday, rice with watery dal, and the same in the evening. Many
do not eat at all in the morning. They say, 'I will not wash my
face until the afternoon', because they believe that to do so in the
morning makes you hungry. Some people bring home leftovers
from their employers.

*The people in the rich houses always blame the servants if they
themselves lose or forget where they have put something. We have to deal
with that. If servants are unjustly accused, women will go to the police
station and say, 'It is not our fault if we are poor. Why should we be
blamed?' If a woman is sick and cannot go to work, and the employer
refuses to pay, 10 or 15 women will go to that employer and ask why he
or she will not pay the wage. In Indiranagar, people know there is a
union, so they will take more care and not make mischief without good
cause. If a domestic worker is ill-treated, we will go and have a dharna
outside the house of her employer. In that way, knowledge of our work
spreads, and more women come to join us.*

*The government organised a week-long programme for domestic
workers. Part of this was to arrange that servants go and register with
the police station and leave their photographs there. We opposed that
and had an alternative programme. We said 'If the servants must do
that, then so must the employer also. Our names and addresses are
with the employers. Let that be enough.'*

One boy was living in the house where the employer was not
giving him proper food. The hungry child stole a chappati. To
teach him a lesson, the employer poured boiling water over his
hands. She then locked him in for three days. The wound became
infected, and he had to be admitted to hospital. (Curiously, I had

heard an almost identical story when talking to older women in Britain who had worked as domestic servants in Edwardian England.) The story appeared in the newspaper, and the women went and sat outside the employer's house. *We threw tomatoes and mud at the whitewashed wall. The police had to arrest her. She is now on bail, and the union is filing a case against her.*

There was another case, a 12-year-old girl. Her employers had a ring, which they had locked away in an upstairs bureau. They looked for it downstairs, and when they couldn't find it, immediately called the police, who arrested the girl.

We came to hear about it late in the night. Women should not be kept in police stations overnight. The girl was kept there, harassed and molested by the police. We had her released, and sat outside the police station. We broke some of the windows. After two years, the police have come to know there is a union, so they have now filed a case against us. When the girl was released, the employers admitted that they had found the ring. We have now filed a case against those employers. The child had been beaten up by them, and then again by the police.

Most of the women in Lakshmipuram are domestic workers. The area is close to a 'residential area' (it is significant that only the middle classes 'reside'; the poor merely live). Sarojimma goes with me to some of the neighbours. Yellamma works four hours a day, from six to ten in the morning, in three houses; she gets Rs40, 60 and 60 respectively, per month. Madevi works in four houses, from six to twelve each morning; at each house she collects Rs60. Philomena, a much younger woman, works in two houses, for Rs70 and 100. Muniyamma, who looks after her grandchild so her daughter can work, serves in one house for Rs150 a month.

The income has improved, but is still meagre. This reflects the low value placed on the labour of women workers. Sarojimma says they are now working towards a basic income of Rs300–400 a month for a four-hour working day. Here, in Lakshmipuram, wages have risen perceptibly over the past few years. Sarojimma says that the union sends a representative with the worker to meet the prospective employer; 'like that, the employers also get to be interviewed by the workers'.

Sarojimma is now completely fearless, capable of confronting officials, police, bureaucrats, goondas. She speaks at public meetings, and with 1,200 other domestic workers, joined a march of almost 100,000 urban poor in Bangalore in May 1993. Women like her are not few in India now; a strength born of oppression and injustice, and made more powerful by complete incorruptibility. Sarojimma will accept only improvements that have been won for all the women. She is a symbol of the stirring in what has been seen traditionally as the fatalistic torpor of the poor in India. The powerful defenders of vested interests ignore the questions and demands posed by Sarojimma and the many thousands like her at their peril.

9. Bombay

The Parsees of Bombay

When people refer to the diversity and richness of India's cultures, they mean a vast range of religions and belief systems, varying from the animism of the Adivasis of central India to the Westernised elite of Delhi; from Jains to Syrian Christians, from the banalised Hinduism of the BJP to the devout sense of dharma of the fishing communities in Orissa, from the impoverished Muslim communities in Hyderabad to the Pathans settled in Bombay. In Bombay, I met some Parsees, a leading exponent of a liberation theology for Islam and, most surprisingly of all, some tribal people living out a degraded form of their traditional culture in Borivali National Park in the heart of Bombay.

Although Bombay is the most 'Westernised' city in India, and indeed likes to think of itself as both sophisticated and cosmopolitan, it nevertheless contains worlds within worlds, enclosed communities, which cling to ancient faiths and cosmologies, defying the advance of 'modernisation'.

The elderly Parsees sit on concrete benches on the thin tongue of land at Nariman Point, and watch the sun spill its dying light on to the Arabian Sea. The wind plays in the white sarees of the women, which flap around their bodies like agitated ghosts, while their pale faces remain fixed on the dissolving disc of the sun. They appear to the observer to present a spectacle of intense melancholy. Not so, says Khojeste Mistry, of the Zoroastrian Studies Unit at Cama Institute. *You mistake for melancholy the reverence of Zoroastrians for the element of fire. What you are witnessing is an act of worship.*

And yet the Parsees of Bombay are dwindling in number. There are now about 80,000, and they are an ageing minority in this city of youth and exuberance. They have lost the vigour which produced so many Parsee entrepreneurs and social reformers in the colonial period, as well as efficient assistants to the British administration. *My grandmother's generation still regret the departure of the British,* says Manek Mistry, a young teacher. *She would always refer to Queen Victoria as 'apni ranee', our queen.*

Many Parsees now feel they live in a hostile environment; and as they stand at the edge of the road waiting for a pause in the relentless polluting traffic, it is easy to understand their repugnance at the phenomenal growth of Bombay. The impression they give is of having come down in the world, of having made a dignified retreat from it. This is certainly borne out in visits to their homes; the 'colonies', often built by charitable trusts at subsidised rents, are ornate buildings, in once-quiet suburbs of Bombay, now under siege from the swirling tide of dispossessed humanity. The stone buildings are crumbling, beyond restoration, attacked by too many monsoon rains. The sober interiors, with carved darkwood Victorian furniture, tiled floors, engraved glass screens and garlanded images of Zarathustra, have a genteel archaic air; the courteous English and ceremonious manners of the Parsees only reinforce the sense of being stranded in time. *The Parsees no longer produce industrialists like Tata, Godrej and Mafatlal*, says Manek Mistry. *Most young Parsee boys want a safe job in government service, or want to emigrate, especially to North America. It is the women who are more ambitious now, a driving force in the community. I suppose some of the most enterprising men have gone abroad. There is a Parsee male brain drain. Parsees are now a diasporic community – in Britain, North America, Australia. This can lead to dilution of the faith. We are trying to establish worldwide networks to rekindle a sense of our common identity. Even in Iran, people who were forcibly converted to Islam are now reconverting.*

The Parsees are Zoroastrians who have been in India since the twelfth century, when they fled Iran under persecution from Islam. Previously, Zoroastrianism had been the state religion of Iran. They landed at Sanjan in Gujarat, and asked permission of King Jadavrana to settle there. In reply, he sent them a jar of milk filled to the brim, indicating that there was no room. In response, the leader of the Parsees placed some sugar and gold in the jar. It did not overflow. He returned it to the king. They were allowed to settle, provided they did not seek converts; and the gold of the Parsees mixed with the people; there was no overflow. The Zoroastrians have never attempted to convert others. This probably helps to account for the acceptance they have gained: they have not been perceived as a threat by any other religious group.

There is much discussion within the community about the cause of the decline in numbers. Some say it is because the young are too concerned with material comfort, and delay marriage until they are 35 or 40; others say it is a consequence of inbreeding, which produces imbalances – a mixture of geniuses and sickly children. Some blame the decline of belief in the dignity of labour 'My grandfather was a carpenter', one Parsee said. 'The last thing he wanted for his sons was to see them adorn an office chair. Now that is the height of ambition for most Parsee parents.' Certainly the Parsees are the most highly educated group in India – around 60 per cent have degrees.

Other people complain of a lack of leadership, the weakening of commitment to the faith. 'The average Parsee can quote more freely from the Bible and other religions than from our own scriptures.' Then there is a factionalism that divides conservatives from reformers. 'Some people want conversions; they want anybody to be admitted to the Fire temples. They even want to change the way in which we dispose of the dead.' Perhaps the most well-known aspect of Zoroastrianism is the way in which the dead are exposed to the vultures in the Towers of Silence. Burial or cremation are not permitted because this pollutes the most sacred of the elements of the earth.

The present crisis has led directly to much creative and energetic work at the Centre for Zoroastrian Studies. Khojeste Mistry insists that youth are coming back to the faith, reacting in turn against the neglect of its basic tenets by their parents' generation. Indeed, there is much in Zoroastrianism that ought to make it profoundly appealing to the declining years of the millennium. *You don't have to fast or sit on a mountaintop. It isn't a life-denying faith. It is the only religion to promote spirituality through the creation of wealth. It says that spiritual and material well-being are inseparable. The difference betwen Zoroastrianism and Judaism, for instance, is that Judaism believes that good and evil issue from the same God. We see the Lord of Wisdom as responsible for all the good in the world. He is not responsible for the evil. There is no wrath of God in Zoroastrianism. We see evil, pain and even death as the temporary triumph of evil over good. We postulate that darkness cannot come from light. Light is at the heart of our religious imagery. If humankind consciously promotes the good, it will be possible to vanquish the lie; theoretically, even death can be conquered. Zoroastrians have never killed in the name of religion.*

We have a common ethnic origin; we are of Iranian stock. Khojeste Mistry stresses that many elements of other world religions are of Zoroastrian origin: heaven and hell, the resurrection of the body, the day of judgement, all extend through Judaism into Christianity. The teachers of Plato and Socrates were Zoroastrian magi; and magi greeted the birth of Jesus. Zoroastrianism was the state religion of Iran for a thousand years; only the priests became too powerful, too overwhelming. Islam appeared then like a breath of fresh air.

The faith has always been ecologically aware, more akin to Buddhism than Christianity or Islam in that respect. There are prayers for water, earth, mountains. *If rituals require the plucking of fruits, we apologise to the plant or tree for doing so. We have a profound respect for nature; there is nothing of the Christian idea that humanity has dominion over the rest of creation. We also have a powerful commitment to social justice. Wealth is a virtue, but it must be shared. Zoroastrianism is in sympathetic accord with the most humane form of capitalism.* As evidence of the enterprise of Parsees, it is pointed out that the first three non-British MPs in the House of Commons were all Parsees, one a Conservative, one Liberal and the third Communist.

Although ethnicity is transmitted through the male line, Parsee women are among the most emancipated in India, and increasingly they exceed men in professional competence and attainment. Bapsy Dastur is characteristic of the new generation; a strong-minded and enthusiastic member of the Zoroastrian Studies Group, she is a solicitor. Significantly, she says that when she tried to enter the legal profession she had far more trouble from male colleagues than resistance among her own people. Her experience echoes that of many younger Zoroastrians: *We have reacted against the blind mechanistic faith of our parents, against the lack of living awareness of its deeper meaning. When I used to ask my elders why we had to wear the sudreh kusti – the sacred thread and garment – they used to say 'Because it's good for you', with no explanation; the kind of response to enrage the young. At school I dabbled in other religions, Shivism, Hinduism, Theosophy and Christian Science. Yet I could never accept a God who inflicted sorrow and death upon humanity. What appeals to me most in our own tradition is that God is good, and bad things come, not from him, but from evil external to him.*

We are now finding a renaissance of Zoroastrianism, with young people eager to find out more. At one time, I even refused to go to the Fire Temple, because I didn't know the reason why we were expected to go. We have started a club, bringing together Zoroastrians from all over the world. Everywhere, there has been a rekindling of interest in our roots.'

This was borne out by Aspi Mistry, who tells that when his brother-in-law was in Tehran, he went into a small shop, and there, in a dark corner, he noticed a picture of Zarathustra. He looked at the shopkeeper and asked him if he was a Zoroastrian. 'Oh no', he said, 'I'm a Muslim'; and he put two fingers to his temple, to indicate that he was a Muslim only at gunpoint.

Adi Doctor lives at Dadar, in a pleasant suburb in central Bombay; the compound is sequestered, shielded by sheltering trees. The flat is cool and quiet. Unmarried, Adi Doctor lives with his mother and sister; until three years ago he was employed in the Bank of India, but gave it up to devote himself to the study of Zoroastrianism. He insists that he is in the mainstream of Zoroastrian tradition, although he is perceived as a conservative, because he still wears the head-covering, the topi, that Parsees are scripturally enjoined to wear at all times.

He abhors those who say 'Parsees must change with the times', because 'we are not talking about social customs, but eternal truths'. Some people don't even have the initiation ceremony for children, the navjote, when they are invested with the girdle and garment, the sudreh kusti, which they should keep until death. The term comes from the Avesta word 'kush', which means circuit, to protect the individual from the evil in nature. It has to be continuously recharged like a battery. It should be made of wool from Pashmira sheep; wool absorbs all the vibrations of the environment, physical and ultra-physical pollution.

Adi Doctor regrets that many Parsees do not want to know their history. Awareness of the past helps to illuminate the present. *The violence in Azerbaijan at the time of the dissolution of the Soviet Union makes more sense if you know that Russian and Iranian Azerbaijan are the same country, and have as much claim to be reunited as former East and West Germany did. All this area was part of the old Sassanian Empire, all Zoroastrian. It was the Zoroastrian kings of Iran who first gave the Christians shelter from Roman persecution. They gave them Armenia. Ultimately, the Crusades enabled Armenia to become the first part of Iran to be Christian.*

Azerbaijan is a Persian word, meaning land of fire. In Azerbaijan many fire temples consecrated by the Iranian kings have been excavated. The spark of the old religion gave the Azerbaijan/Armenia conflict an extra edge. Many people in the old Soviet Union continued to practise Zoroastrianism, although after official persecution of religion, it went underground. Many kept fires burning in basements and cellars. The same is true of Kurdistan; no wonder the Islamic powers won't grant them autonomy. Many Zoroastrians are externally Muslims, but still wear the sacred girdle. In fact, Shi'ism is a shadow of the old Zoroastrian faith. When Iraq went to war with Iran, it is significant that Saddam Hussein invoked a battle in which the Arabs had defeated Zoroastrians.

At the time of the Shah, in 1926, under the Pahlevi dynasty (Pahlevi is the name of the old spoken language of Iran, as opposed to Avesta, the scriptural language), there was a great revival in ancient Iranian culture, religion, civilisation. There were once 300 million Zoroastrians, extending from the Tigris and Euphrates to China, including the Asian republics of what was the Soviet Union.

Zoroastrianism has survived 3,500 years. To those who worry about dwindling numbers, Adi Doctor says *When we first came to India 1,000 years ago, what were our numbers then? The first census was taken in 1871. The population of Parsees in India has never been higher than 125,000. At the beginning of this century it was down to 70,000. We should not panic. It may be that nature limited the rise in our population as part of some divine scheme of things.*

Khojeste Mistry complains that there is no leadership in the contemporary Parsee community. *Until the eighteenth century, priests were the leaders. In the nineteenth century, Parsees were the first community in India to avail themselves of Western technology. They became industrialists, lawyers, doctors, accountants. This gave them a headstart over other communities, and they had the favour of the colonial power, many becoming more British than the British. They were merchant princes, but the religious feeling weakened. Their secular power rose, but that didn't produce leadership. Bombay would not be Bombay without the Parsees.*

Indeed, the celebrated Taj Hotel in Bombay was the creation of Jamsetji Tata, who, having been refused admission at the Apollo Hotel, which was at that time reserved 'for Europeans only', bought some reclaimed land at Apollo Bunder, and constructed the Taj Hotel, facing the harbour. It was the first building in Bombay to be lighted with electricity; Jamsetji Tata bought much of the equipment himself – a soda and ice-making unit, washing and polishing machines, lifts and an electric generator. It opened in 1903; and while the hotel to which the illustrious Parsee was refused admission is now a market, the Taj continues to be one of the most distinctive and luxurious hotels in the world.

Since independence, says Khojeste Mistry, *our elite business and professional people have become anti-Parsee. The Parsee identity took a beating; possibly because of our closeness to the British. If you talk of Parsee identity, you are branded a communalist. Yet if you know who you are, you become a better citizen. My conflict with the business elite is that I say we should rediscover our roots, and that will make us more patriotic Indians.*

We promote material well-being, but if it becomes excessive, it can stifle the community. Selfishness has invaded our people as a direct result of lack of religious awareness. It is sad that our educated and powerful have no vision. Youth is our salvation: we are producing a new generation of technocrats and professionals. The old always bemoan the next generation. They complain that we don't have so many doctors and lawyers coming up; but we have more computer analysts, more scientists, architects. There are few manual workers, it is true; but there is no serious unemployment. There is a small element of layabouts, and a few poor. But in fact, a West German sociologist called the Parsees 'the richest community in the world, with a welfare system second to none'. Over half our population live in subsidised housing, most of it far better than that of any other group in Bombay. Free education, medical benefits, welfare from womb to Tower of Silence. Yet there is a growing group of poor. That comes from bad application of resources; the trustees of our many Parsee charities have become blasé and indifferent.

Adi Doctor says that the first step to salvation is to speak the truth, whatever the consequences. The trouble with Parsees is that they imbibed culture, etiquette and customs from others. *For a thousand years, we had covered our heads; under the influence of the British, we learned to doff our caps. Yet we are called bigots, fanatics, communalists, when we advocate simply observing the tenets of our faith. Our people are digging their own graves. Thirty per cent of Parsees would probably prefer cremation to the Towers of Silence. The latest fashion is for people to donate their bodies to hospitals for medical science; there is a false delicacy about vultures devouring our bodies.*

In Bombay, there were colonies of Parsees. Certain areas were known to be Parsee areas – the Fort area, Victoria Terminus, Flora Fountain, with pockets at Grant Road and Tardev. Now many have moved out to Borivali, Virar, Bandra and Andheri. When he speaks, it is reminiscent of Jews in London talking about the old areas of Jewish settlement in the East End, and the movement to Hendon, Golders Green and Edgware; with the difference that the Jews were fleeing poverty, while for the Parsees it has been a gentle going down in the world, a faded gentility that has driven them out of the centre of Bombay.

The average Parsee has little creativity today; if you ask them to define themselves, most will say 'Zoroastrianism is good words, thoughts and deeds'. They rarely have more than two children. Women are the culprits – they want to follow careers, they see children as encumbrances.

Manek Mistry is in his thirties. A botanist, he sees himself as Indian first and Parsee second. *Parsees are my community, Zoroastrianism is my religion. When the Parsees left Iran, one group went to China, and another to India. There is no trace of those who went to China; why should those in India have survived? It shows there is nothing immutable about our fate. Because of inbreeding in the Indian Parsees, there is now a blood deficiency in many people, G-6 PD. There are only a few million in the world who suffer from this; there is one small Greek island where the community inbred for generations. I expect the Parsees to disappear, because of not making converts and because of increasing intermarriage.*

The Parsees were highly valued by the British, because of their adaptability. They were translators for the British – the name Dubhash is common, meaning bilingual. Some sold liquor, Ginwala, Daruwaval; as well as names like Doctor, Contractor, Motorwala. Mistry means foreman, one of the most common names. Not all were honourable. Some landlords used force to make tribals work on their lands. In the villages in the last century Parsees kept tribal mistresses, their children were called d'vasdas.

Late evening. The city is chaotic, full of the tumult of home-going crowds and traffic congestion. Secluded from the clamour behind bhendi trees and gnarled banyans, the old Parsees remember the time when they always performed kusti on returning home from the office, reciting the sacred Avesta formulae and retying the girdle in two reef-knots, praying before eating, and observing complete silence while they ate, when they greeted their elders as 'sahibji'; when the British would employ only Parsees in the cash departments of the banks, because they were the only Indians considered sufficiently trustworthy.

One might have thought that the optimistic tenets of Zoroastrianism which animate its energetic young believers would be singularly appropriate for the end of the twentieth century: the idea of spiritual salvation through material wealth, the deep respect for nature and ecology, the faith that evil can be vanquished. It seems a pity that the prohibition on conversions should deprive the spiritually hungry of the world from sharing the blessings of so unaggressive and humane a faith.

Liberation Theology for Islam

Bombay suffered more than any other city in India from the violence that followed the destruction by Hindu communalists of the mosque at Ayodhya in December 1992. This came as a great shock to many in Bombay, who had always been proud that their city is the most cosmopolitan and sophisticated in India. They love to compare it favourably with Delhi: in spite of the rapid growth of Delhi, it is still essentially a provincial town that goes to bed at nine at night, while in Bombay everything is available round the clock. The outbreak of killing and looting that afflicted Byculla, Bombay Central, Mahim, Jogeshwari and many other places in early January 1993 claimed hundreds of lives. It seemed impossible to account for it, in this, the most advanced, the richest city in India.

It may be that the very 'advanced' standard of Bombay was one of the precipitating causes. Bombay, with the jewelled horseshoe of Marine Drive, the elegant structures of Malabar Hill, the grandiose remnants of the Raj buildings of Victoria Terminus, the Law Courts and University, suggests a city which can hold its own with any metropolis in the world. Perhaps here we see the form of development to which the government has committed India at its most florid and exuberant. Here, a city of migrants, uprooted from desperate and familiar rural poverty, find that they have exchanged one form of dispossession for another. They confront the market economy in its most naked form. Far from being an aberrant recrudescence of archaic obscurantism, it may be that what occurred in Bombay and elsewhere after Ayodhya is actually a consequence of accelerating 'modernisation', and the assault upon identity which comes with it; conflicts that can only be made worse, divisions that can only be accentuated by the present unsustainable and inequitable development path to which the country's present leaders are now committed. To say this is no idle opportunistic attack on liberalisation; the centralising power implied by an entity called 'the global economy' is self-explanatory; and those disadvantaged on the periphery, how will they reclaim their broken autonomy and damaged sense of worth, if not by returning to their roots, whether these are regional, ethnic or religious? The success of the BJP/Shiv Sena alliance in the State elections of Maharashtra in February 1995 seems to confirm the symbiotic relationship between 'development' and fundamentalism.

Those who are desperately seeking to avoid such reactions must fight on two levels: they must struggle, not only against the most obvious embodiment of communalism – the BJP, RSS, VHP combine, as well as its Islamic equivalent – but also against the relentless pressures dictated by the international financial institutions, which are themselves a form of fundamentalism. For the West now imposes its structural adjustment programmes on more than 70 countries in the world – identical prescriptions that bear no relation to the existing circumstances of the country under consideration, but are dictated by Western ideology and self-interest. All are characterised by policies that actually exacerbate social inequality: decreased government social spending, privatisation, industrialisation, increased exports to service debts to the West.

These fundamentalisms are not unconnected; indeed they feed upon each other, creating a spiral of dispossession and violence. To intervene is therefore doubly difficult. This only reinforces the will of people like Asgar Ali Engineer and those who support EKTA, the movement for unity in Bombay – activists, intellec-

tuals, film-makers, workers, slum-dwellers, students – in their de-
termination to resist.

Author of *Liberation Theology for Islam*, Asgar Ali Engineer
works out of a small cramped office at Andheri. He speaks pas-
sionately of the effects of the present policies upon India, effects
that elites do not see, and which make their apparent espousal of
secularism doomed and an act of the greatest hypocrisy.

*In India, as elsewhere, the imposition of a valueless capitalism is a
source of growing hatred between people. Feudalism, of course, was
never just. But it was not based upon money and commerce alone. Even
a ruler had a certain dharma, he was the protector of religion. Even the
rich landowners and estate holders indulged in charity, so that the
sufferings of others were diminished. Deep human values were there,
and it was this that made such societies last for so long. Religion was
the embodiment of these values. Capitalist culture in Iran sought to
destroy it. Where money is everything, a reaction is bound to come.
Look at Egypt. Look at Algeria; there, socialism had also created a
corrupt elite. It is the poor people in Algeria who support fundamentalism because they suffered most, while the elite got the benefit.*

*It is the same in India. The backlash is coming from the poorer
sections. They think that their suffering comes from the destruction of
old values; if these are restored, everything will be all right again. In
Iran under the Shah, Islam had been neglected. Revive Islam, the
belief went, and corruption and money and immorality will go, and
the country will regain its old glory. Khomeini was also talking about
social justice. The Communists – who also had this as their theme –
were marginalised when the revolution occurred. They were wiped out.
Why? Because they had no respect for the sensibilities of the people.
There were some Iranian students here at the time. They were Marxists. They talked to me, and as events unfolded, they came to realise
that they had performed a disservice to the people of Iran.*

*For a new consciousness to emerge, it must respect the sensibilities
of the people. They will not even listen to you if you do not ... Life is
not determined by economics, but by other things as well – cultural
and religious traditions. Where what you are working for is harmful
to tradition, go circumspectly. Do not launch an outright attack.*

*I fight against many traditions, but I do so cautiously, so as not to
hurt people, and always with reference to the Koran. For instance,
with the status of women. Many Muslims think women have an inferior status that is God-given, that they have no equal rights. When I
quote Koranic verses to refute this, they are shocked, because they
must then acknowledge that they are going against God. Then they
appreciate what they are doing is wrong. But you must take the belief
of the people as the root of your work.*

In the 1980s I was in Pakistan, at a conference of progressive writers. I was talking about liberation theology in Islam. They were aghast. 'You want to take us back to the Middle Ages.' No, not go back, not take you back. Liberate the future with the help of religion. I told them that there is the problem of the masses, which will become your problem also, if you do not take into account their sensibility. There is no safe haven for you if you mount an attack on religion ... You must relate to the society in which you live. Attack religion and be isolated, or be hypocritical. You must have a proper strategy, even if you don't believe in religion. You must not alienate the masses, and make reactionaries that way.

Social justice is central to the Koran, if not to present-day Islamic society. 'Do justice' is a commitment. The closest thing to piety is not prayer or fasting: doing justice is closest to piety. I told them, 'To counter the fundamentalism of Zia, this is what you must do – bring out those contradictions that are also within the Koranic tradition.'

Similarly, rationalists in India do not understand, nor do Marxists, nor Westernisers. They cling to the dogmas of nineteenth-century rationalism, even though these secular dogmas are not appropriate in post-industrial society. Ethics cannot be rational. You cannot impose atheism, as the Soviet Union discovered. Rationalists hate spirituality, which is their error; for spirituality is an essential component of human experience. This is not, of course, the same thing as religious dogma. Quite the reverse – it is often opposed to it.

Naturally, when we speak in this way, we receive superficial criticism, accusations of wanting 'to go back to the past'. But there are certain problems and concepts that cannot be answered with science. Dialogues, interrogations between rationalism and spirituality are always necessary. If I am religious, deeply, I'll be respectful of the religion of others, I won't hate Hinduism or Christianity. Through my own faith, I appreciate the essence of other religions. But if I am dogmatic, orthodox, this will block and blind me to others.

Each religion puts certain values at the centre of its beliefs, values that do not contradict those of other religions, but are complementary to them. For instance, Buddhism has the removal of suffering and compassion; in Hinduism there is non-violence; love in Christianity; social justice and equality in Islam. Where do these conflict? In fact, they cannot exist without each other. Without compassion, you can't have non-violence; without love, you can't have social justice. If we develop this position, we will forget dogmas.

Of course all religions become institutionalised, but factors other than religious ones play a part in this institutionalising process – powerful establishments, vested interests appropriate the religion; hence its ossification. It is not only religion that makes people rigid, it is also self-interest. Institutionalisation is harmful, because it denies the religion it institutionalises. Islam is liberating of humanity; but when institutionalised, it becomes an oppression. 'Go back to the Koran, and then you will know your duty in the world.' No word in the Koran shows disrespect to other religions. It enjoins to hold all prophets in equal respect. It attacks corruption, attacks those religious leaders who were corrupt for their own interests, amassing wealth – that is not an attack on Christianity or Judaism.

When Westernisation is imposed, whether in Iran or India, people live in a dichotomy. There is a split consciousness. They may live at a high standard of material comfort, but they experience a conflict and mental agony because of their duties. They are Westernised in appearance, but they may well become obscurantist in other ways.

If there is a creative synthesis between modernisation (which is not the same thing as Westernisation) and tradition, then there is liberation. But Westernisation plus tradition creates a dichotomy which comes out as obscurantist, reactionary, fundamentalist. I have many Westernised friends who smoke, drink and womanise; but at the first sign of trouble, they run to some fakir or babu. Their religion then becomes a superstition. The highly Westernised become obscurantist, and can no longer appreciate the spirit of religion. Symptoms of this are seen socially: our festivals have become noisy and showy, instruments of Western interests, like conspicuous consumption. Those reeling under the impact of the West take part in order to satisfy their conscience, not as acts of piety.

What we say may remain as empty words, until their meaning is wakened by some crisis. And crises have come, because we have become monolithic, monocultural. We are unused to other sensibilities. We have to work as active agents of God, to open up each other's perception of the underlying sameness of all great faiths.

The Warlis of Borivali National Park

Although Bombay is the first point of destination for many visitors to India, few remain there more than a few days. Bombay is one of the most splendid cities in the world. Its beauty lies not so much in its material fabric, despite the decayed imperial grandeur of some of its architecture: its extraordinary pulse and energy, its beauty are wholly human. People who visit India either bypass the poor, on their way to some conventional scenic amenity, or they are so repelled that they go home appalled by the injustice and cruelty of India. I know people who say 'How can you bear to go there?' as though even to visit such a place of monstrous social injustice were somehow to encourage it.

Even such meagre touristic attractions as Bombay offers are nearly always misperceived, their meaning not understood. This is the essence of a tourism which presses upon the world as yet another mutation of colonialism: other cultures do not exist for themselves, but only for the delight and distraction of visitors. Their existence remains secondary to their capacity to separate tourists from their foreign exchange.

I went with Sarah d'Mello to the 70 hectares of forest land in north Bombay, known as the Borivali National Park. Sarah d'Mello is from a privileged family, and is a former headmistress of an exclusive girls' school. She gave up her position to work with some of the excluded and marginalised of her own city. There are many like her all over India, people who follow a tradition of renunciation and dedication to simplicity and to social improvement. Their work is rarely celebrated. It does not fill the columns of the newspapers and magazines; but in aggregate, it constitutes a powerful resistance against social and economic violence, both traditional and modern.

The extensive national park is so only on paper; and the rights of those who live in it have never been settled. This is a major misfortune for the Adivasis, or tribal people, many of whom have lived here for hundreds of years.

The melancholy decline of the forest inhabitants of India began with the British, whose ingenuity in extracting revenue introduced the money economy into a society that had until then been completely self-reliant. The subsequent rulers of India have shown little more mercy to the life of the Adivasis than their colonial predecessors.

There are now an estimated 1,600 people living in the national park, but there may well be more. Some are descendants of the original inhabitants; others migrated here two or three generations ago, coming to the shelter of the urban forest as the rural hinterland in which they formerly lived became more treeless and incapable of supporting them. More recently, others, non-Adivasis, have come here, some of whom were moved out of the slums of Bombay through evictions and demolitions.

The park is a wildlife sanctuary and tourist attraction. On Sundays, it is a picnic site for Bombay people, who have few such amenities within reach of the city. In spite of this, the condition of the Adivasis has been ignored, although they are close to the centre of India's richest city.

Sarah d'Mello surveyed as many of the park-dwellers as could be contacted by her small group of researchers. None of the children had been immunised; many were malnourished, and most had intestinal worms. Scabies and lice were common. Most mothers were anaemic. Leprosy and alcoholism had taken a severe toll. Many had never seen a doctor; few knew their age. Their way of life, symbiotic with the rich luxuriant growth of the forest, had become degraded as the forest itself was invaded, and as they were denied access to the forest produce which sustained them and which they sustained.

In the area designated national park, the cattle and goats of the people were confiscated, since these were considered a threat to growing things. Their small padi-fields on the lower reaches of the park were declared illegal. They became stigmatised – as in so many other places in India – as encroachers and despoilers of the environment. That they had tended and nurtured the forests for millennia did not interfere with this stern judgment.

None of the people in the forest has a ration card, which means that although they are among the poorest, they have no access to subsidised food through the public distribution system. They must walk 7 or 8 kilometres to buy in the market, where even the coarsest grain is Rs8 a kilo. Some survive through the brewing of *daru*, illegal liquor, and many of the men are addicted. Daru is made from palm-sap, molasses, sometimes with the addition of battery fluid and chemicals. Each still has its own recipe; many stills are owned by people from outside the forest. Some people sell bundles of twigs for firewood, both to the illicit stills, and in the market outside the forest boundary, although they are, in theory, forbidden to touch anything that grows.

In the post-monsoon period, when the vegetation is lush and grows quickly, people cultivate patches of vegetables, half concealed by the high grasses: a few square metres, with a canopy of creepers about 1.5 metres high, and *kakri* and *shirali* – cucumbers and gourds – ripening on the vines. If these vegetable plots are discovered by forest officials, they demand a bribe of 100 rupees. If the cultivator cannot pay, the vegetable patch may be burnt.

One member of each Adivasi family is supposed, by law, to be employed by the Forest Department at 700 rupees a month; but the work remains irregular and casual. The vast majority of people are without occupation, although traditional forest skills are remembered by some, and this helps them survive on such produce as they can harvest – mushrooms, land-crabs, tubers like *suran*, and broad green-leaf vegetables which grow wild, chicha and bamboo shoots, which have always been a standby food in the leanest times of the year. Other plants are used for their medicinal properties, traditional remedies against fever, cough or diarrhoea.

The Adivasis are always exploited, not only by the Forest Department, whose dedication to conservation of the forest remains entirely subordinate to the conservation of their own privilege. As prices rise, forest officers pressure the Adivasis with unofficial fines and bribes in order to maintain their own standard of living. They also take money from herders of goats and buffaloes, who are then permitted to graze their animals in the park. The damage done by the animals to the tender shoots and young trees is then blamed upon the Adivasis.

In the park are the Kanheri caves. These vast stone Buddhist cavities, mouths of rock exhaling a dank ancient breath of the earth, date from as long ago as the second or third century AD. They are reached by a series of stone steps. Here, women sell vegetables, fruits and drinking water to tourists, at 50 paise a tumblerful. Dwarkabhai has six children, and she earns between Rs30 and 40 a day, selling *peru* (guavas), which she buys each day from the market at Borivali Sation. In her tray of fruits she has stuck a bright turquoise peacock feather. She came from Dahanu, 100 kilometres away, at the time of her marriage. Life in the forest is precarious: there is no source of clean water, no electricity. When the women hear the jeep of the Forest Officer coming up the slope, they must run and hide their goods, or these will be confiscated.

A school and medical facilities have been recently established by volunteer groups in some *padas* (villages) in the park. In one village, Sarah d'Mello found Pintia, a four-year-old boy who had been abandoned. He was badly malnourished and eating mud and grass. His mother had died and his father had deserted him. He is now looked after in the village, and is fed each day in the school, where the older children are taught to cook. They grow their own vegetables in the school compound and use these to make their midday meal.

The forest trees soar above the new season's growth: tamarind, gulmohar, *jamun*, *pangara*, *karanji*. The people are Warlis, and have made their houses in traditional style: a rough platform of stones bound with mitti. Part of this forms a veranda, and part is then the floor of the interior. The walls are of karvi, thin wooden sticks, held in place with red earth from the forest floor, and fitted into a frame of more sturdy wood. The eaves of the roof hang low, and the roof itself is of dry palm leaves, held in place by a rough lattice of twigs and branches. Laxmi says that they have always harvested the produce of the forest carefully, and never damage trees. The Adivasis know exactly how much they can take for the survival of both themselves and the trees. The care of the forest should be given over to the Adivasis; yet they are persecuted as though they were the agents of damaging an environment, of which the cool sweet-smelling houses are the living tissue. But now, if they use wood to construct their homes, they must give Rs1000 to the forest officials.

Dhumpada is a small village which can be reached only by crossing a stream, about 8 metres wide, shallow, but running clear and fast after the rains. On the opposite side of this nalla, the village offers a view of great scenic beauty and the utmost human desolation. From this village a five-year-old was taken last year by a panther. She was badly mauled and died. The parents received compensation from the Forest Department.

Ramdas has lived in this place all his life, and has never been to Bombay. He is in his fifties, prematurely old, with a sheen of silver stubble on his face. His legs bear the marks of early malnutrition. His hut consists of a single room, with floor of beaten earth; a stove, made of three bricks. It contains a fire of small twigs. A pot of rice simmers; there are also some chappatis and watery vegetables. A little shrine stands at the base of the wall: a flame burns in a little earthenware lamp, and the white heart of a coconut shines in the darkness. Apart from a string of clothes and a bedroll, there is nothing else in the hut. Ramdas and his wife, Draupadi, who is blind in one eye, have the air of resigned neglect that afflicts people whose children have predeceased them. All five of their children died; four in infancy, but the last one, a girl in her teens, died recently, of what they call, vaguely, 'fever'. Ramdas earns a few rupees by collecting wood and selling it in the market. If an official catches him, he will be fined.

It was not like this before, the people say. *We had our own fields, we grew vegetables for our own use, with some left over to sell in the market. We had our own cattle, a farmhouse. Everything was taken from us when this became parkland.* Madhu is a woman in her sixties, who cultivated rice in her field; *suddenly*, she said, *we went from having everything we needed to having nothing at all*. If any notice was ever given to the people of the planned expropriation of their means of livelihood, it never reached them; nor was there any compensation, or alternative means of making a living.

The government of Maharashtra and the Forest Department have offered to 'relocate' the forest-dwellers in a small settlement outside the perimeter, in a kind of purpose-built township. Nothing could be more inimical to the well-being of the Adivasis. Suresh Warelkar sells wood and water, and alu leaves which fetch R1 for four leaves. The Warelkars were Mahadev *Kolis*, fish-vendors, but with the building up of Bombay and pollution of the sea, they were displaced and came here fifty years ago.

In one of the villages, no one is working today because it is the festival when the people place pots of food on the rooftops for the sustenance of the souls of their dead. They sometimes leave a jar of daru or some bidis – anything the deceased is known to have liked. They believe that the souls return in the form of crows; and until the crows have eaten some of the food, the people will not touch it. The Adivasis here have been completely Hinduised; only in more remote areas do strong traces of animism remain.

The Warlis traditionally painted with rice flour on the mud walls of their huts. Those who live in the park have virtually forfeited this skill, apart from one or two older people; they say that the struggle to survive is too arduous, and there is little to celebrate.

It is lunchtime. In the small school, the children sit cross-legged with a metal plate before them. They sing a blessing on the food they are to eat, and which they have prepared. It is almost unbearably poignant to witness their enthusiasm, their bright openness to the world, the spontaneous warmth of smiles that know nothing of the predatory world beyond, the jeopardised livelihood, the compromised future.

Suddenly a motorcycle rickshaw pulls up on the road. Two young couples – one European, one Indian – emerge from the vehicle. They carry bottles of half-consumed Kingfisher beer. They stride up to where the children are singing and demand to know what is going on here. One of the workers with the Adivasi children confronts them. *How dare you intrude into our lives like this? Either you come into the park, or you drink. But don't do both. And what gives you the right to break in upon other people's worship in this disgusting way? What goes on here is not your business. This may be a park, but it is not a human zoo.*

The park has been organised for the benefit of the privileged, for whom ample entertainments are provided – ice-cream stands, tea-stalls, fortified minibuses to go and see the lions. But nothing for the Adivasis, whose land it was, and whose land it remains. The best way to manage the forest would be not by providing out-relief for forest officials, whose indifference to the forest is total, but by entrusting it to the Adivasis, giving them permission to cultivate a small patch of ground for their subsistence with a limited number of domestic animals. This would protect both forest and people. But reflecting faithfully, as it does, the priorities of the powerful, the supremely dispensable element in the existing programme of conservation is the poor. Sarah d'Mello and those who work with her say that the solution to what look like intractable problems are actually very simple, and quite close to hand; but no one sees them because their eyes are fixed on the far horizon, looking for help from outside, grants from aid agencies, money from abroad.

In the injustice to the already impoverished, we may see, in microcosm, the meaning of the sudden concern for the environment which the rich have recently discovered. Nature, it seems, must be preserved as an amenity for the already advantaged. In this process, it is, once again, the poor who will pay, through exclusion and marginalisation, the further degradation of a life already pushed to the very edge of subsistence.

10. Curses Ancient and Modern

Leprosy

There are now known to be at least four million cases of leprosy in India, perhaps one-quarter of the world's total. In Bombay, those who solicit charity by exhibiting their mutilations to passers-by, bear terrible burdens of rejection and abandonment by their families; like the woman who left her three children so that they should not be contaminated by the prejudice of which they would also be victims. She walked from her village in Marathwada to Aurangabad, worked as vegetable seller until she could afford the train journey to Bombay. She sits in the glare of the May sun on the sidewalk, arms raised, head lowered, her fingers worn to coarse stumps. One day, she says, her children may throw a coin into the hessian rag she spreads on the pavement before her. If they do, they will certainly never recognise her. Sometimes, she dreams that they will seek her out, find her and take her home; only now she has no home, no family. Bereaved of her loved ones by her own sickness which, she says, is a living death, she can only wait for this life to pass: the heroic renunciation of those she loved more than her effaced limbs must be rewarded, she says; a woman of such quiet dignity and courage. No one looks beyond the damaged face and deformed limbs at the passionate, intelligent, sorrowing intensity of her deep, expressive eyes.

There is no such thing as a 'leper'. There are only people who suffer from leprosy. Spreading this more positive view is made more difficult by the persistence of the word, which is used in common speech against any socially stigmatised group or individual. Nor is it helped by all the untreated patients on the streets of Third World cities, whose mutilations appear to confirm that there is something both irremediable and cursed about such an affliction; and who are driven to make a 'livelihood' out of the disease.

In Bombay, there are an estimated 100,000 people with leprosy. Indeed, whole outcast communities exist, for the most part distilling illegal liquor, notably at Pushpavihar in north Bombay. At Churchgate Station, the city's busiest terminus, the lights flash 'Leprosy is a curable disease; it is not hereditary.' Below the sign sits a man whose stumps are bandaged with dingy gauze. The money chinks in his metal beaker as the home-going crowds pass by. Life expectancy is not shortened by leprosy. It used to be said that the curse is life, not death.

Alert-India is one of seven organisations in Bombay involved in the fight against leprosy, working in two wards with a combined population of 1.2 million. The work has involved house-to-house surveys, treatment of those discovered to be affected, and education. In the slums, the incidence of cases may reach 20 per thousand, compared with a city average of 10 or 12, and a lower rate in the rural areas. The persistence of social shame, the fear of being abandoned by community, neighbours and family, are powerful incentives to concealment, and indeed the greatest barrier to the effective treatment of what is readily curable.

Leprosy is known to be at least 2,500 years old. Originally found in India and China, it was taken by the army of Alexander the Great to Greece, from where it spread slowly throughout Europe. There are traces of it in Egyptian mummies, while the last indigenous case recorded in Britain was in 1798.

There was no medical breakthrough until the Norwegian Hansen isolated the bacillus in 1873; but it has only been during the past half-century, since the mix of drugs that can cure leprosy has become widely available, that hopes of total eradication programmes have risen. The Indian government aims, optimistically, to eliminate leprosy by the year 2000. As more research is undertaken, more cases are detected. This reflects the success of the screening programmes.

Dr K.P. Manek, now working for Alert-India, was originally in general practice in Bombay. The first time he diagnosed leprosy, he admits he went home and scrubbed his hands, boiled his syringes. *I was a medical graduate and I also was full of fear and prejudice, so what could you expect from people whose only instruction had come from tradition and the folklore of fate and divine retribution?* There is, he insists, no need for anyone to be crippled or debilitated by leprosy, if it is detected early enough. *All the deformities that you see on the streets of Bombay are preventable, and most cases can be cured within a matter of months.*

In the slum areas there are many obstacles to effective diagnosis. There is no pain, people do not feel ill. Where material survival is the major concern of the people, treatment of a disease which is not immediately disabling takes second place to providing themselves and their families with an income for basic sustenance. A small patch on the arm that does not even itch – this is often the first manifestation – seems a trifling complaint to slum-dwellers.

143

The best propaganda is a cured patient, says Dr Manek. As the antique, deep-rooted prejudice is slowly dispelled, more and more people refer themselves to the clinics run by Alert-India. They also come with other skin ailments – allergies, fungal infections, and a form of skin-blanching called polymorphic light corruption, which many mistake for the beginnings of leprosy. When a case is diagnosed, all other members of the family are contacted. Only about 25 per cent of patients are infectious, while 95 per cent of the population are resistant. It can be spread to those who are susceptible by skin contact, or it may be airborne. As yet, there is no vaccine.

The most common early symptoms are patches on the skin and loss of sensation. Leprosy is an infection of the peripheral nervous system: the nerves affected are in the cool areas of the skin – elbows, neck, feet. The danger of deformities comes from the loss of feeling. People may cut or burn themselves without experiencing any pain. Women at cooking stoves are especially vulnerable. They may receive severe scalds without being aware of them. The wounds may then fester or suffer further injury, which can lead to even greater damage.

You don't realise what a powerful warning system pain is until you can no longer feel it. As the disease advances, the hand becomes claw-like, and the nerves are affected. The eyelids won't close. There may be resorption of fingers and toes; motor and sensory functions are impaired. Blindness and mutilation occur as a result of loss of sensation.

Leprosy affects only human beings, unlike the TB bacillus to which it bears some resemblance. The bacillus cannot survive for long outside the body, and is killed by sunlight. The incubation period is two to five years. It responds to most of the drugs used against TB. It cannot be cultivated in a laboratory. There are two forms: lepromatous and tubercular, the latter producing nodules on the skin.

However thoroughly the slum districts of Bombay are surveyed, there are always some people who drop out of treatment: they may go back to their village or leave the treatment programme for other reasons. Some patients are so desperate for money that they will sell their drugs to others. Most of the burnt-out cases on Bombay's streets have come from villages, where they will probably have been discriminated against, denied access to the well, ostracised or even driven out. There are five self-settled communities in Bombay, but it is clearly impossible and undesirable forcibly to sequester people. In any case, leprosy can be socially concealed: the visible deformity rate is only 2 per cent.

At Ghatkopar, a busy industrial area in north Bombay, Alert-

India is holding its weekly clinic. A long blue-washed room in a corner of the compound of a hospital. Here, an effort is made to normalise, to make ordinary, what has always been regarded with such horror and superstition. There is a long queue of the poor, anxious and patient; one of those interminable queues in India, where a frieze of waiting humanity stands in line, never quite knowing whether its basic needs will ever be supplied. They carry documents in little plastic carrier-bags, so that they are secure against mildew or rats. One man, cured of leprosy 20 years ago, shows me the printed programme of an official prize-giving ceremony at which he was on display to demonstrate the curability of the disease. He is very proud to have been distinguished in this way. Other people have sheaves of old prescriptions, doctors' notes, ration cards, certificates of registration – all the sad official papers which the poor need to earn the right to be wherever they are, and the attention to which they are entitled.

Among the patients today one woman is a chairmaker, another a rag-picker, a tailor, a barber, the young son of a millworker, an employee of May and Baker, a worker at the Compton Greaves electrical factory, a peon in a government office. One 13-year-old has been sent by his teacher who noticed patches on his skin. There is a man who had dropped out of treatment for some time because he had to return to Bihar when his father died. Some of the people who come here have done so as a last resort, having gone to private doctors, where they paid for expensive ointments, creams and antibiotics which had no effect. Others have come from more distant parts of the city, unwilling to be seen visiting a leprosy clinic in their own neighbourhood. The patients are a cross-section of the industrial suburb, clearly no more deserving of the curse of God than anyone else in this vast city; indeed, many of them have already suffered in many other ways: the family from Solapur who migrated to Bombay when they lost their land to a moneylender, the people driven from Nasik by drought, the woman living on the pavement with her three children, abandoned by her husband. A dark-skinned woman in a violet saree is nursing a pink plastic doll. She sits, rocking to and fro, holding its pink face close to her dark one. Rejected by her family in the village, the doll is her child and consolation.

There is a big specialist hospital near Bombay Central Station for more severely affected people. Such centres are necessary as refuges against the prejudice of the majority. Some patients have been denied treatment at other hospitals if they have a history of leprosy. Even casualty departments have been known to turn accident cases away if there is some obvious evidence of leprosy. Pregnant women in labour have been refused entry to maternity wards. Acworth Hospital even has a separate crematorium, although it is against the law to discriminate against leprosy patients. Dr Manek speaks of the need to educate the medical profession, many of whom, whatever their level of professional competence, often lack the human sympathies to overcome traditional, deep-rooted aversions.

Because there is a higher incidence of leprosy among the poorest, Alert-India has been extending its operations to cover more general health-awareness programmes. Like so many other former 'ineradicable scourges', its presence will recede most rapidly by changing the living conditions of the poor, by giving them access to clean water, proper nutrition and education. It is significant that, given the new economic policy of the government, the kind of social spending that would achieve these goals is under threat.

Latapi, the Mexican leprologist, points out:

Leprosy cannot be completely rooted out by physicians and control offices and leprosaria and propaganda: it will disappear when the cultural and economic factors change, because leprosy is the thermometer of civilisation.

Whatever the altered social and economic context in which India's poor must now survive, the idea of a divine scourge dies hard. The superstition and prejudice surrounding leprosy may have been mitigated by the efforts of people like Dr Manek and the Alert-India teams; but prejudice and superstition are not so easily dispelled. Indeed, they readily take up their abode in some new area of human experience.

In the 1990s this new abode is AIDS, which, like leprosy before it, has also been seen as a curse, a visitation of God, a moral stigma. AIDS, like leprosy, is an immunological disorder; and while it remains incurable and is, as yet, of disputed provenance, the sufferers are blamed for the anguish it brings, just as generations of leprosy sufferers were. In that sense, AIDS patients risk becoming the 'lepers' of the millennium.

A Cry From the Streets

Something about the young man made me hesitate before avoiding his approach in Delhi's Connaught Place. Perhaps it was an unusual air of dejection, a sadness strange among those whose purpose in the heart of the Delhi tourist area – dealing, selling or hustling – generally compels them to adopt an air of cheerful honesty.

His face had a haunted, sleepless look, his eyes were sore with weeping. He said 'Apse paise mangta nahin. Apse thode batchit kar sakunga.' I'm not looking for money, I just want to talk to you. 'Why, what's wrong?'

From his shirt pocket, he took a letter, handwritten and dated one week earlier, from the All India Institute of Medical Sciences. He had, it appeared, presented himself as a blood donor, and the terse, clinical note stated that he had been 'detected' as affected by the HIV I/HIV II virus, and also as a carrier of Hepatitis B.

Mukesh is a graduate of Lucknow University, one among hundreds of thousands of unemployed graduates in India. He had come to Delhi to work in the canteen of a military base in the capital, with the help of an uncle who is in the army. He earns Rs1,500 a month ($50), but with accommodation and food included he considered this a reasonable employment, even though it in no way corresponds to his abilities or training. An able, intelligent man, now 24, he nevertheless showed complete ignorance, both about the means of transmission of the virus, and about the likely consequences for his health.

For him, the letter was a simple sentence of death. *When will I die?* he asked. *Will it be soon? Will I fall down in the street? I don't know what to do. How can I tell my family? It will kill my mother. She has done everything for me. She loves me too much. Shall I kill myself first?*

He was still stunned by the news and by the unceremonious way in which he had learned it. He was trembling with apprehension and confusion. I asked him about his life. He had been in Delhi for three years. Yes, he had been with prostitutes. Yes, he had also had sexual relations with men. One of these is married, with a family. *When I told him what had happened, he was very angry, cursed me and told me never to go near him again. My other friend was more understanding. He advised me to go home and die with my family.*

Mukesh is the eldest of four children. He is, he says, the favourite of his mother. *She loves me too much. When I am at home, every few minutes she wants to kiss me. She does not let me from her sight. How can I go home and tell her she must not touch me without getting the disease?*

He is also reluctant to tell his mother because he knows that she will sell all her jewellery and the little land she has in order to pay for medical treatment, to find a cure, when there is none. *That would not be fair to my sister and two younger brothers. I do not want them to curse my memory. It is better to die alone.*

His eyes fill with tears. I take his hand, and say to him that being

147

HIV positive is not immediately life-threatening. It can take eight or ten years before it develops into AIDS. If he looks after himself, eats and rests well, there is no reason why he should not continue to lead a reasonably normal life. There is no risk to others through daily contact, through touch or through a mother's kisses. The essential thing is to abstain from unprotected sex. He had never heard of the expression, and did not understand what it meant.

A grievous personal tragedy. Yet at the same time, emblematic of much that has gone wrong in these vast, swollen, cruel cities. For Delhi is the destination of waves of migrants, overwhelmingly male, forced, for economic reasons, to leave the home-place and those they love, in order to send home remittances upon which thousands of villages in Bihar and parts of Uttar Pradesh depend for their survival.

Delhi is a place of raw, male energy and suppressed sexuality. There are, inevitably, fateful consequences of these forced migrations, of families amputated of their loved ones, of involuntary separations, as men from distant villages find themselves alone in a strange environment for alien purposes of which they are not the true beneficiaries. A life of nothing but exile and labour is not a dignified one for a human being; particularly when, in the city, the images of lurid sexuality are all-pervasive, on cinema posters, hoardings, advertisements, in books and magazines on sale everywhere.

All this is of little comfort to Mukesh, as he surveys the wreckage of his young life. All I could say to him was that death awaits us all, and that although his own life may now be shorter than he might once have expected, this does not necessarily mean that it must be filled with hopelessness and despair. He should perhaps see the remaining years as an opportunity to achieve something of lasting good, for his family or for others afflicted as he now is. Within himself he will surely find the strength and courage to continue. I told him that I knew people in Delhi who counsel and work with HIV patients, and that they would certainly be able to help him. He said he had resolved to go home to the small town near Kanpur, initially for a ten-day visit, but would say nothing immediately to his family. He would break the news gently to them, over a period of months.

I went back to my room, deeply saddened by the desolation of the young man's life. I turned on the TV, where Star television was showing a tired American serial celebrating the unreal lives of the super-rich. How poignant that India should be able to afford to buy in this cultural junk, while living flesh and blood is perishing and wasted on the streets of its cities.

I met Mukesh several times after this first encounter. We spoke about his feelings, his changes of mood, as he swung from optimism to violent despair. He had had a quarrel with his aunt, and had told her what was wrong. She ordered him to leave the house. He went to lodge with the family of a friend from the same town in Uttar Pradesh. His friend and his wife welcomed him, and took him into their house, which was little more than a hut on the pavement. He gave up his job in the army canteen. He had spoken of going home, but made no effort to do so. Little by little, he looked more neglected, was becoming more indifferent to what would happen.

I took him to a meeting of the AIDS Bhedbhav Virodh (ABV), the Anti-Discrimination Group which meets once a week on the roof of the Indian Coffee House in the heart of Delhi, where waiters in colonial livery serve coffee and snacks to those who pause on their way home from work. He was apprehensive about meeting them. *What will they think of me? How can I face them.*

Sister Shalini and a group of people from the Indian Social Institute, together with other sympathisers and social activists, are available on Wednesday evenings to meet with and discuss the plight of anyone who needs help; and then pass them on to counsellors and befrienders. A steady stream of young people come to the meetings: they want to do something, create public awareness, have an exhibition, perform street-plays, hold a demonstration, educate people about the reality of AIDS, and to break down the taboo which threatens to turn the illness into another major disaster for India.

There is no evil in India which does not call forth resistance to itself: the work of the AIDS Bhedbhav Virodh brings support and succour to many people as desperate as Mukesh.

As a result of our meetings, I had asked him if he would mind if I wrote a newspaper article based on his story. I would then be in a position to help him with the money I received. He said he had no objection, but then I heard nothing from him for some time. I assumed he had found someone to confide in through the Anti-Discrimination Group.

One cold night in November, I caught sight of him in Connaught Place. He looked thin and miserable. His clothes were shabby and dirty. He had, he said, been sick. He had given up his job, and was living entirely on the charity of his friends. He had not gone home; he was not yet ready to face his family.

I gave him the thousand rupees from the newspaper article, and went with him while he bought new trousers and a new jacket to keep warm against the cold of the Delhi winter. He had found a new job, working in the market from six o'clock in the morning till two in the afternoon, earning about 80 rupees a day ($2.50). He is in regular contact with one of the doctors recommended by the ABV, and has been befriended by a sympathetic gay man in the group. The last time I saw him, he said that he at last felt strong enough to go home and talk with his mother. I hugged him and wished him good luck. After that, I left Delhi. I did not know his address and doubted that I would ever see him again.

But I did. I was in Delhi for two days in April 1995. He was on the back of a motorbike when he saw me. He is thinner. He has a cough, but is working, selling watches on the sidewalk. He has been home and told his father, who told him that whatever happens, he will be welcomed and cared for there.

Brown Sugar

India has for centuries been one of the world's principal producers of opium. While cultivation was encouraged by the Moghul Empire, the systematic growing of opium was imposed upon subsistence farmers by the British, especially in Bihar. That the opium was 'needed' so that it could be forced upon the Chinese in order to finance the British addiction to tea is one of the lesser ironies of colonial history. This early version of crop substitution had far-reaching consequences for the lives of the growers. It transformed their culture, disrupted their traditions. Those, in the UN and elsewhere, who are now talking of crop substitution might perhaps reflect upon the violence with which the growing of opium had been imposed in the first place.

Until the 1970s, Britain depended upon India for its supply of morphine. This has changed since Australia, using advanced technology for harvesting and processing, has captured much of the global market for morphine. This switch has presented growing problems to the Indian government, which has been cutting the official area of cultivation for over a decade, although these cuts remain mainly on paper. There has been inadequate provision for the farmers to find any alternative source of income. Since the government also drastically cut the commission paid to buyers, one result is that considerable quantities of heroin have leaked into the unofficial market; and there are now tens of thousands of addicts on the streets of every major city in India.

Many traditional cultures in India have used drugs – opium, *bhang*, cannabis – in ceremonial or religious rites. Secularisation has invaded once sacred rituals, and in some cases the sacredness has vanished, leaving only dependency and habit. Opium was never a problem before the British came; and only with the more recent process of 'modernisation' has it become the spectacular affliction which India has witnessed in the past decade.

There are many organisations in Bombay concerned with drugs: most of these help the well-to-do, college students, middle-class women hooked on tranquillisers to combat loneliness. Some use religious conversion as a therapy, which effectively creates a new, if less physically damaging, dependency upon the faith to which the individual is converted.

There is a high lapse rate, however; the presence of heroin in Bombay, especially in its most accessible form, 'brown sugar', is highly visible. The drug is easily available. Very little has been done for the majority of addicts, who are the poor. It has been estimated that there are 70,000 or 80,000 addicts in Bombay alone. They can be seen everywhere: young children with a piece of silver paper and a match on any railway station, ragged self-neglected young men on the pavements, the flashy dealers who loiter around the tourist hotels. Bombay, a place of enormous energy and creativity, is equally the site of bottomless despair: we met one young man, Vinod, who had put his hands in front of a train, so that he would no longer be able to smoke.

SPARC (Society for the Promotion of Area Resource Centres), famous for its work with pavement-dwellers, is one of the best-known organisations which has set up a detoxification centre for the poor of the slum communities. It also serves as a research centre. The municipality gave it a ward in an old hospital at Andheri in north Bombay. There, they have space for about 15 patients at any one time. This initiative has been so successful that it has now been extended nationally.

Detoxification is now relatively simple, says Dr Dayal Mirchandani, who left private practice to work with the SPARC group. *Using clonodine, we can alleviate the signs and symptoms of opium withdrawal. It can even be done at home, if the environment is right.* In private nursing homes in Bombay, the charge for detoxification can be anything from Rs1,000 to Rs50,000.

We offer unconditional detox, says Gabriel Britto, director of the project. *Some treatment centres place conditions. Some are concerned about the visible 'success-rate', because they have to impress donor agencies. Nor do we believe in making the process of detoxification punitive. If withdrawal can be made painless with modern medication, what point is there in making people suffer?*

Molly Charles, who lives on the premises, says, *Some people object that addicts use detox to cut down the cost of their habit – after detox, you can get the same effect with a smaller quantity of heroin. To us, that's an advantage. When the rich become addicted,*

151

they lose all drive, but the poor are driven by their addiction; they become very inventive in the ways they get the money to feed it.

If you stigmatise addiction, exaggerate the problem, you are creating a greater role for the experts, but doing very little for those you're supposed to be helping. Britto claims that Western methods of treating addiction as though it were an individual problem are not helpful in India. *It is a social issue, one of the many that confront us here. It is an aspect of development in one sense, because 'development' itself generates dependency on the Western financial and banking system, dependency on Western lifestyle, addiction to its goods and services. Development means the death of self-reliance; and so do drugs.*

Many of the people who come to the detoxification centre have other problems – TB, malnutrition, respiratory disorders. These are also treated. *We also have to deal with the effects of adulteration of the drug before it reaches street-level. You might find anything – chalk, sawdust, rat poison – added to make up the weight.*

Psychotherapy is available for those addicts who need it, but as psychotherapist Dipti Behda admits, *Poor people whose basic needs are not even met do not give a high priority to 'just talking', which is how they see it. It means the sacrifice of a day's wages, which may make the difference between whether or not they eat.*

Among the people in the plain colour-washed ward are Rehnat Khan, an 18-year-old, who was introduced to drugs by his elderly neighbour whose hut was an *adda*, or distribution point, in the Bandra slum where he lives. He tells how his parents forced him to come here. They tied him up so that he could not run away. He left school when he was nine, and has worked selling night-dresses in the market close to the station. For this, he was getting Rs70–80 a day, all of which he was spending on brown sugar. His father works on the railway, and has visited him since he came here. He has promised to take him back home after detoxification.

Mohammed Hanif is 22. He is married, and has a child of four months. He has been addicted to brown sugar for three years, but says that the birth of his daughter has given him the motive to give it up. He works as a polisher of old furniture, which his employers sell at great profit. He started smoking charas as a teenager, and then went on to chasing the dragon. His wife's family come from Gujarat, and they will return there when he is clean; that way, he hopes to be free of companions who share his addiction. In his slum, the community organised to attack the drug dealers. They went to the police, but they were in the pay of the slumlords. The people took sticks and knives, and broke the addas themselves. Later, they publicly explained why they had done it; and the narcotics squad raided the area, and closed down the dealers.

Naresh is 28, a melancholy figure who looks much older. He says his mother died when he was a baby. He was an alcoholic, and his wife left him. He could no longer continue his work as a diamond cutter, for which he was being paid Rs1000 a month. He lives with his sister and her three children; she has been abandoned by her husband. There are, he says, worse things in Bombay than addiction; and poverty is one of them.

The aim of the SPARC group is to train former addicts within the slums, so that they can take over the rehabilitation and prevention work themselves. Das lives at Cheetah Camp in north Bombay, a community of Dalits from Tamil Nadu and Muslims. Over the years, they have built up the community on what was marshy, polluted land, so that now it is one of the best-organised slums in Bombay. The work of Das is to prevent the young from becoming addicted. He is based among adolescent workers, like Radhakrishnan, 15, the only earner in his family, and who does *zari*, embroidery work, sewing sequins on to fabric for women's sarees. Radhakrishnan says he learned to do embroidery from his father; he has been able to do it since he was three years old. He left school at ten, when he started work. In the same workshop is Yacub, 13; Raju, 16; Kumar, 19. Some youngsters work part-time after school. They say that drugs are available in Cheetah Camp in spite of the vigilance of the community. Das also supports the families of those who have been through detoxification, to help them prevent a relapse into addiction. *In Cheetah Camp, the community supports are there. It isn't the same for those who live on the footpaths and have no roots. But these are stable, solid communities.*

SPARC works closely with Apnalaya after-care centre at Malad, 2 kilometres from the detoxification ward. Sujata Ganega has always worked with youth in the Bombay slums, and she became aware of the drugs problem in 1985, when there was absolutely no provision for the poor. The request for help came from the community itself. *At that time, the total provision of hospital beds in Bombay for drug addicts was about a dozen. The building at Malad was empty, so we organised it as a short-stay centre for rehabilitation, where the people stay for two or three months before returning home. There is a structured programme of work, discussion, reflexion and recreation. The referral system is informal, including parents, youth groups, addicts themselves. There is prejudice in the community. People say 'Why help addicts?' They've seen them on the road, they accept the stereotypes, that they're criminals and beggars.* Apnalaya has a TB clinic and a general clinic for the community itself, so that people do not think their health is being neglected for the sake of the addicts.

Viraf Irani works at Apnalaya. A Parsee, he had a good job as cargo-handler at the airport but he lost it because of his addiction. His wife left him and took their child. He lived on the streets of Bombay, neglected himself, became dirty and emaciated. One day on his way to meet the dealer, he saw an addict on the pavement in a state of extreme dereliction. *He was in rags, there were sores on his body crawling with maggots. And yet he was still able to chase the dragon. On my way back, I saw the Municipal van: this boy had been covered with a white cloth, and the attendants were picking him, swinging him by his arms and legs into the van, with the rest of the human garbage. And I realised that is how I would end if I didn't do something about it. I decided I would not let that happen to me.*

Of the residents, the youngest is a boy of 14, abandoned on the pavements of Bombay when he was a baby; the oldest a man in his fifties who was a vegetable vendor. Kishore is 23; his bladder has been weakened by long drug use, and he is sometimes incontinent. He shows his knuckles, he has beaten them against the wall in frustration and rage until they bleed.

During the recovery period, strong feelings are released; there is a return of sexual feeling, and powerful attachments are formed. Santosh has just completed three months here. He found himself a job as a carpenter, but his father would not let him take it – he insists that his son should work as a peon in an office. Nando is a cobbler. He had been on brown sugar for eight years. He returned home last week to his wife and children. He says that when you are deeply involved in drugs, it is like a passionate love-affair. Nothing can reach you, no one can turn you from it, even those to whom you are most deeply attached. Prakash tells of a long progression, from dropping out of school, 'solution' (glue-sniffing), alcohol, ganja and charas, before he started on brown sugar. It seemed to be part of the culture of the boys he spent his time with. *You tell yourself it's under control,* he says. *You think you can stop if you want to. Then one day, you realise that it isn't true. You've lost yourself to something more powerful than you are.*

Whatever wrongs and evils exist in India, whether communalism, casteism and untouchability, dowry deaths, child labour, corruption, abuse of human rights, poverty and social injustice, there is always resistance, people not merely fighting, but creating new visions of what might be, in the place of the cruelties against which they struggle. It is this aspect of India – not merely the Mother Teresas, those tending the multiple casualties of its social and economic system – but the unknown, uncelebrated women and men inspired by Gandhi and those who followed him, seeking not only the recovery of lost visions and dispelled dreams but the reanimation of these in the contemporary context.

11. Bhim, Rajasthan: Fighting Feudalism

Dev Dungri

Environmental degradation is not simply something that happens to the landscape: the lives of people are also tragically altered. The damaged, crumbling hills of the Aravalli range in Rajasthan create a strange, surreal landscape, in which specks of mica wink and glitter in the shadowless sun. In the stony glare, the only colour is the sleek black of cattle, and the vivid lime-green or lemon-yellow of a woman's saree, as she almost runs beneath her burden of fodder or fuel.

A parched, unrestful place, which depends for its survival on remittances from the seasonal migration of the men. It is just before Divali. The men have returned for the festival. It is a moment to celebrate for those who have come back safely. Each year, from this area, there will be some who do not return, whose lives have been claimed by careless construction companies in the cities, or by accidents in well-deepening schemes in the countryside.

The land is poor, supports only one rainfed crop in the year – wheat, maize, jowar. An unexpected shower in October made people rush to sow their empty fields again in the hope of another crop: a fine down of green hovers over the barren land. Most people have only small parcels of land, which provide them with a scant subsistence for less than half the year. The rest of the time, the men, no longer secure in their home-place, must go wherever work is to be found – to Ahmedabad, Baroda, Delhi, even to Libya and the Gulf.

After Divali, these will become villages of women and children. This is a wheat-eating area; rice is a luxury for feast-days. In the lean season, many will eat only roti with salt and red chilli. The only men who stay are those who have a skill that can be employed locally – masons, constructing ever more opulent houses in Bhim for the banias, the merchants and moneylenders, who have grown rich lending to the poor. The banias are also migrants, travelling to Bombay, Delhi or Bangalore in search of richer pickings than anything to be had from the desperately poor people of this exhausted area. Their houses stand empty in Bhim for much

155

of the year, houses with terraces and arcades, two or three storeys, with long views over the desolate landscape.

The only other source of employment is government works, whether by direct employment or special schemes. There is no surplus land, and there is so little fuel that the people cannot even bake the clay tiles with which they roof their houses.

A still, slow place that speaks of oppression and poverty, a fitting social expression of the stony hills. Even the trucks that pass through on Highway Eight from Bombay to Delhi speed through, leaving the noise and smell of exploitation. One driver we travelled with had set out from Ahmedabad 12 hours earlier; he would reach Delhi within 16 hours, without stopping. He was carrying a consignment of fresh vegetables for the Delhi market. He boasted that he could drive for three days and nights without sleep. For this he is paid Rs1,000 a month ($33). The evidence of overwork lies scattered all over Highway Eight: a moment's distraction, an overturned truck, splinters of glass, the rusting vehicle in the ditch; and the bodies of the dead under faded cloth.

Dev Dungri, a collection of small villages lost between the Pink City and the City of Lakes, Jaipur and Udaipur, lies in the shadow of two disintegrating hills, where even the gods have deserted the barren slopes. Here, six years ago the Mazdoor Kisan Shakti Sangathan (MKSS, Farm Labourers Strength through Unity) was formed by a group of people who had come to live here with the intention of helping the people to organise. At the time, they had no very clear idea of their project; all they knew was that the lives of the villagers were scarred by poverty and injustice.

They had intended to spend the first year getting to know the people, and then consider what to do. In the event, they were overtaken by the famine year of 1987; and the work they have done has been dictated by the need of the people, who have lived and died for generations in voiceless penury.

Aruna Roy had been with the Indian Administrative Service for ten years, and had worked in Tilonia, the celebrated rural development centre in Rajasthan. Nikhil had lived in Washington, where his father was air attaché. Shankar, who comes from a village close to Bhim, has done just about everything. From a family of small farmers, his father was a *patwari* who died of alcohol poisoning when Shankar was 14. His mother worked as a daily wage-labourer. Having struggled to complete his Bachelor's degree, he was rejected by the army. He sold kerosene, set up a *pekora* stall, minded chickens and acted as chowkidar, made *namkeen*, worked in an oil-mill, a slate factory, an ice factory, before joining the Adult Literacy Association in Ajmer; from there, he became involved in puppetry and street theatre.

The house where they live at Dev Dungri belongs to Shankar's cousin: a mud-plastered stone grey that takes on the hue of the changing sunlight – pale rose at dawn, fiercely colourless at midday, gentle gold-grey at dusk, and silver under the low sparkle of the Rajasthan stars. Their life is one of complete simplicity; the food is vegetables, dal and chappatis. There is no electricity. Water comes from the well. All are paid Rs22 a day, which is the official minimum wage in rural Rajasthan, according to a State government Act.

When they came here, all were motivated by the desire to get back to what non-government organisations ought to be. 'So many of them have become professional structures, modelled on the hierarchies of business' says Aruna Roy. Their friends predicted that nothing would come of it. In fact, what they have achieved with the people in seven years is an extraordinary comment, both on existing forms of charity and NGOs in India, and the desperate need which these fail to touch, or alleviate only partially. Here, there is no foreign money: the people have funded everything themselves. Out of their poverty they have found what is necessary to commit themselves to hope, to the future. That is popular mobilisation. And the lives of the activists entwine themselves with those of the people they serve.

Mohan Singh, now in his late fifties: a sheen of white stubble on his angular chin, a white moustache and white head-cloth. He formerly had two bighas of land, where he grew channa and wheat. In famine years, there would be work on relief schemes, although the wages were always far below the official minimum. Some people worked all day for Rs5 or 6, and there was a record of one man paid 95 paise per day (3 cents). The official minimum wage of Rs22 is in fact a maximum. The unofficial minimum is now about Rs14. The people of this area had been more or less written off by the authorities: powerless, exploited and hitherto unorganised, they have been easy to cheat, and have accepted injustice and oppression as though these, too, were part of the cruel landscape.

The trees, says Mohan Singh, *went about 30 years ago. People were forced to cut them to sell them in the market-place for firewood, since they had no other livelihood.* In that sense, those who blame the poor for deforestation are right: but their poverty is scarcely self-inflicted. *Even so, we never cut big trees now, just cactus and* bambool, *and then not to destroy them, only to lop. We use* dhokra *for house-building, cactus also for charcoal. We cut and prune* deshi *bambool, and use the leaves as fodder for goats. What is left serves as fuel.*

The people of the desert have many skills. They build their own houses, of stone, earth and wood, and bake their own hand-made tiles. They apply fresh earth and cowdung to the floor twice a year. The houses are scrupulously clean. The chulha is built of the same material as the floor, flame-hardened with time. Mohan Singh, like many older people, regrets the changing values of the desert people. People have become more mercenary, more materialistic, he says. *They are less innocent. Then, we were all brothers.* It is important to separate the element of truth from that of nostalgia in their comment on changes brought by 'modernisation'. *Today,* says Mohan Singh, *if I want money from my brother, I'll have to mortgage my land.* And in truth, that is precisely what happened. The parables are often only thinly veiled reality. Mohan Singh mortgaged his land, like so many people, although they do not often speak openly about it.

Loss of land usually begins with a loan. The interest rate is so high that repayment becomes impossible, 3 per cent a month, compounded every six months. The creditors then convert the loan into mortgage, under what local people say is a 'call system': the land is now mortgaged to the moneylender, and no further interest is added. But all the benefits from the land then go to the creditor, on condition that the loan is paid within five or six years. If not, the land is then considered to belong to the moneylender. Mohan Singh in fact lost his land to his brother.

Sawai Singh also mortgaged part of his land ten years ago, although some still remains. His son has gone as a stonemason to the quarries near Bhilwari. There, working and living conditions are so bad that the quarry owners try to get their workers bonded to them, by offering large loans which they can never repay. Udhay Singh went to Delhi as a construction worker. He has also migrated seasonally to Pali, where there is a garment-dyeing factory; there, he worked as a chowkidar. His son stayed at school until the tenth standard, but since then his life, too, has been a wandering one, in search of work.

Rainfall here is around 400–450mm a year; but much of it comes in short bursts, so there is considerable run-off from the treeless hillsides. Last year, eight or nine men from the district were killed in deep well-digging in Gujarat. In well construction, they are lowered by winch in a bucket, and sometimes the bucket drops. A young man in the village of Sohangad was crippled for life in one such accident. 'Of course we don't want to go.' One man who has not worked for ten months, and owns a tea-stall in Ahmedabad, is reluctant to depart when all the men go after Divali. He has TB. Those who go with construction gangs must pay the contractors Rs3 a day. The men put off the departure until there is no other way. The women remain, villages of seasonal widows. Children, too, must work: at eight or nine, they will work in small hotels in Bhim or other market towns. The parents may be given Rs100; in effect, they are selling their children, who are often given food and nothing else in the little roadside *darbars*.

In the famine year of 1987, the cattle died, and the men migrated for the whole year. The children were hungry and without warm clothing for the cold of winter. Aruna says at that time, when they first came to the area, the people thought they must be rich, or that they would buy land to open a factory. *Their hope was that we could supply money or jobs. We had neither to give.*

A neighbour from Dev Dungri passes by, curious to meet the foreigner who is staying in the little village. He has a government job, looking after 50 kilometres of road in the district, reporting faults, pot-holes, damaged surfaces. Employed by the Public Works Department, he receives Rs1,800 a month. The work is going to be privatised, so even this level of government security for a few privileged people in the area will cease. I asked how many children he has. He said 'None. I have six girls.' Then he said proudly that he had managed to hold the marriage ceremony for all six on the same day, in order to spare the expense of six separate marriage-feasts. The youngest is eight. Girl children are valued in this region, because so much of the work in the fields is done by women.

Shankar tells how one of the public works projects in the famine year was to deepen the *tallab*, or reservoir. The full wage was never paid. This, they discovered, was actually government policy. The justification is that money that comes for famine relief should be spread as widely as possible. If half the amount is paid, work can be given to twice as many people. The official simply pays as much or little as he chooses.

Responsibility for getting the work done has devolved upon the workers, who are told they will get the same amount whether they do the work or not. Some work gets done, but less than should be; and then the officials are justified in paying less. People perceive the work, not as a creation of assets for the community, but as a formality. They see the labour as not producing anything, and they take it in the same spirit as the officials. It undermines their commitment. They know it is fraudulent.

Shankar says they decided to campaign for the full minimum wage. The struggle was not new. *Tilonia had filed a petition in the High Court on this issue in 1982, after the famine year of 1981;*

claiming that underpayment was economic coercion and an infringement of basic rights. The petition was upheld, but the judgment was not clear, and there were loopholes which the Rajasthan government used.

It was our policy not to adopt a high profile but to fight locally, with strong, clear examples. We would pick one local site and follow it through. We didn't use our contacts in local or national government, at least not at first. We did later. When you see the full forces ranged against you, you realise you cannot afford to be too pure, or you'll be defeated. They are quite ruthless.

The question arose, who should be given famine work? The poor said they had not the slightest chance of getting on to the muster rolls. Those who got onto the list were relatives of officials, patwaris, managers of the works. There was one famine relief works where the wife of my uncle, who is a schoolteacher, had got on to the roll. She was cut off. The family came and screamed at me; but at least that helped to establish that we were on the side of the poor, not influenced by relatives and so on. We got the poor put on the rolls. We didn't draw up a list, we urged the poor to present themselves and ask why they were not on the rolls. So 75 people went.

We got involved with one particular work-site. We decided on the wage issue, and to focus on the Department of Famine Relief, because the reason they gave for paying less than the minimum wage was that people don't work, therefore no one gets the minimum wage. They make it sound logical. We said 'Give one example where someone could do the full work and get the minimum wage.' They couldn't provide one.

The work is only for a very limited period, 15 days or so. One labourer is chosen as supervisor for the site, the mate he is called. He is the fall-guy. He is not a government servant, officials have no responsibility for him. If there should be an outcry over corruption, he can be removed, he has nothing to lose. 'He is one of you', they will tell the workers; so they get him to do the dirty work for them.

We began to understand the intricacies of the whole thing. The mate, the sarpanch, the patwari, the junior engineer – we talked to everyone, and then we said 'You appoint the supervisor, because it is lack of supervision that prevents the work from being done. Choose someone out of the department itself, not the mate; then we can be sure he will be responsible for overseeing the work.' We said 'We will set up the labour gangs, and work out a model of how much work will be done. We will measure the work and any shortfall will be reported back.'

So they appointed somebody. We got people into working groups, and persuaded them to work as hard as they were supposed to. The workers said 'We'll never get the minimum wage.' 'Yes, but let us try.' So we had 140 workers on one site, an irrigation tank at Dadirapat.

We broke them up into gangs of 20 people. Previously, they would have taken the whole 140, measured the amount of work done in the 15 days, and divided it by 140. Actually they didn't even do that, they just said to the people 'This is your wage.'

So we had a full-time government servant to tell the people how much they should do daily. He measured the amount of work and told them exactly what was expected. The people worked hard, exceeded the fixed amount.

At the end of the 15 days, no one came. All 140 went to the tehsil and asked for someone to measure the amount of work completed. The junior engineer came and did it. The work should be measured within seven days of completion; previously, six or twelve months had elapsed. Payments were due to be made for that work the day before Holi [a major spring festival]; *a day when everybody needs money.*

When the workers came to be paid, they were offered Rs6 a day. The officials were trying to destroy our credibility, as well as people's self-respect for the work they'd done. At first, they wouldn't take the money, because they'd agreed not to accept less than the minimum. Officials got the husbands or wives of the workers to take the money: they told them everybody else had taken it, and if they didn't, they would lose it. Everybody accepted, except a hard-core group of six, Mohan Singh and his wife and four others.

We kept the issue alive, but we couldn't mobilise on a large scale. It happened that an official team came to inspect the famine relief work. The situation was very bad. People turned up from all the neighbouring villages. The inspection team arrived in a cavalcade of 15 vehicles, and they were astonished to find 600 people waiting for them. They were informed of how bad things were: the Public Distribution System has little grain, there is no work, the wages are below the unofficial minimum. One woman had made a roti out of thorns, and she brought it to show them. Her family had been eating rotis made of a mixture of thorns and grain. That created a dramatic stir. They took it and said they would examine it for its nutritional content. The local administration were worried when they saw the crowd – they'd never seen such a mass of angry people before.

During that time, we had got to know a man from Sohangad, Lal Singh, who became one of our most committed supporters. Sohangad is in the feudal belt: it was there that we were to take up the land issue the following year.

The next year was officially not one of drought. Yet there was drought. In fact, they declared many villages famine-afflicted but there was no money left. In macro-economic terms, they had spent money: there was an effective transport system for when the grain actually came. This prevented endemic hunger from translating into pure famine. Their principle was that there must be no famine deaths. They are not bothered about malnutrition, or hunger-related sickness; as long as no one could say people had died of hunger, they would be in the clear. Five sacks of grain were sent to each *panchayat* office. The local patwari could release grain as necessary, to prevent famine deaths.

We decided we would compare the situation that year when things were slightly better. There was no government work. So what could the people mobilise against? We decided to initiate a people's study, a survey comparing a year of drought with a year of official non-drought. We would then present our findings to Famine Department officials. We took 15 villages. The people got very involved. We called the Famine Commissioner and the Joint Secretary of Famine Relief in the central government, to whom the people from each village presented their findings.

Even in years of good rainfall, people still need work for several months to buy the food they cannot produce. The survey defined those people with no regular income as below the poverty line. Those who had enough to eat from their own fields for 10 of the 12 months were excluded as being self-reliant. Those who had to migrate and those who derived only three or four months' grain from their land were defined as poor.

The poor were found to be three-quarters of the population. The rural elite say, 'There is no poverty; every family has one member in the police or the army. They drink their money away.' The rich have never wanted for ingenious explanations as to why poverty is the fault of the poor.

People were now in a position to use statistics to counter such myths. The poor had a self-image defined by the elite. Now an alternative version to the stereotype was being put forward. Local government servants and the elite disputed the findings. 'All right', they were told, 'choose any village and go from door to door. We will say nothing. See for yourselves.'

Lack of self-esteem renders people impotent, says Nikhil Dev. It prevents mobilisation. The karmic law has always been blamed in the past; but modernisation has brought its own form of karma that reinforces tradition. But that, too, is double-edged: when we talk to people about the country's indebtedness to the World Bank, they know what we mean, because that is a direct parallel to their own experience of the moneylender. There is an instant understanding, which the elite do not have.

This is one of the crucial elements in our struggle. We are local, totally based in and totally of the locality. Yet we cannot ignore national and international developments. We make the linkages wher-

ever we can. It can be translated into the idiom and experience of the people here. Aruna Roy talks of being 'bi-cultural', rooted in India yet also exposed to Western-style education and acculturation.

While the struggle over the minimum wage was going on, the land issue arose in dramatic form, in the village of Sohangad. This is fundamental. There was one jaghirdar who owned five or six villages; Sohangad was one of them.

For a long time, individuals had tried to protest, but there had been no organised collective resistance. It was a familiar form of domination: the jaghirdar took half the produce of everybody's field, many of which yielded little anyway. If anyone took wood or earth for building, any commodity, he always demanded half, even when they had taken it from the commons, which he also claimed as his own.

At that time, there was a government programme, Preshasan Gao Ki Or – Land to the Village. One-day camps were held, where government officials went to the panchayat headquarters to sort out local land issues. In Rajasthan, there is wasteland available for distribution, especially at election times. The land is poor, not very productive. Officials exhibited lists of government land available, and allotted it to those eligible. A new scheme had been introduced, nijavan, or personal forestry, where people would be given a plot of wasteland to plant trees, the produce of which would be theirs on a 25-year lease. This was an acknowledgement by the government that they could not do forestry; their schemes had failed. It was also a means of privatising all but the legal commons. When the Act was passed, it was assumed that the better-off would be more likely to plant trees than the poor, so the bigger, richer landlords were entitled to larger allotments. The poor would get a maximum of 5 bighas. If companies took on the wasteland, they could have it for forest-based industry.

Around Dev Dungri, many middle-class people were applying for wasteland, not for development but to build houses. It was also valuable as grazing land; many affluent people took large tracts.

In Sohangad, we used the opportunity to see how much land the jaghirdar owned, and how much more he was appropriating, because lists had to be posted saying which plots were available; all plots and their owners had to be shown. He had effective control over a large tract of government land. People filled in forms applying for that land. They agreed to send in all the application forms together, because they knew there was bound to be a confrontation. Forty filled in the forms. The jaghirdar got a real shock. Such a thing had never happened before. 'Marenge, marenge, zamin nahin chor denge', said Hari Singh, the jaghirdar to Lal Singh. 'We'll die before we give up our land.' But the people held fast.

The jaghirdar put pressure on the villagers. He tried to break them into two groups. He threatened them. He mobilised the Rajput, landowning lobby. Although he was a small crude jaghirdar, he had connections to ministers in the State government and the local bureaucracy. Rajputs are everywhere, the tehsildar also was a Rajput, and they stuck together on this issue.

This was when we first realised we would have to use some of our connections. We had a new understanding of the social forces against us; and we considered that our friends who shared our convictions should support grassroots initiatives.

On the allotment committee was the local sarpanch, the Block Development Officer, the Forest Ranger and the tehsildar, the local MLA and the Sub-Divisional Magistrate (SDM) in the chair. Within the administration, the Sub-Divisional Officer (SDO) supported us, because he was from a Scheduled Tribe background so he was alienated from the Rajput lobby. That gave us an ally. He had already been threatened by Hari Singh, the jaghirdar.

Hari Singh thought he had popular support: it is amazing how power can convince itself that the people love those who wield it. *When he saw the strength of our support, the banias – the local trading lobby – also organised. The Rajput lobby fixed on a date when the Assembly was in session, and the MLA could not be present, thereby making the allotment illegal. They thought any decisions would fizzle out. The Rajputs decided they would apply for land in the names of Scheduled Caste people, who would get precedence over the numerically dominant Rawats, who are among the Other Backward Castes. Hari Singh had control over the Scheduled Caste people; they were terrified of him. So he got their thumbprints on blank pieces of paper: they would be the ostensible applicants for the land, and he would take it. Aruna continues, We had to develop an appropriate response. We decided to register a women's society. It had to be a collective allotment, because individuals would have been scared to do it. So the women of Sohangad registered. In front of women, Hari Singh would not fight. Rajput women are in purdah, so they would not be able to apply. We moved the battle on to a different terrain. A women's co-operative was formed in secret, and the allotment was made at the level of the Collector in Udaipur. He let the SDO know when the papers were ready and fixed a date for handing over possession.*

The tehsildar informed Hari Singh, who ranted and raved and swore revenge. His people went with guns and swords to the village that night. The gang had come to terrorise, not to kill. The cry went up in the village, and all the women came running. The attackers ran away, and a confrontation was avoided. If they had met, it would certainly have ended in bloodshed.

Hari Singh sent messages threatening death, to us too. Whenever we went to Sohangad, the villagers always came back with us, taking us by roundabout paths to avoid ambush. The police eventually came five days after the confrontation. It was a tense time. Hari Singh tried to turn the issue into a caste struggle, Rajputs against Rawats. We called a cross-caste meeting of the villagers; and out of that meeting the Sangathan was born in May 1990.

Twenty-five hectares of land in Sohangad were allotted to the women. The society got over one lakh rupees from the National Wasteland Development Board. The women did fantastic work on the land. As a result, the whole area woke up to the fact that the jaghirdar could be taken on and defeated. That it was done without violence was really our good luck. That women had taken on such a role – there was no history of this in Rajasthan – came as a shock to the feudal system. Rajasthan, where five years ago the case of sati had made such macabre history, where child marriages and women's oppression have always been part of the social landscape. Our modes of working were quite unexpected to the ruling classes.

We visited Sohangad one evening at sunset. The village is several kilometres off the main road, down a rough dusty track. Cows follow the beaten paths across the fields; a young man is making rope as he follows them. The compounds of the houses are stacked with fodder; chaff mingles with the dust in the rocky waterless landscape. The men had returned for Divali, and there was an air of hopeful expectation at the coming festival. Babu Singh invites us into his house and offers a glass of buffalo milk. He is a mason, and does not migrate. In his house, there is now electricity: a bare bulb throws its light over the plain whitewashed interior. He acquired 6 bighas of land 18 months ago. Formerly he used to go to Delhi, where he earned Rs50 a day on construction work, dangerous, dirty work.

The women go with us to the 25 hectares of land which they have cultivated and worked on for the past three years. It has been transformed. There are 6,000 kilos of standing fodder, which is shared between the 60 or 70 women of the co-operative. The land is not good: stone and rocks jut through the thin soil. But digging trenches and channels has prevented the water from running off; and the planting of trees and shrubs has stabilised the rough land, and permitted the growth of grasses, flowers and small fruit trees: ghudi, bamboo, gulmohar, mulberry trees and ber for fodder. There is a hedge of cactus around the land to prevent stray animals from grazing. We climb on to a big promontory of rock which gives a view over the whole region: the distant patches of forest, the dry rocky earth, the small settlements. Most of this land was claimed by Hari Singh. The only problem here now is snakes in the undergrowth – *kraits* and cobras. There is, say the women, now a strong resource-base in the village; this has given a new cohesiveness to the community: there is always a reason to meet, argue and debate. They have transformed the landscape and their own fortunes; a living witness of what is possible once the community gains control over its own resources.

This strengthened people, who realised that by doing relief work they really might be able to earn the Rs22 a day they were entitled to. This led to the next issue: the strength from one victory feeds the next struggle. In May 1990, the Sangathan took two resolutions; first, that we would not accept less than the minimum wage for government work, and second, that we would not take part in corruption by paying bribes. This was the ethical base on which the Sangathan was founded.

In June 1990, Sohangad formed a group of workers who refused the payment of less than the unofficial minimum, which had gone up from Rs11 to Rs14. On various sites in the area – road-building, tallab-mending – 310 people refused to take the wage. After one week, the authorities tried to pay. No one took it. A week later, all 300 went to Bhim to demand payment of the minimum wage. The SDM absented himself. We thought we would stay, spend the night in the tehsil building. We said we would wait until the SDM did come. They were mostly women, about 180 women, maybe 60 or 70 men. Two or three policemen were sitting around. They telegraphed the police station, saying we would not allow them to shut the office door. Five or six came in a jeep, wielding lathis, and began using them on the women. I was on the phone to the SDM, telling him what was happening, and outside a roar went up. I said to him, 'You'd better come.' The police were about to be lynched. One woman had been beaten about the head and was bleeding profusely. There were about eight cops and 300 people. Their lathis had been taken away and broken. They stood no chance against the anger of the people. We tried to come between them, but they were uncontrollable in their anger.

The first thing was to be heard. Chunni Singh had a brainwave. He yelled 'Mazdoor ki Sangh Shakti Sangathan'; we are a non-violent movement. There was a pause. We said 'Let us have two minutes' silence to condemn the police attack.' In the silence, people calmed down.

The SDM turned up, and the Irrigation Department official. Although the people got no satisfaction, they learned that this is how you get a response. They stayed all night; then decided if there was no agreement to pay after one week, they would go on hunger strike.

Nothing happened. After a week, eleven people offered to go on hunger strike. Two or three more joined each day until there were 17, two of them over 60. We had no experience of this. It was foolish. There were too many; the energy required to look after 17 was too much. Four days passed. The MLA called the Collector and said, 'On no account pay them.' He recognised us, a strong anti-feudal force, not to be supported. He organised the riot police, a whole truckload of them came to confront us, and intimidate us. The people were not scared. The riot police didn't know what to do, they marched up and down. On the sixth day, the Collector came from Udaipur. He was worried about the elderly people. The medical equipment they had to test our physical strength each day was inadequate.

There was a dramatic meeting between him and the Sangathan. In the end he said, 'We will pay you to your satisfaction after three days.' We lifted the hunger strike, because we believed him. Nothing was paid. All Bhim was electrified; we had support from everywhere, even the trading community.

We had been defeated. But the struggle had to go on. Next time, we resolved to take up a smaller, more manageable case. In fact, it has become a legal battle in the High Court at Jodhpur. It is still going on. But Supreme Court battles are not felt by the people as their struggle.

Next year, the government work scheme employed two of our activists from Dev Dungri as labourers, Narayan and Devilal. They gave notice to the sarpanch, saying they expected a full quota of work and full minimum wage, and a review of the work to ensure that their demands were fulfilled. It was a road-building project. No one came, either to determine the nature of the work or to review it.

They had decided to pay Rs11 for 15 different kinds of work on which people were employed under the scheme. That was in February. By April nothing had happened. We met all the officials, even the Secretary of Special Schemes in Jaipur. They said they could do nothing, because it was an issue of policy.

On 1 May we decided to sit on a dharna outside the SDO's office. On 29 April, there had been an inquiry where workers had deposed publicly. The sarpanch never turned up. The officials drove to his house and held the inquiry there. The project director found in our favour. There were 400 people outside. The report was sent to the Collector. By this time, the area had been transferred under new district boundaries. The Collector said, 'I can't deal with it.' He sent it back to the old Collector. He sent it back to the new one. It seemed doomed to be lost in the bureaucratic labyrinth.

The dharna became a hunger strike, a fast unto death. Five people sat, one from each area. It was a huge affair, two or three hundred people present day and night. Food was supplied by the people, and the workers gave money. There was a row of ten chulhas, people

*cooking in pairs; a vendor who sold mint gave us a bouquet of mint
each day. Even the local jailer gave us Rs10 and a few kilos of
wheat. At the level of officials, all Class Four staff were with us; they
passed information on to us, the wireless messages and police communications. The CID were there to watch us. One of them was a cousin
of one of the hunger strikers.*

*The Secretary of the Rural Development Department looks after the
employment programme. We urged him to send a team, which he did,
including the Project Director of the Divisional Rural Development
Authority (DRDA) from Udaipur. We were very angry. They said the
poor do not work, and that is why they do not get the full minimum
wage. We said 'If you have come with these preconceived notions,
you'd better go straight back. If you don't believe there is any reason
for the agitation, why have you come?'*

*They said 'The fault is the sarpanch's, but you chose him.' Aruna
launched into him. She said 'Are you responsible for your ministers or
your Prime Minister?' He was publicly berated. The local officials
laughed. We said, 'Why do you laugh at people who have nothing to
eat? What is so funny about it?' Lal Singh then said, 'We have
understood you very well, and you have understood our cause. Instead of playing around like this, why don't you shoot us? All you
want is our death. Shoot us dead.' Nikhil said, 'This is a government
programme for the poor. Why do you have to come all the way from
Delhi to investigate it?'*

*The MLA, representative of the people, never met us. It was the
election of 1991. The Chief Minister came to address a meeting at
Bhim. Officials were afraid we would disrupt the meeting. We said we
would indeed do that unless a meeting was arranged with him. He
came to the place where we were sitting on strike. He had met us
once before and said to us, 'I'll send you to Andhra and you can
become Naxalites.' To Aruna, he said, 'You should be working for
literacy programmes instead of this.' He knew Nikhil's father. This
time, he said he would do his best. He told the SDO to take the
papers and follow him. It was such a small issue: 12 people, a matter
of Rs1500. Yet it had become a full policy issue.*

*He consulted various secretaries, who were against minimum wages
being paid. The word came back. No. Then news came that the police
were coming from Jaipur to take the people away. The Chief Secretary's
daughter-in-law was a friend of ours, and she gave us the tip-off.*

*That night, we resolved no one should sleep. The hunger strikers
were placed in the middle of the area we were occupying, the men
next, then the women on the outside. We formed a tight, cohesive
band, stripped the armbands off the hunger strikers. They said 'Send
us the hunger strikers for a medical check-up.' It was midnight.*

Within minutes 150 constables surrounded us, with helmets, shields and lathis. The Additional Superintendent of Police was there. 'We want to talk to you.' We switched on the microphone. All Bhim was sleeping. The women have a wailing sound which they use in a crisis, and they started wailing over the mike. We also had a dhool, a drum on which people make a war-beat at such times. The cops broke the mike and smashed the lightbulbs. There was pandemonium. They had been instructed not to touch Aruna. They lifted the men and the village women. By this time, all Bhim had woken up, and more and more people were coming. The police had gone 100 kilometres before they realised they hadn't got two of the hunger strikers. They came back and demanded the handover of the others.

Next day they thought the agitation would end. Instead, 700 people gathered. There had been a strong reaction in the villages. After eight days, news came from Delhi: the Union Secretary for Rural Develoment had made a statement that if the minimum wage was not paid by the government of Rajasthan, the next grant of 100 crores would be stopped.

We mobilised people from the villages and went to the SDO. 'Until you pay, no one leaves this place.' At four o'clock the payments were made. The agitation came to an end.

The sarpanch was a liquor dealer, a crook. Later, he got an attack of severe paralysis. See, the people said, if you are evil and oppress the poor, this is what happens to you. The SDO opened one of his files one day and there was a cobra in it. People felt for once justice had been on the side of the poor.

But in order to win such a partial and local victory, so much effort had been required. And of course, there are no final victories. It will happen over again next time. Only the people have learned, both their own power and the tactics for such struggles. Next time, they say, we will not make the same errors.

The Struggle for Sangawas

In the rural areas of India, there is a network of interlocking oppressions, which means that any effort to resist must be fought on several fronts at the same time. One of the most powerful allies of the existing power structure is alcohol, whether legally or illicitly brewed and sold: it undermines communities, and saps strength that might otherwise go into social and political struggle.

In recent years, many women have concentrated on banishing drink from their villages and communities. The work of the women in Tamil Nadu is justly well known. But all over India, there have been similar, less celebrated efforts. What happened in Sangawas, a village of about 200 families, 20 kilometres from Bhim, is characteristic.

It is a Monday morning in November. In the shade of the neem tree that shields the village from the Ahmedabad–Delhi highway, the people gather to talk of their victory over one of the greatest enemies of the poor.

The government auctions out areas of Rajasthan each year to liquor contractors, who will guarantee to raise a fixed amount. The excise money from liquor is the second largest source of revenue for the government of Rajasthan. In addition to the legal liquor, locally brewed *khati*, made of gur and *mahua* flowers and leaves, is also sold; sales which the government does its best to suppress.

In Sangawas, the government was supplying liquor to an unlicensed shop. The thikedar, or contractor, takes a licence for fewer outlets than he actually controls, and the undeclared shops provide him with his profit. The women of Sangawas had tried to get rid of the liquor shop which was in the centre of the village, close to the handpump. The drinkers fought and quarrelled every day, and normal village life was disrupted. The women are severe. Jaiti says that the misery of men who must spend more than half the year as migrant labour is no excuse. *It was the children who went hungry, the women who were beaten.* Khiribhai, a thin woman who sits with her saree shielding her sad eyes, says, *Even our utensils were sold for liquor. My husband must have spent a lakh of rupees. We women had to put mud on our heads, go labouring for a few rupees to feed our children. We could not migrate like the men. Some days, we could give them only half a roti to eat. Women already do two jobs – we work in the fields and we work in the home. As well as that, we had to earn money.* The women show their ankles, bare of the silver ornaments which have been sold to buy food.

In May 1992, some of the women went to a fair organised by the Mazdoor Kisan Shakti Sangathan (MKSS). The women knew that the Sangathan had helped the women of Sohangad wrest land from the jaghirdar, and had gained minimum wages for a government works programme. At the *mela*, the women met the Collector, and they spoke with his wife, telling her, 'Come and see how wretched our lives are made by that shop.'

The Collector ordered the shop to close. On the day it was shut down, the police warned the owner that they were coming, so that he could hide his liquor, which he then started to sell from his own house. Things became worse. The drinkers terrorised the whole village when they were drunk. The people went to the Deputy Inspector of Police. He gave them to understand that if they beat up the dealer, he would not bring a case against them.

For the first time, the women stood up to the drinkers. To their surprise, they ran away. The women then met the liquor vendor. 'The shop is illegal.' The thikedar responded by getting a licence from the government that legalised his business, and he started trading again.

After two months, they returned to the Collector. He again suspended the licence, this time on the grounds that it was a threat to law and order.

Then the Collector was transferred. The thikedar again got a legal permit. The women said, 'Legal or not, we're not having it.' They met and agreed to stop any vehicle that came with liquor. The contractor's jeep arrived. It was immediately surrounded by 40 or 50 women. They said, 'You are causing fights, brother against brother.' The contractor pushed Jaiti. She caught him by the collar, and the women gave him and his assistant a thrashing.

The contractor lodged a case with the police. The employee who had been beaten up was a man from a Scheduled Caste. Assault upon an Untouchable is a serious offence in Rajasthan, and carries a long jail sentence. With no mention of liquor, he filed a case under the Scheduled Caste Atrocity Act against the women; most of the women themselves are from Scheduled Castes.

When the police came to the village, they singled out the leaders of the anti-liquor agitation, including Sawai Singh, one of the Sangathan's most active members, and accused them of assault upon the Scheduled Caste man. When they were told they were being arrested, the people said, 'Four won't go, 400 will. To use the Scheduled Caste Atrocity Act for another reason is an abuse of the law.' The police could not arrest those named, and went away.

The women went to the Superintendent of Police and the Collector, and told them that if they persisted with the case, the consequences would be tremendous. The whole Sangathan would organise in support of the people. The Superintendent ordered his Deputy to return to the village and find out what really had happened.

The Deputy was unsympathetic, in the pay of the contractor, and he tried to show that the women had been the aggressors. *We said to him, 'We will not allow liquor in at any cost. We are also Scheduled Caste women. If you misuse the law to transform the case into the issue of assault upon an individual from a Scheduled Caste, we too will use the law to say the thikedar has abused us.' The women said, 'If you persist, we will start an anti-liquor movement that will spread to the whole region'.*

The three main liquor contractors in the region took fright at this, and they went to the office of the Sangathan. *We have to give the government the sum we have promised. We will close the shop in Sangawas, if you will let us open it elsewhere.* The representatives of the Sangathan said, *If the villagers elsewhere have no objection, we have none. But if they do not want it, we shall support them. If this movement begins, we shall lose everything. We will withdraw from Sangawas, but do not spread the agitation.* The MKSS repeated that where there was opposition from the people, they would support it.

The government speaks with two voices, says Jaiti. *They say 'Do not drink', yet they give contracts to promote drinking. When we addressed the government, they said 'We need money from liquor for development that will help you.'* Jaiti said, *'First you destroy us, then you give us development. You destroy us to the worth of one rupee, and then give us back 25 paise. We don't want such development.*

On 2 October 1993, birth anniversary of Mahatma Gandhi, 1,200 people assembled and passed three resolutions: wherever there are illegal shops, the people will press for closure; wherever a village opposes legal shops, a movement will take place to close them; and where illegal liquor is brewed, the Sangathan will break the *matkis* and take the people to the government and demand that alternative employment be found for them.

There is peace in the village now, says Jaiti, *but there is still poverty.* The only other employment is a small tobacco factory, employing about 25 people at Rs15 a day. The rest of the men must still leave. The women ask, *Why should we raise our children only to see them depart? Many people in the village are in debt. Others have mortgaged their land, or have sold it, because they have been unable to repay loans which they took if their men failed to migrate one season, or if they couldn't go because of sickness.*

The women say they have achieved apnavishwas, self-esteem, from the struggle. This may help them fight for a better life for their children, who are already working in the 'hotels' of Bhim, on building works, on other people's fields. *Their childhood has been stolen.* Some will go to the stone and marble quarries, where they may become bonded. *We have no choice. To feed a family of seven or eight people, it costs at least Rs50 a day. Some days, we eat only roti with salt and chilli.*

Sawai Singh has prepared breakfast in his small one-room house built of mitti and thatch: chappatis of wheat and maize, a little dish of spinach and *methi*, a glass of buffalo's milk; an enormous sacrifice for his guests. He shows us a photograph of his most recent job: driving a huge 80-ton tanker from Bombay to Baroda. The vehicle has 74 wheels and can carry weight up to 400 tons.

As we leave, the people stand with us on the edge of the highway waiting for a truck that will go back to Dev Dungri. They say, *We have won a victory, but we have not won the war against poverty and injustice. We are still led by the blind and governed by the deaf.*

Shopping for Necessities

In spite of these victories, poverty remains relentless. The next step for the MKSS was the attempt to bring within reach of the people fair prices for the basic necessities of life.

I never thought I would ever see a shop that brought tears to my eyes. That isn't strictly true: I have often felt like weeping at the vanities and superfluities on sale in the bazaars of the world, while the needs of so many people remain unanswered.

But this is different. The MKSS have opened two shops in the area, the principal one in the market town of Bhim, a market centre upon which about 70,000–80,000 people in the town and neighbouring villages depend. Bhim itself is not a spectacularly attractive place: a bus stand, rows of shops, grimy rocky streets where pigs roam; some nomads, beggars from a Scheduled Caste who also perform. The spacious houses of banias tower over all other buildings.

The shop that has been set up by the MKSS is a plain building, a concrete shell really, open to the street. It is a fair-price shop, providing daily household goods, not only far more cheaply than the surrounding traders, but even more cheaply than the subsidised shops of the Public Distribution System; and the quality is much better.

The place is busy all day, besieged by the poor from the villages around Bhim, the people who contributed to make it possible, and who now have their reward in low-priced, wholesome, unadulterated fare. The MKSS grind their own spices and lal mirch (red pepper), because in many shops dust and powdered red brick are often added. Setting up the store was the least of the problems: striking against the vested interests of the existing traders was the real issue.

The shop is unadorned, and without decorative display: sacks of moong, urad, channa, rice; dried coconut, potatoes, onions; packets of matches, candles, soap, spices, chilli, *gira, haldi, dhania,* garlic and ginger. The prices are chalked up on a blackboard. From time to time, one of the workers takes the microphone and calls out the prices to the whole thoroughfare. The crowd around the MKSS shop contrasts with the almost empty stores of the banias. A crude metal scoop, metal scales, a wooden counter. Above, the symbol of the MKSS: two fists, of man and woman together, emblem of the joint struggle against the violence of poverty.

The capital for the shop came from interest-free loans from members of the Sangathan, loans of Rs10, returnable after two years; other money came from sympathisers and friends, including gifts and donations, which provided a capital of Rs50,000. It is a commercial enterprise, and has to be self-supporting. The profit goes back into the shop, and the enterprise is being extended to some of the bigger villages in the area.

It emerged out of the mela in May 1992, which was really a rally to celebrate the various victories of the Sangathan. People had made and contributed things to the mela, and the idea arose that a victory over wages was not sufficient to tackle poverty. A decision was taken to influence the market, the very instrument by which the system measures everything, to provide better-quality and cheaper products to the poor. *This time, we decided to play the game by the rules laid down by those with wealth and power. It is a different kind of strategy; sometimes confrontation is necessary, at others work by stealth; yet again, by more open forms of struggle on the terrain which they are supposed to be defending.*

Resistance from the traders was strong. They tried to prevent the suppliers from furnishing the shop with goods; they even tried to divert trucks carrying supplies. They sought to intimidate the poor into buying from them – they had them in their power through loans and debts. In every way open to them, they tried to prevent the scheme from being effective. The MKSS had to find alternative sources of supply, even if this meant going all the way to Beawar, the biggest town in the area, in order to circumvent the cartel set up by the local traders.

They have exceeded their highest expectations. It is one of the bravest and most simple of initiatives, and so successful that the MKSS have decided to extend it.

Nikhil Dev says, *The macropolicy, dictated by the World Bank and IMF, involves 'targeting' the Public Distribution System. It means privatisation, contracting out; it is a recipe for corruption. We are taking over one ration-shop in the area; since we are already undercutting ration-shops in some items, there is no reason why we should not deliver more effectively than the government-run shops. In this sense, we feel there is a potential for taking over administration of the 'reforms' dictated by the Western financial institutions, and instead of using them against the poor, using them for purposes which are the opposite of those intended – in favour of the poor. We are also thinking of organising labour collectives to compete for contracts.*

The small group at Dev Dungri is one of the most active and effective I have met. The need for such work is only too apparent in the landscape you pass through on the road back to Beawar: the collapsed treeless flanks of the hills display an obscenely shocking nudity. Everywhere the debris sparkles with mica; pink-grey sand and soil, rocks and cactus and stunted trees with thorny bleached branches and flattened tops. Some hills are jagged with boulders, and landfalls spilling at their base; other hills have been rounded and softened by their emptiness. Here and there is a splash of bougainvillaea, the brilliant dyes of the fabrics, head-dress of gold, lime and scarlet, which shine like hope in the barren monochrome, just as the work of the MKSS glows in the forgotten feudal social landscape of central Rajasthan.

12. Andhra Pradesh

The Lacquer Bangle-makers of Hyderabad

A community of about 500 families – about 3,500 people – live on a piece of land adjoining the great Mecca Masjid in the old city of Hyderabad. The area is reached from one side through a green-painted wooden gate from the courtyard of the mosque itself, beneath a yellow-stone arch and minarets. To the right, the four towers of the Charminar can be seen – 56 metres high, fretted carved stone – constructed in the 1590s as a thanksgiving for the end of an outbreak of plague.

The heart of the densely packed commercial centre of Hyderabad: a long-established Muslim community, created over 40 years ago, when Urdu-speakers from parts of what are now Maharashtra and Karnataka found refuge in Hyderabad before it had become part of Andhra Pradesh, a state defined linguistically by Telugu.

What was originally a squatter settlement has become a settled community; although crowded and densely built, most of the houses are now of concrete and the area has been paved. The people pay a nominal ground-rent of Rs2.50 a month to the mosque, but some who have become well-to-do now rent their property, as homes or workshops, to others.

The principal occupations are the making of lacquer bangles, quilts and zari (embroidery work). Both women and men are involved in a complex division of labour in making the lacquer bangles. Men heat, colour and shape the lacquer and make the bangles; women and girls heat the coloured glass beads and stones and press them with their thumb into the warm lacquer. Every woman worker has a black calloused scar on her thumb, where it has become hardened by the pressure of hot glass over the years; the young girls have inflamed and tender marks, because their skin has not yet become insensitive to the heat.

It is mid-morning. Every house stands open to the street, and in each one, groups of women and children are working. They sit over a metal chulha, sometimes home-made out of an empty Palmolein tin: an opening at the bottom of the tin, a grille of a few strips of metal, a lining of rough clay, on which a charcoal fire burns constantly. Above this a metal plate; on it, the beads – green, red, plain crystal, yellow. The women pick up the beads one by one with a pair of metal tweezers, and press them into the lacquer, forming floral designs of their own making – perhaps 80 or more beads go into each piece. The bead must be pressed in before it goes cold or it will not stick. Their hands move dexterously; the hardened thumb embeds each stone deep into the cooling lacquer.

Shaheen has five children: together she and her two daughters make five dozen bangles a day. Her son does embroidery in a nearby workshop: she shows a sample of his work, pale pink cloth with motifs of leaves and stars in gold thread. Shaheen's husband has a job in a machine-tools factory but is on a daily wage, and work is not available every day. They have lived here for over 30 years, having come originally from Bidar in Karnataka.

Shaheen's house is small: a single room, about 9 feet high, and 10 feet by 10: a small washing area, a cooking stove, vessels on shelves built into the concrete. There is a big metal cupboard, but no other furniture, apart from bamboo mats on the stone floor. There is no ventilation; and Hyderabad is one of the hottest parts of India in summer. The lower half of the room is whitewashed, the upper part blue. The family's clothes are strung out on a string diagonally hung across the room.

Naseem is 12. She sits over the chulha, deftly picking up the beads and pressing them into the pink lacquer. She goes to school for one or two hours a day, a school run by a women's group, Saathi, and held in a room in a corner of the mosque compound. This is a welcome break in her 12-hour working day. Naseem gives me a bangle and the tweezers to see if I can do the intricate work. The first bead gets too cold and falls out. The second burns my thumb and I drop it. Naseem laughs and says 'You'd soon get used to it.'

Although there is drainage and paving in the slum, there are no toilet facilities. Its great advantage is its proximity to the commercial and business centre of Hyderabad. The markets exist locally. The work can be done at home, and can be collected and delivered to the house, even though the girls and women are grossly underpaid for what they produce. Indeed, out of this unpromising place comes some of the most delicate and beautiful work imaginable.

Nearby, Hamid and Mehmud Khan, brothers in their twenties, are doing zari work. They make the designs for the front of the *kamiz* themselves, and take their inspiration from the pages of fashion magazines. They have only to see a design to be able to reproduce it. They learned the work from the owner of a shop, who sells all the materials. He takes 20 per cent commission for the work he gives out. They are paid according to the complexity of the design: some pieces require hundreds of sequins and pearls, as well as the complicated stitching. They pay for the beads, sequins, silver and gold thread; and receive on average Rs500 for a garment, which will sell for about Rs800 in the shops. Occasionally, if it is especially intricate, one kamiz may sell for Rs2,000 or more.

Their profit comes to about Rs100 a day, and for this they work 12 hours. Both have been working since they were 12 or 13. The material is stretched and tied on to a wooden frame, so that it is taut and ready for the decorative work. They crouch beside the frame. The needle is of wood, with a sharp metal point, with which they push the thread through the fabric. Hamid has three small children; the little boy sits close to his father, plucking channa from a bunch of greenery in his hand. The family all live in this one room: at night, the wooden frame is folded, and seven adults and three children sleep here. The mother says it costs Rs100 a day to feed ten people.

The mother tells how they came to Hyderabad from what is now Maharashtra, after the police action in 1948: Muslim atrocities against Hindus, before the Nizam was ousted in 1957, were avenged with much bloodshed, and many Muslims found refuge in the city. In 1992–3, after the demolition of the mosque at Ayodhya, there was no trouble here. Muslim–Hindu segregation is, however, almost complete in the Old City.

Next door, two young men, also brothers, Hakim and Hussein, are working to the sound of a cassette playing Hindi film songs. They are making the bangles into which the beads will be pressed later. Lacquer is a mixture of translucent greenish gum and titanium. They melt the lacquer over a charcoal fire, colour it and draw it into strips which are then reinforced with two metal rings. The metal rings themselves are heated and expanded to the desired size on a cone, which matches them to the ring of lacquer. The two young men make the bangles and their profit is Rs100 a day.

Hamida, a woman whose husband has deserted her, lives with her brother. She has five children, three of whom help her. They are working on blue-coloured bangles with gold beads. They will make Rs24 for a dozen bangles, and make five dozen a day.

The slum is congested: vegetable carts clutter the narrow lanes, women are washing around the public taps, beating the garments on stone slabs. Others sell *papad* and pekoras, a few guavas or bananas, to those too busy to prepare a midday meal. People are carrying the results of their labour to the shopkeepers or workshops.

A school for young children has been set up in the tomb of a mullah, an elevated stone tomb covered with a green gold-embroidered cloth, a stone floor. About a dozen children sit with slates and chalk.

On a veranda outside their rented hut, three girls, the youngest aged ten, plaits tied in a lustrous loop, a child with a new-moon smile, are working over their tiny stove; all bear the stigma of their labour on the thumb. They are using gold- and silver-coloured stones which, being metal, retain the heat even more than glass. This family also came from Maharashtra. Sujida, the ten-year-old, spends four hours a day at the school run by Saathi, and eight hours working. They make five dozen bangles a day, Rs3 a pair. Sukravi, the mother, has nine children. Two girls are married. Sukravi is prematurely worn. Too old to work now, she says she has to depend on her children for her food. Her son works in a bedmaker's shop next door.

This is a small *godown*, or warehouse, owned by four brothers who live in an adjacent building. In the narrow space of the godown is a heap of waste cotton which is bought from the mills for Rs12 a kilo. A machine – which cost Rs15,000 – shreds the coarse cotton into softer down. The lint and dust coat everything with a fine white beard. Sukravi's son feeds the cotton into the machine: he wears a handkerchief around his nose and mouth. The cotton blanches his hair, face and body. The quilts are filled with the softened cotton and roughly stitched. Later, the women will re-stitch them more competently. They make five or six a day, a profit of Rs20 or 30 on each.

Mohamed Yusup and his 15-year old son work together in a rented workshop. They sit one on each side of a rectangular metal plate. In the middle is a cavity with a charcoal fire, the heat from which keeps the plate permanently hot. To make the lacquer, they use a mixture of gum and titanium powder. The gum is melted and kneaded with the powder till it has the consistency of nan bread. Then it is shaped into a long thick cylinder, and allowed to harden. There are, explains the man, various qualities of gum. The *sanjira* they use is the most expensive.

To make the lacquer bangles, the hardened fawn-coloured cylinder is melted once more, this time over the charcoal fire, until it becomes pliable again. Then to the hot melting lacquer, a lilac colouring agent is added, in the form of a rectangular block on a stick, which melts on to the hot lacquer, coating it evenly. The lacquer is then extruded with the help of an iron on the hot plate, cut into the desired length and flattened into the shape of a bangle. The metal plate is oiled before the lacquer is rolled so that it does not stick. The strip is then passed over to the 15-year-old, who closes it into a circle, holds it once more over the fire, and presses two metal circles – which have previously also been heated over the fire – to strengthen the bangle. Left to cool, these bangles will be collected by the owner, who will then give them out to women and girls for the insertion of the beads.

The metal reinforcement rings are checked for size, and then pounded and made flat with a heavy piece of iron on a kind of anvil. The metal strips are stuck into the lacquer and then pressed with the thumbs. Father and son work with great concentration; neither gets burnt. They make five dozen bangles a day. Mohamed Yusup and his family came here from Jabalpur in Madhya Pradesh 40 years ago. The 15-year-old, the oldest of five, has been working with him since he was ten.

They buy charcoal at Rs5 a kilo and use up to 4 kilos a day. Two kilos of lacquer will make 12 dozen bangles. They work from nine o'clock in the morning till nine at night, with half an hour for a meal at 2 p.m. The room is rented for Rs250 a month: a bare floor, a lightbulb, a metal stand with tools and a cupboard, and an earthen jug of drinking water.

Opposite Mohamed Yusup live two sisters, both without husbands. They look after Yusup's three youngest children, and at the same time make cotton-filled rasai, or quilts. Today they are making quilts for babies: the fill the rasai with cotton, stitch it into squares, so that the cotton is evenly spread, and then sew a gauzy frill around each piece, about 1 metre square. They get R1 per piece and do 20 a day. For adult-sized quilts, the payment is Rs8 a piece. Taherabee tells how they came here from Madhya Pradesh 40 years ago, to avoid the language riots at the time of the reorganisation of the States of India. As we are talking, the owner comes to collect the previous day's consignment. He checks that all 20 pieces have been duly completed and hands over two 10-rupee notes. Taherabee says that her husband took another wife and left her. She pays rent of Rs250 a month and Rs2.50 to the *masjid*. She says she is a poor woman, but is thankful that their position on masjid land gives them security. She eats whatever is available; and gets a little extra for looking after her neighbour's children for whom the workshop would be a danger.

Mohamed Osman works with more expensive stones. He sells four bangles for Rs25, but the stones which the shop-owner delivers are semi-precious and worth several hundred rupees. The four bangles sell for up to Rs400 in the shops. He makes the bangles and sets the stones, and can deliver 60 a day, 15 sets of four. He mixes the titanium with the superior lacquer (Rs280 a kilo), a toffee-coloured gum. Titanium costs Rs120 a kilo. He says that although he is doing high-quality work, he cannot start a business on his own account because he lacks the capital necessary for the raw materials. He has eight children, and he does not want them to do this work. He wants them to get an education so they will do something better. He says there is often a delay in getting payment from the supplier. Other members of his family help do the expensive work; the cheaper bangles he subcontracts to some of the women in the neighbourhood.

In the next workshop, four boys, between 11 and 15, are working over two wooden frames doing zari work: beautiful, elaborate designs with sequins and gold thread, following with a sharp wooden-handled needle the pattern that has been printed on to the fine material. The boys are highly skilled and relatively well paid: 200 rupees a week, although to get this they must often work from 8 a.m. to 10 p.m., with half an hour's break for meals. They have a day off 'sometimes'.

Nearby, an old man is making ceremonial topees with his wife and son: embroidered material which they sew on to a cardboard frame, adding three loops of imitation pearls and a red bead at the front. They can make 20 a day and are paid Rs15 per person.

This is by no means one of the poorest communities. In the narrow streets, sagging powerlines hang over the low roofs, and the TV aerials suggest a community that has attained a certain level of material well-being, because of its proximity to the market. The lanes around the masjid are full of shops selling the fine objects that come out of the slum. The people here have developed their skills out of necessity, under conditions of extreme adversity. When they came here, all say they had nothing. And indeed, their skill and inventiveness are not undignified; what is disgraceful is the shamefully low price they receive for their labour; but to achieve these modest monetary rewards requires the sacrifice of the childhood of their young, the impairment of their health. Saathi recently ran an eye camp here. Out of 500 people who attended, 200, mainly children, were found to have severe eye problems because of the long hours of close intricate work, the smoky unventilated houses, the need to use poor lighting only sparingly, and the absence of natural light in many workplaces.

Seema has been working with Saathi for two years. She says their greatest achievement has been to establish a school in an outbuilding of the mosque. Around 70 children come, not always regularly, from 10 a.m. till 2 p.m., and then mostly as a break in their labour. *Seventy-five per cent of the children did not go to* school. One typical example is of a very intelligent eight-year-old who desperately wants to learn. He works 12 hours a day for a perfume-seller, for Rs150 a month. His family had borrowed Rs200 for a wedding from the perfume-seller, and was paying back most of the boy's salary in interest on this money. We approached him about releasing the boy for a few hours a day. He said 'I have to get back my money.'

Initially, parents resisted the idea of school. The community has gained its economic advancement because of the pooled labour of the whole family. The contribution of children has been vital. The family collude with exploitation because that is their only hope. But we have made headway. We have classes for women in the evenings, and more and more are becoming literate. Our teacher is a woman from the community. The children themselves have been transformed. They now come looking clean and neat, and they save some of their money for new clothes. Now the men have come to us and said 'When are you going to get a master for us?' So we now have literacy classes for men at nine in the evening after work is finished.

The Old City generally starts late: the shops open around 11 a.m., but stay open late into the night. Even the doctors' clinics open only at 9 p.m., and go on till midnight or later. Originally, the school was in the mullah's tomb; but when the girls had their periods they could not attend; so only some of the smallest children go there now, and the masjid has given us this room.

The economic gains do not do away with deprivation. Children deprived of sleep, of play, of education, women confined in cramped, unhealthy conditions, rarely going out: this is the price of their fragile place in the market. It isn't that children should not help with the family economy, it is a question of degree. The capacity to make and create beautiful things and to contribute to the work of society is one thing; to work 14 hours a day in a dark room over intricate zari is another matter.

Saathi is devoted to resolving precisely this dilemma: how to release women and children from exploitation and damaging destruction of health without forfeiting the skills and dignity which have made out of this community of refugees a proud and competent people with a strong sense of function and purpose.

Andhra Pradesh Civil Liberties Committee (APCLC)

At the Second World Conference on Human Rights in Vienna, June 1993, the APCLC made the following submission through K.G. Kannabiran and G. Haragopal.

We, the representatives of the APCLC, wish to draw the attention of the world body to alarming trends which seem to have almost missed the attention of the Conference. The world in general, in our perception, is entering into one of the worst phases of a human rights crisis. This is particularly true of most of the developing countries of the world. This crisis stems not only from a lack of commitment to and conviction of human rights by respective governments but also from a model of development that is being thrust upon them by the industrialised world backed by international financial institutions. This has gained even more support and legitimacy because of the collapse of the socialist world. The world-view that is being pushed through has been de-emphasising the welfare role of the State, resulting in the abandonment of egalitarian goals that inspired the world during the first half of this century.

These developments have very serious implications for the present and future of human rights. The large millions of the people will have to undergo further hardships. If the present model is ruthlessly pursued the way it is being done, there is no hope for the poor and oppressed at the end of the tunnel. The United Nations and human rights bodies should grow alive to this situation as it is heading for a violent violation of the preamble and the spirit of the Universal Declaration of Human Rights.

It has become increasingly clear in recent years to observers of human rights in Kashmir and Punjab that the abuse of power by agents of the State, particularly in such forms as fake 'encounters' with 'terrorists', disappearances, torture and extra-judicial killings, has been taking place against a developmental background, in which regard for human life itself is being diminished. The distinguished Indian commentator Rajni Kothari spoke to me of the dispensability of the poor: 'With an unprecedented expansion of the middle class itself, and the growing importance of technology in place of labour, it has become politically feasible to explicitly exclude the poor from the social process.' In this analysis, it is only to be expected that the millions of poor, displaced and disfranchised people will challenge the legitimacy of their exclusion; social militancy, struggles against exploitation, as well as movements for regional autonomy and for the recognition of ethnic differences, will increasingly be branded as 'terrorism'.

To find out what experience had informed the understanding of the APCLC, I went to Andhra Pradesh to meet human rights lawyers and defenders of some of the most desperately impoverished people in India, people driven into the arms of 'extremists' and 'Naxalites' by extremes of dispossession.

K.G. Kannabiran is the former President of the APCLC; a veteran fighter for the rights of the poor. I met him at a time when particular energy is required to fight the overtly anti-egalitarian thrust of the new economic policy.

We started by talking about evictions of slum-dwellers in Hyderabad. *People in the slums do not move readily, even though they are evicted frequently by thugs in the pay of government. They go through the courts as a self-defence mechanism. Even so, atrocities are frequent against slum-dwellers; rowdies and the police directed by the occupying power structure do their work. They are all land grabbers. The institutions against land-grabbing simply do not function. In the municipal building, there is a specific Office for the Redressing of Land-Grabbing. But it is staffed by personnel who think the poor should not have land. All their life they have protected the rich against the poor. How can it function effectively? The High Court judge in charge of land reform dealt with it so effectively that there is no land left for distribution to the poor. The Land-Grabbing Office is illusion, a mockery. It exists to deceive people.*

In theory, India has the most perfect laws. Child labour, bonded labour were abolished in 1950, Untouchability was abolished with independence. All those things are still in existence. Governments continue to pass acts abolishing Untouchability, for civil rights, protection for Dalits, the Atrocities against Scheduled Castes Act – none of these things would be necessary if the Constitution were observed.

Passing laws is one thing, but the police structure is still colonial, with a bit of feudal culture thrown in. The police and their mentality are part of the legacy of the British. The police never support the poor. On the contrary; the police are actively destroying the constitutional structure so visibly that it makes me very angry. They have become so brutal that they are part of a cannibalised institution. They kill their own kind without mercy or examination or thought. And they resent any comment on it at all. Every day the police indulge in heinous crimes, all vindicated in the name of law and order. The majority of people do not have the courage to stop these injustices. If a poor man is done to death in a police station, there is no protest.

The courts are also like that: dead institutions. Like Bleak House, devoid of both the pathos and humour. The levers of all our institutions are in the hands of those who have no sense. They think that the labour of the poor is to be appropriated by them and no one else. They may occasionally react paternalistically, dole out pity.

In reaction to the new economic policy, I feel stress must now be laid on the Constitution: in a normless world we must cling to something. Ignoring the Constitution means the debate cannot be effective. The new economic policy is against the Constitution: it is against social justice. It is on this anti-Constitutional aspect that it must be fought; otherwise we are only playing at radical politics.

Everything becomes discredited. All the workings of our institutions are a phantom play. Going to the High Court every day and working for the trade unions is a phantom activity; nothing is certain, you cannot grasp or feel anything. Sometimes I feel like Don Quixote. Nobody listens. People are interested in their salaries, their conditions of service, the luxuries that come with their position. No one exhibits any commitment to the Constitution or any genuine concern for the poor and needy. A righteous anger against injustice is absent. It has reached a pathetic state, when a High Court judge goes to the press saying, 'I have disposed of so many cases and so many commissions of inquiry.' But he won't have the courage to say, 'I have done justice in so many cases.'

It seems the West defeated Hitler, but then perfected his methods to a fine art. Human rights documents are signed by nations which have not the slightest respect for human rights. At the UN meeting in Vienna, I was astonished that country after country known for violating human rights appeared on the podium and asserted that no such violations occurred in their countries. Human rights have become a weapon in the hands of the US to implement the Monroe Doctrine. They play on every schism in every country to foster the fortunes of their sympathisers and do not care who perishes in the process.

We suggested in Vienna that there is no point in depending upon governments for human rights. An alternative popular movement is needed to oversee and safeguard the rights of people. Governments have a stake in the perpetuation of arms dumping, for instance; how can they care? We should transcend this governmental mode of dealing with conflict.

Governments always feel beleaguered. They fear the people are always in insurrection against them. They are frightened, and frightened because they fear justice.

The year 1969 was a watershed in India in the development of what we see now. Mrs Gandhi was in a real economic crisis, and she could think of nothing better than to call populist rhetoric to her assistance. What she said was that the directive principles of state policy should take precedence over human rights. She portrayed it as a conflict between courts and Parliament, in which Parliament was progressive and the courts regressive.

To be fair to her, the directive principle she meant was of a state which she saw as the Indian equivalent of a welfare state: the Constitu-

tion spoke of the fundamental duties of the State to protect livelihood, weaker sections, primary education, reduction of unemployment and so forth. Since these things are pro-people, it provided Mrs Gandhi with fodder to bombard the J.P. Movement and the Leftist parties; and thereby, she came back to power. She was in a deep economic crisis. The Naxalite movement was flourishing and she could not control it. She would have been embarrassed to attack the JP Movement, because Narayan was a national figure.

The Naxalites were butchered; 1,500 in Andhra. The leaders were liquidated. There was a State of Emergency in Andhra in 1969. Even so, not all the Naxalite areas could be controlled. It was a problem for her, because her power-base was eroding. In 1975, the Emergency was the last resort.

At that time, K.G. Kannabiran was the only lawyer fighting for the detainees. Other lawyers were afraid, an honest fear that they would be interned. Any lawyer appearing for the detainees would be questioned and taken into custody within two days. Kannabiran says that the Andhra police are the worst in India. Three of his colleagues in the APCLC have been shot by police. The vice-president of the committee, a doctor, was shot dead in his surgery. Kannabiran himself receives regular anonymous letters threatening death. He says he is not afraid. He has been doing the work for 30 years and sees no reason to cease now.

The most pernicious argument is status-quo-ism: with all its injustices, the present system is the best we can expect. Those injustices are seen as irremediable. There is an attempt to establish what is unjust as inevitable and unalterable.

Indira Gandhi thought Emergency was the answer. Rajiv came up with the idea of Clean Government. He was just a playboy who knew nothing. Narasimha Rao is doing all the things Indira did without the aid of Emergency, because they are acceptable to the class that is not their victim. To keep its privileges, that class will accept anything that must be done to others.

Narasimha Rao talks of democratic principles. His role is that of wolf in sheep's clothing. Inside the party, his role is to survive; outside, it is to protect the ruling classes, like the big landlord he is.

What I deplore now is the absence even of a perception of injustice. It is terrifying. The prospects in every way are frightening. When you close all forms of redress, people in general become either indifferent or afraid. Violence then becomes the only way of telling people what is happening. Our government has never responded to political protest: protest therefore continues and becomes exacerbated. A new generation comes along and sees nothing has changed in spite of protest, and they draw their own conclusions. Ten years ago there was protest in Kashmir. Now we see protest with AK rifles. Now many groups have arms; this is no longer a monopoly of government. Vocal insurrection has become armed insurrection. People then do not understand why bridges are bombed and buildings dynamited. Government has lost the capacity both of listening and of responding.

In India, with its oppressive, hierarchical caste structure, there is no concept of social justice. There is no indigenous human rights concept because of a Brahminical order. You cannot talk of Indian human rights. Whether the idea was born in the East or the West does not matter. Oppressive structures must be resisted. You must try to implement your work in an insurgent manner; that is, to use your own concepts and fight on the basis of those concepts. I try to operate by a form of insurgent jurisprudence – juristic principles used against the rulers, just as the bourgeoisie used them against the aristocracy of England. Feudal laws can be used effectively against the feudal system itself.

In India, Congress leaders were versed in Western liberalism and principles of justice, and by them they fought the British. Similarly, by now saying that the Constitution must be enforced, we become rebellious. The Constitution says that India shall be a socialist democratic republic, and bring about change in society whereby economic, political and social justice will prevail, and human dignity be restored.

If you plead to restore the objectives of the Constitution you are labelled an extremist. When lawyers speak of the advantages of the new economic policy, they are undermining the Constitution. We are, alas, unfortunate revolutionaries, who are merely fighting to retain the Constitution.

The politics of the people and the human rights movement must be integrated, or the human rights movement becomes merely a crime auditor of the government. Most human rights bodies say so many people were killed, etc. They want to keep out of politics. The result is, you maintain an audit of crimes committed by the State, without integrating it into the politics of the people that will enable them to fight for their right to overthrow the order. You don't call murders by their name, they become 'human rights violations'. Murders by the police become 'custodial deaths'. Radical movements find their leaders are often killed, like Niyogi, or they become outlawed and go underground and they are then not effective.

13. Chattisgarh: The Chattisgarh Liberation Front

The Legacy of Shankar Guha Niyogi

Bhilai is in the region of Chattisgarh, about 60 kilometres from Raipur in Madhya Pradesh, in the very centre of India. You follow the Bombay–Calcutta Highway Six, a road bordered by desolate tamarinds blighted by pollution from traffic and industry. A cloud from a cement factory creates a permanent shadow across the countryside of what used to be known as the rice-bowl of India, where the sweet basmati rice has traditionally been grown. The Kedia distillery sends its indescribable smell of chemicals and malt across the countryside, as its waste pollutes the drinking water of the surrounding area.

The Bhilai steel plant is visible from afar, and the multi-coloured trails of smoke from it numerous chimneys stripe the sky with rose, violet and pale grey. Outside the entrance to the huge plant – the biggest in Asia – is a black marble monument to Soviet–Indian friendship, constructed with Soviet technology in the 1950s. The colonies of permanent workers are in neatly spaced three-storey buildings, surrounded by grass and beds of canna lilies. These workers now form a privileged caste; the produce of their labour – the enormous output from the steel plant – becomes the basic material of hundreds of small steel plants and units, the workers of which have none of the advantages of the huge state-owned complex. Many of these use dangerous and dirty technologies; the workers are employed casually, even though many have been with the same company for 15 or 20 years: they have no sickness benefit, no security of labour; and they live in hutments and slums.

The small plants make all kinds of steel goods, from cooking vessels to auto parts; their workers must do overtime without pay; there are many accidents, and no compensation is given for death. In some factories the deaths of workers have been denied, and the bodies never found. It was with the unorganised sector that Shankar Guha Niyogi began his work in the 1970s, creating a trade union for those thought to be beyond the scope of union activity. Starting with the workers in the opencast iron mines, he

188

later shifted to the exploited industrial sector. It was the success of this work which was to lead directly to his murder in 1991.*

He had been leading a strike of casual and contract workers of the industries dependent upon the Bhilai steel plant. Far from making wild or extravagant demands, the workers were simply asking for implementation of the law of the land, for recognition of the regular nature of their work.

Niyogi was shot through the open window as he slept in his modest room in Bhilai in September 1991. He had been warned that a conspiracy of BJP politicians, industrialists and senior police officials planned to take his life. Later, after an investigation by the Federal Bureau of Investigation an industrialist was arrested but allowed to escape from jail. Since then, there has been no action by the authorities.

But the workers have continued their strike. Now in its fourth year, many who are totally without resource other than their labour power have maintained their solidarity. Their struggle is against terms of employment which are contrary to the law of India. By a strange paradox, it has now become subversive to work for the implementation of laws and ideals enshrined in the Constitution of India.

Some of the workers sit in the union office at Bhilai; a small room with a portrait of Niyogi on the wall. Their faith in the justice of their cause and their solidarity offer sad reminders to people from the West that the cruelty and oppression which once united our people in struggle have not disappeared from the world; and poignant echoes of our own history are heard in their testimony of tenacity and hope.

The dignity of the workers is impressive, the more so because most are thin, undernourished, oppressed. How have they survived for four years without income? Y.K. Chandrakar was a skilled worker at Raipur Alloys before the lockout. He lives in a small hut with his wife and two children, without running water or electricity. They manage because his wife is educated and she gives tuition in maths and English. Mohammad Rizwad Ahmad joined Raipur Alloys in 1985. He is from Bihar, and has three children; he has not seen his family since the strike began. The company works three shifts a day; there is a core workforce, but the majority are contract labour. His family were living here with him, but they had to go back to Bihar when the workers were

---

* For further discussion of Niyogi, see Jeremy Seabrook, *Victims of Development*, London, Verso, 1994.

dismissed following the strike; they have a little land where they grow wheat and maize. His wife has a machine, and makes clothes. The family eat once a day.

Sanjay Kumar Prasad was with Simplex. Sanjay says that labour makes up just 1.5 per cent of the total costs of Simplex, which is notorious for low pay and casual employment. Many of the companies are diversifying, following the new liberalisation regime in India. Simplex is building a fruit-processing plant, for the export of mango and tomato juice.

The little dusty towns on the road to the iron ore mines where the Chattisgarh Mukti Morcha (CMM, Chattisgarh Liberation Front) began, are the scene of that energetic search for livelihood that characterises all communities in India; women in dark sarees sway beneath their burden of fodder – vast headloads that conceal the upper portion of their body – or gnarled branches of firewood or pitchers of water. A man on a cycle carries a goat around his shoulders, like a fur stole. In places where the river widens out so that there is access to its shallow banks from the road, trucks stand in the water up to the rim of their wheels like cattle. An extraordinary image: the transfer of traditional practice to new forms of conveyance. Similarly, in the rice-fields, the people wear traditionally designed broad-brimmed hats with strips of bamboo, but the shade is provided not by grass now but by strips of polythene.

Nine months after the death of Niyogi, the dismissed and locked-out workers held a demonstration on the railway line at Bhilai to press for some progress in the negotiations between the union and the industrialists. The CMM has always been peaceful: among the basic tenets of faith of Niyogi's organisation was non-violence inspired by Gandhi.

Of course, says Laxman, a member of the union, *the government of Madhya Pradesh was BJP at that time.* [Since then it has reverted to Congress (I), a party with no more sympathy for the workers than its communalist predecessor.] *They were not interested in listening to the voice of the workers. We had maintained our peaceful agitation for two years. We sat down on the railway track on 1 July 1992 because we wanted the government to hear our demands. We decided we would stop the trains that day. There were about 5,000 demonstrators. The government officials came at one o'clock in the afternoon and told us to vacate the track or to accept the consequences. The government had said it would arrange a meeting between the industrialists and the workers. The Collectors of three districts and the Commissioner of Raipur had prepared a draft agenda to which the industrialists refused to talk to the workers. Only after that was direct peaceful action decided upon.*

At five in the afternoon the police fired on the crowd, killing 16 people and wounding many more. Such was the discipline that no panic ensued. Quite the contrary. The people remained where they were, seated on the railway line.

The movement of the CMM is symbolic; it is a movement of liberation rather than simply a trade union; but a movement which recognises the centrality of livelihood. Activities are not limited to the workplace, or even simply to workers: its members include released bonded labourers, women, child labour, tribal people.

The very existence of the CMM is seen as a threat to the government's new policy of retrenchment and liberalisation. The State and Central governments both support the policy, directed by the International Monetary Fund and World Bank, of greater 'flexibility' of labour, exit policy and privatisation. The government is afraid that union success in Chattisgarh might give heart to other labour struggles all over India, at a time when it has been judged expedient not to extend protection to the un-organised workers of India, who are among the most exploited and humiliated people on earth, but to withdraw these advantages from the organised sector, a mere 9 per cent of the workforce.

Although there are many eager recruits to take the place of the sacked workers, these have neither the skills nor the discipline – partly a consequence of union influence – to carry out the work. When exports are crucial to the new policy, many companies have found that with the loss of their reliable workers, the quality of their production has suffered, the delivery dates have been delayed, and organisation within the industrial unit has fallen apart. On the other hand, some companies have used the opportunity for further mechanisation, so that fewer workers will be needed.

Dalli Rajhara is the site of the opencast iron ore mines, a bleak settlement on the ravaged hills. The rocks here have the highest ore content of any in India; the rest dust colours everything, buildings, vegetation, faces, so that the whole town appears to be rusty.

The people who worked in the mines were some of the most helpless and overworked in a country where exploitation in one form or another has reached a high state of perfection. Before Niyogi began his work in this district, the people were living below subsistence wages; they had become dependent upon alcohol; life was violent and without hope. One of the principal campaigns in the early days was an anti-liquor movement, which gained Niyogi the enmity of those friends of the people, the liquor-lords.

Now the town shows all the signs of the improvements which

the people have achieved by their efforts. What used to be dark impoverished huts have been extended to create more ample houses, constructed mainly of the red earth itself, with locally made tiles, surrounded by enclosures and gardens, and with screens to prevent the rain from washing the walls away. I visited some of the workers who belong to the CMM. Everywhere, I was received with courtesy and warmth, and the people spoke proudly of achievements which they will not give up, no matter what pressures are placed upon them by the employers, by their private armies, by the government, by the orders of Western financial institutions. 'Consciousness', they say, 'is irreversible. You can take away material things, but you cannot impair an understanding that arises out of triumph over adversity.'

Phaugaram is a native of Chattisgarh. He still has one acre of land, 5 kilometres from Dalli Rajhara. He says that 20 years ago they worked up to 16 hours for a daily wage of Rs4.50, starting soon after three in the morning and going on until seven at night. He worked in the Danitola mine, where Niyogi also worked. The INTUC trade union was there – the union of the Communist Party – but it had become inert and corrupt. Now people work from seven in the morning till three in the afternoon and get Rs82 a day. This is how they have been able to extend the houses and construct gardens. The work is still arduous: men and women bring the ore from the mines to the spot where it is broken with a hammer, and then reload the lorries which take it away to the plants for smelting. Those who transport the ore carry it on their heads in baskets, loads of between 30 to 50 kilos a time, walking up to 3 kilometres. Workers who wash the ore now clean 10 tons a day; formerly they washed up to 30 tons. Phaugaran has three children. Before the CMM was formed, they ate rice and salt as the main meal of the day; in the mid-1970s there had been drought and famine. Now half his daily income will buy three meals, including eggs, dried fish, mutton and chicken occasionally, as well as the daily rice, dal and vegetables.

The union built a hospital at Dalli Rajhara by voluntary labour. Each day, there is a steady flow of people suffering from respiratory diseases, infections and injuries sustained at work, as well as pregnant women. This is one of the most tangible achievements of the CMM. Since the strike began, the hospital kitchen has been providing one meal a day for employees who are withholding their labour. Each day, 20 or 30 men will be fed there; the union provides a limited quantity of rice to the families of the strikers. On this occasion, the men are former employees of the Kedia distillery and Simplex works. Their courage and hope are deeply affecting. With all the power and wealth of the owners, politicians and police against them, they have nothing but the being together, the support and solidarity of this bleak isolated mining town: the priceless consolation of collective struggle – something which the rulers of the rich countries of the West have worked so hard to undermine and destroy.

The landscape around Dalli Rajhara has been convulsed by mining activity; red terraces in the hills mark the passage of the roads where the trucks take the excavated heart of the mountain to the works at Bhilai. The mines are at present still government-owned, run by the Steel Authority of India. Earlier plans for mechanisation had been rejected by the workers in favour of a plan of semi-mechanisation which would not throw the miners out of work. The Steel Authority accepted the plan of the workers. But with the new liberalisation programme, there is no longer any constraint on the upgrading of technology, even if this means the degradation of the workers. The workers say the government wants to install automatic conveyor belts – that is, to disinter the plan which had been thrown out by earlier union negotiation.

Tham Singh is also from Chattisgarh, his home place – 85 kilometres from Dalli Rajhara. His was a family of landless labourers. He worked for Rs2 or 3 a day, and his father became a bonded labourer. When Tham Singh was 12 his father died and he inherited the bondage for the loan which had still not been paid off. He ran away to Dalli Rajhara to work in the mines, which turned out to be at that time only a slightly more refined form of bondage. He is now retired, a not very robust-looking man in vest and pants sitting on a wooden bed in his house, giving no sign of the epic of oppression and exploitation which his life has been. When he came here, he worked as a stone-breaker, Rs4 for a 16-hour day. Five members of his family worked in the mines. After the organising of the CMM, and the struggle for a living wage, he was paid Rs82 a day – a more than 20-fold increase. The workers must break a minimum of 4,500 kilos of stone per day. There is constant risk of injury, from cuts and wounds from flying stone. In the mines there was no drinking water; only water from the opencast mines or from the rust-coloured nalla. After the struggle of Niyogi in the early 1970s, the workers did receive some benefits; for one thing, they were issued with ration cards, which entitle them to subsidised rice and wheat, sugar and kerosene. Even so, the ration-shops do not receive enough for the allocation to the people; quite often the rice is taken by officials and sold on the open market. In any case, the heavy labour in the opencast mines requires a higher ration of rice than comes through the subsidised system.

Tham Singh's son has just died. He became ill through working in the mines for many years, inhaling the dust. His father says simply, *We shall struggle until we die. Too many of those we have loved have died prematurely of old age, injury or avoidable sickness; too many in childbirth, too many children in the mines.* Keeping faith with remembered flesh and blood feeds their proud and fierce commitment.

The houses are dignified; we sit on metal and plastic-string chairs in the little garden of Baluram Thakur; the enclosure has a thornbush gate to prevent animals from escaping. In the little garden there are tomatoes, beans and custard apples. There is a pile of baskets from the mine, stained red with the iron dust. The women are preparing the evening meal on the veranda under the roof. They now have electricity here. Baluram Thakur earns Rs1700 a month as a welder. There are four adults and four children in the house. Baluram Thakur and his brother Krishnabhai say that all they need is enough for a decent living. Simple living was also one of Niyogi's basic Gandhian principles. They know a deadly secret here, which is that enough is as good as a feast; a heretical attitude in a world where a quickening industrialism denies the possibility of sufficiency, and keeps the people of the West on the rack by having substituted for enough a superfluity without end, without meaning and without satisfaction. How do the people of this remote part of India know? They say it is obvious.

But their children will not work in the mines. There are no jobs; indeed, there has been a voluntary retirement scheme: 1,900 have taken voluntary retirement in the past three years. Today 2.7 million tonnes of ore are mined with 5,700 workers, as against 2 million tonnes with 10,000 workers 15 years ago, when Niyogi started work here. Mechanisation is being introduced, and as workers leave they are simply not replaced: when labour achieves a dignified living wage, they are disemployed by the introduction of capital-intensive machinery.

The workers of the CMM know there are no final victories; each achievement is partial, provisional and reversible. It is unbearably poignant to sit in their sweet-smelling compound in the indigo evening warmth and observe the intelligence and understanding of people who have suffered and struggled in ways that may have ceased to be understandable in the West but are part of Western history too.

India, say the workers, needs labour-intensive industry. When the labourers work efficiently and create maximum output, there is no need for machinery, apart from that which relieves people from

194

degrading labour. The supreme endowment of India is its 900 million pairs of hand. We don't want foreign machinery displacing
people; we don't need technology that will disemploy our children.
Can you imagine the levels of violence and despair if we follow that
path and create no work for future generations?

The union has made a survey of unemployed youth in the area;
there are over 17,000 in the immediate district of Dalli Rajhara.
The union wants to be given work in the ancillary industries around
Bhilai. Some of those who have taken voluntary retirement have
purchased land in the villages, going back to the rural occupations
from which they were originally evicted, although this can sustain
only a fraction of the people in the area. *What we need is minimum
mechanisation that will take the stress from the worker; to improve the
lot of the workers, but not to throw out of work – that should be the goal
of Indian Policy.*

Beside the union compound there is a graveyard with a memorial
to those shot by the police during various agitations over the past
15 years. In the union office, there is a shrine to Niyogi; his picture
and chair, garlanded, and an oil lamp perpetually burning. On the
wall of the office the shoes of some of those shot by police in the
late 1970s.

In the South, there are many echoes of the forced industrialisation which occurred in the West: the people are changed from rural
labourers to industrial workers in much the same way. Like the
miners in the early industrial era in Britain, the iron-ore workers of
India have not lost contact with the countryside. Organised resistance to oppression and injustice takes place under similarly hostile
circumstances.

But there are other elements: the process in the South is acceler-
ated; it is buttressed by an established global industrial system, and
by an intensifying displacement of workers by technology. In a
country like India, this threatens consequences far more damaging
than the managed technological change in the West. One thing is
clear, however. The working class has not disappeared from the
world, however elusive its presence may appear now in the West.

Pithora

A worker with the CMM tells this story. *An Adivasi is sitting
peacefully under a tree in a remote jungle village. An extension
worker comes along and says to him 'Do you have land?' 'Yes', says
the Adivasi, and waves his hand, 'all this.' 'Why do you not cultivate
it more?' 'Why?' 'To get more produce.' 'Why?' 'To take it to market.'*

'Why?' 'To get more money.' 'Why?' 'To live more comfortably and more easily, so that you can sit back and relax.' The Adivasi says, 'What am I doing now?'

About 100 kilometres east of Raipur, the jungle has been badly degraded; the people, who are mainly Adivasis, have been denied all rights over the products of the forest. On the day we arrived, eight men had been arrested for growing padi on government land – even though they had been doing so for 20 years. Subsistence, it seems, has become a crime.

The CMM has been helping the children of Adivasi families in this area to acquire skills. People who formally had worked only in the fields of others for Rs5 a day, can, with a useful skill, gain independence and increase their income tenfold. Karan Singh, a young man in his early twenties, has a cycle repair shop on the edge of a small village, overlooking the padi-fields where the rice is almost ready for harvesting; red and gold stems of grain curving gracefully over the dried-out fields. Karan Singh sits on the threshold of the dilapidated hut, straightening the spokes of a wheel. He has two brothers and a sister; by his labour, he is able to earn enough to ensure that the family eats properly. His little workshop is crammed from floor to ceiling with pieces of dismantled cycles – wheels, chains, tyres, bells, pedals. Karan Singh says the bicycle is the most widely used form of transport here; and the rough track is very damaging to the tyres. Karan Singh is happy in the modest security he has achieved. He will soon marry. He has no wish to leave his home-place. He says 'I have all that I need here.'

Not everyone is so fortunate. In the village of Pithora itself, there is a community who make handicrafts of bamboo. They migrated from Orissa 15 years ago. Radheshyam is sitting beneath the veranda of his small hut, with a brother and cousin. They are making vessels for cleaning rice: a kind of woven bamboo pan, a *supa*, in which the women toss the rice in order to sort out bad grains and small stones. The strips of bamboo, finely cut, are held between their toes, and they weave them with a deft hand motion into a taut firm fabric. They are supposed to receive a certain amount of bamboo from the government; it is distributed by the forest officials but it is often unsuitable, and the officials charge extra for it. Naturally, the people go in search of their own material; but if they are caught they will be fined Rs10 for each stalk of bamboo. The officials keep it for themselves.

Each worker can make two or three supas in one day. Once a week, the middleman comes; the workers receive Rs30 for each basket; they have no idea at what price it is sold in the market;

they only know it is a great deal more than they are paid. The three children of Radheshyam's brother learn from their uncle: their mother died of a snakebite, and they must become self-supporting as soon as possible.

In this, the rainy season, life is harder. The middleman does not come, and then they must go from village to village on foot, trying to sell the produce themselves; but this takes time when they could be occupied working. Some of the children make jute rope by hand, twisting it from a hook in the wall of one of the houses.

They came from Orissa because of a series of droughts in the 1960s and 1970s. The people had lost such land as they possessed, and many had become indebted. A long procession of evicted humanity has been set in movement in India as a consequence of human-made disasters, climatic alteration, development projects, industrialised farming. Not all go to the cities; some are internal migrants, artisans who cling to their craft, and settle wherever they can find a supply of the raw materials they need.

Each day they work from six in the morning until midday; they eat and rest for an hour, and work again from early afternoon until evening. Their children cannot go to school because they must learn the craft, take care of the cattle, and help in the fields of those who have land.

Officially, bondage is now abolished in India, although there are still an estimated five million bonded labourers. The Madhya Pradesh government denies that bondage exists in the State. Yet in Pithora, Jairam was bonded to a landlord in order to pay for his marriage: for a loan of Rs550, he was bonded for three years. He received 1½ kilos of padi per day during that time. He has now paid off the loan. He says that people enter bondage all the time, only now it is for a shorter period. They still pay extortionate rates for the loans, but at least there is an end to the term of bondage. In this way, the bonded labourers have as great a vested interest in concealment as the landlords; so both parties collude, under the pretext that it is free labour. *It is the same as the government of India*, says the CMM worker, *they take a loan, they are told what to do by the IMF and World Bank. They do it and pretend India is independent.*

Jairam works in the traditional family occupation, making the rice-baskets, and earns Rs20 a day. He, his wife and their two children live in his brother's house. The house is illegally occupied, because this is common grazing land. The house was brought by his brother for Rs500, although the owner had also constructed it illegally. The lives of many Adivasis are lived on the margins of legality – the land they occupy, the work the do – everything criminalises them.

Beneath a khair tree on the edge of the village, a whole family sits, working with bamboo in the shade. Drupadi is in her thirties. She says that women know how to do everything; she cuts the bamboo into fine strips with a sharp curved knife, just the necessary thickness for weaving. A sweet resinous smell fills the air from the cut bamboo. She earns between Rs20 and 25 a day. The bamboo comes from the jungle, and they pay the forest officials (unofficially) Rs2.50 per stick of bamboo. She used to borrow from middlemen, take a loan to buy the bamboo, but the debts were so great that they could not make a living: the corruption of forest officials is a lesser evil than moneylenders. They buy rice at Rs7 a kilo in the market. The basket for which they are paid Rs25 sells at Rs35 or 40. They can make two a day. Drupadi says they cannot afford to educate their children, because they have to earn as soon as they can. They use mahua leaves to make daru, liquor; and they sell tendu leaves for bidi-making. They also take wood from the forest, although they are careful not to destroy growing trees, and they take honey, both for their own use and for sale. Drupadi says the government is not planting trees to benefit the people; its afforestation schemes are all eucalyptus and teak, for revenue, construction companies and building in the towns. She says in the village there are perhaps 40 or 50 rich farmers and their families, with 70 acres or so. There are 15 times as many poor families.

A small tea-shop in a clearing between the trees: the proprietor brings out a rough bench which he places on the flattened earth outside. His poor shop has few items for sale – some biscuits, bidis, a few packets of soap, candles. The shopkeeper came from a village about 70 kilometres away after a drought; he sold his share of the family land to his brother. He earns Rs20–25 a day, but only 15 or so in the lean season, and he has managed to repurchase 2 of his 2.5 acres with the money he has saved. He has five children, all of them now married.

He says that there is a resident midwife in the village, but no other medical facility. Malaria is common and, what is worse, there have been a large number of cases of cerebral malaria in the past year: when the outbreak occurred, there were no medicines, because the government supply had been sold by one of the employees. The malaria health inspector failed to appear.

As we sit talking with the shopkeeper, a motor cycle roars to a halt in a cloud of dust. A man dismounts and walks unsteadily towards the group with whom we are sitting. Sevak Singh is the sarpanch – chairman of panchayat. He demands to know what we are doing here. The rich farmers are no friends of the CMM, who have disturbed the pattern of domination in the area. The sarpanch stands belligerently and demands to know why we are in 'his' village. He smells strongly of drink. It is four o'clock in the afternoon. He picks a quarrel with the representative of the CMM, and then apologises profusely to me as a visitor. I say that we have come in a spirit of friendship, and then he turns upon me and says that we should have asked his permission, he is the sarpanch. He verbally abuses the shopkeeper and his wife, and they become apologetic and cringe before him. It is an ugly spectacle – the display of naked power of one human being over another; a rare insight, thanks to the sarpanch's uninhibitedness through drink. He orders us out of the village; and then apologetic again, drives off into the dust.

One of the older men who has been observing the scene tells us that no one pays any attention to the sarpanch. How does he get elected then? He has many friends, the man says without further explanation. The sarpanch is always drunk. If a poor man goes to him with a problem, he will demand money for drink. He takes money from people so that they can be allowed to stay on government land. Big landlords encroached illegally, and they try to get pattas (land deeds) issued in their favour. They take money from the poor to permit them to remain on 'their' (stolen) land. The old man is in his seventies; he wears a rag of a turban around his forehead; his teeth are crooked and discoloured by paan; but his eyes are bright and gleam with a keen intelligence. He tells how his father was bonded for 50 years, and his father's brother for 30 years; the family were landless. His father had been indebted for Rs300 (about $10); and the repayment was such that he would never be able to pay back the interest, let alone the principal. He received 1.5 kilos of padi per day. The landlord to whom he was bonded had ten others working for him.

There is a CMM woman worker in the village. She says women are fieldworkers like the men; they earn about Rs10 a day in the preparation of the fields and the harvest season. They are sexually harassed by the rich farmers, manhandled and even raped. If a women fails to bring a dowry when she marries, she may be driven away. If she proves to be barren – in fact, it will never be known if it is she or the man, but it is always assumed to be her fault – she will be thrown out. Women are still treated here as inferiors: there is no woman in the panchayat. The CMM has trained some women – in tailoring, soap making, cycle-brush making; literacy – and tries to arrange loans for women, although this is difficult because government officials delay everything. *We have trained 40 women and 34 fully completed the course, but they have no capital to become self-sufficient, they have to work in the fields. If they do get a loan, their husbands will take it.*

We follow the beaten earth track between Pithora and Sukhri village which is where 28 former long-term bonded labourers live. They were released by a court order about five years ago, in the largest mass release ever recorded in India. All were given compensation of Rs6,250 and a small piece of land on which to build a house; the pattas were issued by the government. Some bought a little land. Even so, this has not been the last word. Some rich farmers pay government officials who then permit them to graze their cattle on the poor people's crops. This destroys the yield, and undermines the livelihood of the poor. The rich farmers then buy the land from them at negligible prices.

The houses here are low with rough verandas supported by bleached tree branches, thatch and tile roofs; an uneven rocky thoroughfare, with grass growing at the side; cows and bullocks lying in the road; dogs, goats and bullock-carts.

Shyamlal tells how his father took a loan from the landowner, a loan that went on increasing because of the high rate of interest. He become bonded, and was in effect a slave. If he came late he was cursed or beaten. There was no limit on the time the landowner could demand of him – 14, 16 hours a day. He had seven children, and received 1.5 kilos of padi, that is about one kilo of rice when the husks are removed. His mother also became bonded, and together they got 3.5 kilos of padi. When they were freed by the High Court, they were given 2 acres of land. They grow rice, some of which they have to sell to buy clothes, so that leaves them nothing to eat in the lean season. They are still fighting for the patta to the land.

The police and forest officials still harass the people. The CMM has helped them to organise; without the CMM, they would have been driven out of the refuge they were able to acquire with the government compensation, evicted by servants of the same government.

When the Supreme Court came here to inquire into bondage, the landlords were given the names of the bonded labourers who came to talk to the officials, so they could deal with them afterwards. This is the reality of life in the countryside: the law is only as good as those who enforce it; and when the officials are corruptible, themselves often ill-paid and insecure, there is simply no way of enacting all the benign legislation on the statute book. The officials have their own private enterprise to augment their income, through extortion, threats and exploitation.

The peace of the village street scene belies the violence beneath; there is a bleached cart tipped up in the street, on which birds perch; crows and pigeons, forest birds, bulbuls and parrots. The warm wind moves the dust, half covering the stones and then revealing them again. Creeper grows over the red roofs with ripe pumpkins and gourds; people sit in the warm evening on a charpoy; a cow serenely eats some of the fodder brought by the women, pausing in its eating to look up; a pink flower sticks coquettishly out of its mouth. Then it goes to lie down under the karanj tree – which provides oil – growing in the middle of the road, and spreading its welcome shade over the houses.

The people here call themselves Agriyas; they believe they came from Agra to Orissa first of all; they were a landowning caste, who had become soldiers in the Kalingan Empire, and they settled in Orissa after the disintegration of the empire, in this tribal belt. The people had no knowledge of money or exploitation. They cultivated the land as self-reliant farmers.

Their houses are arranged in extended families around a roughly constructed central courtyard, where the women prepare food, wash and linger to talk with each other over their household chores. In one house live five brothers all of whom had been bonded. They cultivate the garden behind the buildings; in this late monsoon period, there are *kochai* and *kandi*, vegetables, green vegetables, *sulyari*, lemon, mango and bananas. There is a pond, and a small patch of a pulse called ahar. The sersua tree is used for fodder, there is a small field of maize. Shade is provided by sagoon (Chattisgarhi for teak) trees. Water pumpkins grow by the pond, green silver globes; while an ornamental strip of marigolds provides a splash of brilliant colour among the green.

Beneath the immemorial calm of the village are also ancient struggles and enmities, exploitations which, even when they are officially abolished, live on in subterranean forms. The CMM, however, is persistent. There is only hopeful and continuous struggle. It is a modest achievement, but one from which people derive dignity.

The killing of Niyogi has not destroyed the movement he inspired. His spirit lives on in non-violent but determined commitment to social justice and forms of development that waste neither the material nor the human resources of India.

But the removal of Niyogi has great symbolic meaning. It is part of the common wisdom of all International Monetary Fund and World Bank programmes that government spending should be cut, that exports must increase, that privatisation and devaluation of the currency should occur to make the country more competitive. Increasing social destitution and hunger will be a direct consequence for the poor of India: those who stand in the way of this version of progress are dangerous.

14. The Prospect for India

A number of major shocks in the early 1990s have given a new impulse to the work towards an alternative to the present development path in India. Perhaps the most fateful of these – and not unconnected with many of the others – was the 'shock therapy' (in the words of economists) of the new liberal economic policy. This represented a definitive rejection of India's tradition of self-reliance and *svadeshi*, in favour of dependency upon and growing indebtedness to the West. A second was the the the rise of the fundamentalist BJP and its allies, culminating in the demolition of the mosque at Ayodhya, the subsequent murderous riots, and the riposte of the Bombay bomb blasts early in 1993. A third was the growing assertiveness of those traditionally outside the caste system, the alliance of the poor which voted in the State government of Uttar Pradesh in November 1993.

The West has sought to press home its advantages in India, as elsewhere, in a unipolar world. Its economic fundamentalism now sees no obstacle to perpetual growth and expansion, or to its dissemination in every country in the world, save a few recalcitrants like Iraq and Cuba. One of the most aggressive assertions of this has been the Western definition of human rights, from which economic rights must be rigorously excluded. In a competitive, cut-throat, rat-race system (the elegant imagery speaks for itself), there can be no sentimental concessions to the right to livelihood.

Popular movements in India have countered this narrowing definition of human rights with the radical right to life as the most basic of all human rights. What, they ask, is the point of protecting political and civic rights, when 30,000 children die each day from avoidable disease and malnutrition, when hundreds of thousands of women in the South give birth astride the grave? This creative redefinition of human rights has been one of the major contributions of the Narmada Bachao Andolan (the campaign to save the Narmada Valley from being flooded by the Sardar Sarovar Dam project), the Chilika Bachao Andolan, and all those groups which have taken the right to livelihood argument to its logical conclusion.

More than the idea of a dam, the Narmada movement has questioned not just the dam but the whole issue of development itself. It has confronted the World Bank and the Western financial institutions with the consequences of their actions, and the human and ecological reality of their theories. Further, it has highlighted the malignancy of 'development', a development grafted on to India and countries of the South, without reference to the conditions and traditions of the countries on which it is imposed. And here they have struck at the heart of Western fundamentalism, which has sought to conflate capitalism with cosmos, the workings of one economic system with life itself: a macabre parody designed to conceal the fact that much of the sickness of the modern world – in both North and South – is socially and economically determined, not part of fate, or necessity at all. The karmic law of the West is strictly human-made.

The Indian alternative – decentralised, small-scale, local, Gandhian – instead of being raised as an example to a world threatened by over-development, intensifying industrialisation and social and ecological disintegration, has been occluded by the evangelising fervour of Westernisation and the rise of Hindu fundamentalism.

The vociferous advocates of accelerating commitment to the market-reforms of Congress(I), and the grandiose visions of *Hindutva* (Hindu hegemony), which fed the rise of the communalist parties in the early 1990s, appear to be the principal forces in contention in India. In fact, these bitterly warring oppositions share a devotion to the maintenance of the existing economic order. Their political incompatibilities mask common aims, not the least of which is the perpetuation of social injustice, economic inequalities and privilege. The contortions of the RSS in its commitment to svadeshi were at odds with the welcome offered by the BJP to the entry of the multinationals into India.

The rise of Hindu fundamentalism is not revanchism. It is actually the modernising of Hinduism: the Christianising, Islamicising or Judaising of Hindusim; transforming its tolerant, polymorphous openness into something equivalent to the hierarchies, efficiency and order of more highly organised world religions. Svadeshi in this context is mummery, useful for the BJP to conceal its true purposes: with svadeshi India won't get nuclear bombs, a streamlined state, superindustrialism, discipline and order. But with the BJP it will, as indeed it will with Congress(I).

In a curious way, the rhetoric of all the main forces in contention in India contains an element of truth. As far as Congress(I) goes, surely no one can deny that India is in need of renewal, a salutary cleansing of a somnolent and obstructive bureaucracy.

And when the BJP talks of the need to recuperate something of India's past, who can fail to see that the rejection of Indian tradition, skills and creativity has been a profound insult, not simply to Hindus but to all Indians? The fact that malign ideologies flourish in the presence of real evils neither condones the ideologies nor nullifies the evils. The recovery of something of value from a past that is being junked does not necessarily mean that the BJP is right. For there are other noble traditions which it chooses to pass over in silence, which are in far more urgent need of rehabilitation: the practice of *ahimsa* (non-violence), of self-restraint, respect for all living things, the practice of a joyful austerity, do not belong to the zealots of millennial nostalgia.

As for the institutionalised Left, that too proclaims an archaic and alien creed. This ideology that has withered in its Western heartland continues to bear a strange half-life in India, living on in creaking slogans and threadbare prescriptions. And yet, who will deny that its project of social justice touches the most vital of all the problems besetting India?

We are left with clashing, totalising ideologies, whose common thrust is continuing adherence to existing developmental and economic forces, ideologies which demand untold human sacrifice to their particular variant of revealed truth. Only when the positive elements in each are taken from their dogmatic and inflexible context, and reassembled in another form, will they take on a new vitality and force, something to inspire faith and hope in the future of India.

This is the task of the alternative movement, the aggregate of all the popular initiatives, the resistance to developmental aggression and economic violence, the commitment to communal peace and tolerance. If the alternative is to have the power and the dynamic energy of the present deadly forces now in conflict, it, too, must tell a story of hope and inspiration: not a story of restoration of the glories of an imagined and irrecoverable past, to be attained through the destruction of this place of worship or the building of that temple; and not the fairy-tale promises of wealth and affluence without end, if India will only follow the path indicated by its Western mentors; and not even the mirage that social injustice will melt away if only the State will take control of the production and distribution of the fruits of industrialism.

The existing ideological alternatives within the mainstream are all crusades of fundamentalists, of the perpetuators of mouldering dystopias which belong in the graveyard of all the vain human sacrifices which they have already demanded in their deadly progression across the world. The West imposes its version of a modernised, industrialised humanity, so irresistible that it sweeps all before it. No wonder that people retreat to the only spaces left to them – the apparent safe haven of the past or the tarnished New Jerusalems of an impossible future. The mangled identity and crushed consciousness of people cannot be stifled; and unless these can express themselves, they will emerge in the distortions we have seen in India. In any case, the poor are excluded from these battles, as was shown by the coalition of Dalits, Muslims and the oppressed in Uttar Pradesh, which came, in part, as a response to the cruel alliance of the Brahminical order with Western elitism.

The present task for the alternative movement is to roll back those malignant forces at work, not merely in India but equally in the former Soviet Union and the former Yugoslavia, as well as in those places where the Western way has been imposed, in Brazil, in the Philippines and in most of the countries of Africa, where Western fundamentalist 'reform packages' demand their tribute of human flesh from the poorest and most vulnerable on earth. This is not, however, to absolve the rulers of India from responsibility. It is easy, as Patwant Singh points out, for Indian governments to point to 'the foreign hand' to blame India itself for misgovernance and error.

'The foreign hand' has become part of our political vocabulary, a constant, handy, dependable abstraction to which we could attribute just about everything. The alienation of entire States – troubled by the Centre's policies and prejudices – could be blamed on a foreign hand. If Western powers armed Pakistan, it was seen as a conspiracy of the foreign hand to destabilise us. And even when our own evil, homegrown, religious bigots fanned Bombay's second wave of massacres – within a month of the December 1992 killings – we attributed it to a foreign hand ... We took many steps without prompting by outside powers: the surrender to linguistic jingoism which continues to leave a gory trail as the reorganised States seethe discontentedly over territory, river waters and jobs; the failure to overhaul the administrative system because we liked exercising power from the top – as in the colonial days – with no participatory role for the people below ... We clamped the Emergency too through our own innovative genius, substituting a dictatorship for democracy, and putting to rest democratic aspirations by yearning for dynastic rule. Since dynasties and dictatorships need massive funds, we successfully tried our hand at corruption on a matching scale; by amending the statute more than seventy times to make it easier to keep people in place, by eroding the judiciary and the executive, by encouraging state terrorism, and by using religion to usurp the majority community's votes. Neither Pakistan, the Western powers nor other foreign hands had anything to do with any of this, we did it on our own.*

This is a useful corrective to those who turn India into a perpetual victim, for that itself is part of a colonising inferiorisation: the alibi of what was done to us by others creates the complicity of victims with oppressors. It does not, however, absolve leaders and elites from treacherous, manipulative and cynical collusion with external contemporary centres of power in an 'integrated global economy', an alliance designed to impose a colonial economy upon their own people.

This new alliance of fundamentalisms can be resisted only by elaborating a different kind of faith; and the only fundamental in this faith is its commitment to the sanctity of humanity. That this is what most people already believe and, indeed, practise, was evident in the responses to the violence that shook India, both during the post-Ayodhya riots, and during the bomb-blasts in Bombay, as well as after the earthquake in Maharashtra. For at that moment, human beings did not have to be told to rescue the dying from wrecked buildings. They did not wait for political bosses to direct them to the hospitals to give blood. They tore away with their bare hands at the collapsed masonry to bring out the injured bodies of total strangers. The neighbours in Dharavi or Jogeshwari in Bombay who sheltered one another from the madness of lynch-mobs were not acting because they subscribed to this ideology or because they thought it was in accordance with that dogma. They recognised, instinctively, that all we have is each other, that flesh and blood are our only recourse and only defence against the multiple afflictions of human life on earth.

After four years of the 'new economic policy' in India, the inadequacies of Western economic dogmas were acknowledged even by the Prime Minister. Narasimha Rao declared at the World Economic Forum in Davos in 1994 that there is not just one single way for the development of societies: 'In the new-found enthusiasm for change, governments should not go overboard and plunge large chunks of their people into mass misery;

---

* Patwant Singh, *Of Dreams and Demons*, Rupa and Company, New Delhi, 1994.

they have no right to do so.' Every country has to find its own mode of economic development. 'We cannot have a ready-made formula for economic development. Ready-made prescriptions coming from thousands of miles cannot be accepted.'

Whether this represents a genuine change of heart is unclear: certainly, it was the preamble to jettisoning the 'Exit Policy', the right to hire and fire, which was part of the WB/IMF conditionalities in structural adjustment loans: the shake-out of 'surplus labour' from Indian industry was deemed to be of primary importance in the drive for efficiency and modernisation. However that may be, there has been no calling into question of the need to pay back the foreign debt, which has reached about 40 per cent of national output, while debt servicing takes 31 per cent of national receipts (*Mainstream*, April 1994). As we shall see, the World Bank has learned the art of changing its rhetoric, advocating 'poverty reduction', 'environmental protection' or, more recently, 'popular participation', in response to criticisms levelled against it. It has even expressed 'concern' about public investment (*Times of India*, 13 December 1994), while its central tenet has hitherto been the reduction of public expenditure. All these rhetorical contortions have not been accompanied by the slightest change in practice over the past 50 years. At the same time as Narasimha Rao was talking of the 'mixed economy ... which has saved India, time and again, from political submission and economic dependence', he was supported by the ILO which insisted that the economic structuring programme of India must acquire 'a human face.' But it was also reported that farm products from India are set to reach a value of Rs10,000 crore in 1994 ($2 billion), and that export restrictions on bajra, maize, ragi, jowar and barley are to be lifted. While 40 per cent of the people of India do not have sufficient purchasing power to provide for their needs, 'More emphasis henceforth will be on growing cash crops to make farming more remunerative and make a dent in the international export market' (*Times of India*, 8 April 1994).

These contradictions are unlikely to deflect the Western financial institutions from their purposes, and their role in the global process of filtering wealth from poor to rich, from South to North. But they do suggest that resistance in India to the policies has been far greater than anything anticipated by the government, not least the popular movement against the GATT agreement and its extension from trade in goods into the areas of agriculture, services, intellectual property, finance and banking. India is too complex and pluralist an entity for the abrasive certainties and rigours of the Western way to be imposed without a struggle.

More than this: there is always a discrepancy between what the rulers of India claim to be their policies and what actually happens. As Claude Alvares, author of *Decolonising History,** observes, the celebrated inefficiency of India is perhaps its greatest protection against the assaults on its culture and sensibility now coming from the West. *Nothing works as it should, he says, and that allows people to make their own spaces and refuges within the system. For instance, I've been under threat of arrest for four years: an article I wrote is supposed to have libelled some politician. Well, it's known where I live, I live openly. Only no one bothers. One day, the police came to the office and asked where I was. I was actually sitting at the word processor in the next room. My wife said 'I don't know where he is, he's a freelance journalist, he may be in Delhi somewhere.' 'When will he come?' 'He never tells me.' 'Who is in the other room?' 'Come and see.' She kept her cool. 'Who's he?' With a dismissive wave, she said 'He's the typist.' They went away and I haven't seen them since. So if I'm wanted, I'm not wanted so desperately. When I leave the country, they type your name into the computer when you return. They've never typed my name accurately yet. By the time they've written Claude Alfonso Alvares, they've made at least one mistake.*

This is why those protesting at India signing the GATT agreement are exaggerating. The policy simply cannot be implemented, cannot be policed in India. Let them sign. As in so many things, India says 'Yes, we will do.' But it can never be put into practice. Somebody goes to the US, buys some drug on the market, starts manufacturing it in a small unit. Who is going to stop them selling it at one-tenth the price?

There are so many examples. Of course, it works the other way too – they do not implement the benign welfare legislation either. But it leaves areas of freedom. The inefficiency of the State means the economic 'reforms' will be dispersed, lost in the rambling structures through which they must be carried out.

This view of inefficiency as the salvation of India, however, reckons without the seriousness and attention to detail with which the West imposes its structural adjustments and collects its debts.

Rajni Kothari has identified the next phase in the strategy of the Western financial institutions and Western and Indian governments in their efforts to co-opt dissent. NGOs and popular movements are being flooded with aid money in an effort to neutralise

---

* Claude Alvares, *Decolonising History*, The Other India Publishing House, Goa, 1993.

the sources of resistance to the present policies. This shows up a new fault-line, between those who can and those who cannot be won over, or at least whose crusading edge can or cannot be blunted, by large sums of money. Such NGOs then become parallel business organisations, with elaborate career structures and well-appointed offices, while those which remain true to their base must survive on their own resources and the support of those they represent.

Kothari says, *During the Rajiv and Reagan/Thatcher years, the challenge was identified as coming from the NGOs. Reagan said to the World Bank, 'Why are you working with governments, why not with the market, the private sector?' There has been a shift towards privatisation, and towards the NGOs, which are seen as an extension of the private sector. Both are perceived as means of curbing what little challenge is emerging from Third World governments, and from the intelligentsia. Many Gandhian establishments, labour unions, educational institutions, with all their faults, did form a multiple oppositional thrust. The efforts to co-opt them are highly visible.*

This was borne out by a World Bank seminar in Delhi in January 1994, where the representative of the World Bank asserted that the most 'developed' societies (that means the richest) were those which had a highly evolved and sophisticated civil society: the clearest indication that this is now the target of the Western institutions. I spoke with the Acting Head of the World Bank in India in the autumn of 1993, and it was obvious that the Bank had been severely damaged by its withdrawal from the Narmada Project; and that this had left the government of India to pick up the pieces. Such a situation is clearly unacceptable. In consequence, it is now the policy to devolve responsibility, to coopt popular movements and grassroots initiatives so that they will carry out, or at least soften up the people for, the rigorous policies deemed necessary by the Western financial institutions; they will receive some money, a lot of responsibility and no power. They are to be the executors and implementers of policies which many of them came into being to resist; their purposes are thus subverted, their reasons for existence undermined.

For this reason, as Smitu Kothari of Lokayan points out, there is no reason to romanticise all people's movements, as though they were necessarily a force for good; after all, the RSS is also a social movement. *The best hope for India lies in the richness of its local cultures, its multi-religious, caste, ethnic and social diversity. Pluralism in India is a feature of its social order, not a surface phenomenon, not a division of power as is US pluralism. India is a non-centralised society.*

Vandana Shiva, author of *Staying Alive*, says, *Although there is a massive assault, global, financial, intellectual, to impose a monoculture on India and to destroy its biodiversity, that biodiversity is an integral part of the local cultures of India. Survival of culture and crops are a common cause, the conservation of local seeds is also the struggle of local ways of life, a celebration of particularity and diversity. This is where the resistance is coming from, especially from women, who are more rooted in those cultures. Women are the conservers and protectors of life in all its forms: the colonisation of the seed has a particular resonance for them. Women know there are some things that cannot be bought and sold in the market-place.*

Within India, the efforts to absorb and neutralise dissent are reflected in the movement towards Panchayati Raj, the devolution of power to the traditional Indian community level. This is now government policy. The paradox is that the decentralising of political power should occur at the very moment when economic power is becoming more centralised, globally as well as nationally. This once more implies a devolution of responsibility, but not of power.

Anil Singh, of Voluntary Action Network India (VANI), says, *The 73rd Constitutional Amendment, passed in April 1993, is the law setting up Panchayati Raj. Why, we may wonder, was it passed only now, and not under Rajiv, when it was first brought before Parliament, when he had a two-thirds majority? It didn't succeed, because it was left to a free vote. Yet this minority government passed the bill, all political parties in support, JD [Janata Dal], BJP, Left parties and Congress(I). These are nearly all from upper-middle-class backgrounds: few seriously believe in decentralisation of power. So why did none oppose openly? Narasimha Rao consulted everybody and satisfied everybody. There are also many loopholes. The Central Act says nothing about the Gram Sabha, the general body of the village. There is no power to the Gram Sabha: only the elected representatives can do everything – planning and implementation. We were demanding that more power be given to the Gram Sabha, to make it the supreme body, because elections can be won in all kinds of ways, as we know, through money, intimidation and so on. The electoral process has been discredited. The second aspect is that the government is facing pressure from multilateral agencies to curtail its own budget – the IMF, WB are urging the government to cut its own expenditure. The State, which has already cut education, health and welfare spending in the last two budgets, now thinks it better to give the social sector into the hands of the public, the people, so they will manage it; and if everything goes wrong, people will blame their own local representatives, not the government. They want to develop civil society, to devolve management to NGOs, so they will take responsibility for policies which are increasingly dictated by remote, distant and unaccountable forces. Voluntary organisations are cheap contractors of government; they deliver the goods, therefore voluntary organisations are given more of a role in the Panchayati Raj institution.*

VANI will support the idea of making local institutions more powerful, more effective, because we believe in people's power. Therefore we have pressured State governments to make their legislation more progressive than the State directive dictates. If we can subvert the real intention of the legislation, and make it serve what it says it does, we will have achieved something.

L. C. Jain, who has been working for the achievement of local autonomy for many years, pinpoints the dilemma. *Globalisation destroys self-employment, self-reliance, the life of the non-organised. But with political decentralisation moving forward, there are enough people in India to exert pressure on the political authority in the country to take their interests into account before they barter or bargain them away. If negotiations are carried out by the government without the consent of the people, the government cannot commit the people for ever; if it exceeds its mandate, there is a good case for the government being removed from office. Decentralisation is not only a political development, it also releases a social force for the first time: one-third of the elected seats are for women. This means one million women will enter public affairs. Politicising of women on this scale will have a tremendous influence on the social order. Between 15 and 18 per cent of seats will be reserved for Scheduled Tribes and Scheduled Castes, which means that virtually half the seats will be reserved for disadvantaged groups. Those who say the dominant castes will control it are belabouring an obsolete theory. This new social force will do more for India's development than any cash that can be generated locally or globally; therefore, the space and scope for equity will be vastly expanded and strengthened.*

The centralising forces at work in India are very powerful, and the consequences, in terms of curbing dissent, curtailing local autonomy, infringing individual human rights, in the form of arbitrary arrest, torture and unlawful imprisonment and killings, are plain. R.S. Narula, quoted by Patwant Singh in *Of Dreams and Demons*, says

There are now more killings by our police in one year than there were in 150 years of colonial rule. Deaths due to torture in police custody are continuing unabated and unwept, despite the public outcry of Human Rights Organisations.

The BJP, for all its desire to impose 'Hindutva' upon India, converges with the present policies of Congress(I). Rajni Kothari says,

The people who raided the Golden Temple and sought to impose a technocratic order are the same people as those proposing India's integration into the world economy. They wanted a hegemonical State a propos of its own people – any movement of an ethnic, tribal, regional or grassroot kind must be put down with violence by the emerging Superpower that is India. Against this process is not the Left, nor the Janata Dal, but movements of people, the alliance of Muslims and Dalits, the coming together of the poor and disadvantaged.

Indeed, every political party is now talking of the Dalits. V.P. Singh first raised the issue of reform, in the sense of distributing government jobs more equitably. This met great resistance from the upper-caste youth, and led to violent demonstrations towards the end of the V.P. Singh government. *This, says Anil Singh, effectively splits the Dalit movement, between those who will accept the reforms to the system and those who want more radical change. Do the Dalit leaders want to become like Brahmins, or do they want upliftment for all the poor? Those Dalits who become rich and powerful already treat other Dalits like Untouchables. Within 5 or 10 years Dalits will be ruling in many States. But on the whole, they have no alternative vision. If power is given to the Dalits, they will manage the system. Upper-caste attitudes towards the Dalits are reminiscent of British attitudes towards Independence: these people cannot rule themselves; they're not ready for it. Well they can and they are. The same argument is used of women: women are not capable. Yet women manage their families, even though most mothers are illiterate. The same argument ran through ruling class attitudes to the workers in the West: they cannot rule, they are ignorant, untutored. But they were absorbed into the system. And no doubt, the Dalits could go the same way. For change to occur, there must be both a mass movement and the political education of people.*

One of the most celebrated struggles in India in recent years has been the Narmada Bachao Andolan. It has resisted the construction of a vast series of dams across Gujarat, Maharashtra and Madhya Pradesh which would displace up to 300,000 people; successfully, in the sense that the Andolan has won all the arguments against gigantic industrialised development. It achieved the setting up of the Morse Commission, which declared the project damaging and unnecessary; as a result of its findings, the World Bank withdrew its support from the scheme. But since the government of India is determined to proceed, it must now assume full responsibility. The activists of the Andolan together with the people in the submergence area brought work on the dam to a halt in the monsoon of 1993, by refusing to move out of the area to be flooded. The government set up another review of the project. Work began again before this review had been published.

In April 1994, representatives of the villages in the next submergence area camped for six days outside the Prime Minister's office, and finally gained an interview with him, so that he cannot plead ignorance of the intentions of those resisting the construction of the dam. A satyagraha took place in the same area in May 1994. The Supreme Court has forbidden forcible evictions. About one thousand Adivasi families remained in the submergence area, saying that as the sluice gates are closed, they would rather drown than be displaced. Medha Patkar, leader of the Narmada Bachao Andolan, says that even those who accepted 'rehabilitation' have discovered that there is no land, no money, no adequate compensation for this loss of their livelihood, which means the loss of their lives. They might as well be drowned by development. In December 1994, Medha Patkar was being forcefed in hospital after a long hunger-strike against continued construction. The dam, in however modified a form, will certainly now be built.

But the movement cannot be said to have been a 'failure': this kind of confrontation will become more frequent if the present Indian government does not modify its commitment to the existing development model in more radical ways than mere changes of emphasis and rhetoric. The strengthening of the non-coopted popular movements, the rising consciousness and independence of Dalits, the resistance of those whose resource-base is being enclosed and taken over by the market economy, the reaction of women refusing the violence of 'development', constitute a formidable and growing force.

'Modernisation' is thought to be the same thing as accepting the Western myth of wealth creation, that zero-sum game that gives the illusion of conjuring something out of nothing, the myth that the market and democracy are indivisible, and the myth that the earth can bear unlimited predations upon its resources. The propensity to build empires which has characterised Western civilisation for half a millennium has always rested upon a conviction that they have a mission to convert the world. This continues, although conversion now is no longer to their religious faith but to its bastard offspring, its monotheism of money.

The upsurge of resistance, of people's movements, of indigenous reaction against the present direction of 'development' is not merely a negative rejection. It draws upon profound cultural reservoirs of traditional wisdom, experiential knowledge, ability to survive multiple colonialisms, conquests and invasions. All this represents, not simply another way forward for India, but also hope to a world caught up in the desperately competitive struggle for a form of wealth measured, controlled and manipulated by the West. Levels of violence, social pathology and disease in the richest societies on earth, as well as the intense destruction unleashed by industrialism upon the earth itself and the growing mass of people sunk in voiceless misery suggest that the world is now open to alternatives; and it may find them, here, in India.

Glossary

Hindi words and other terms and expressions used in the text, with explanatory notes.

adda: distribution point
Adivasis: tribals, the original inhabitants of India
agarbatti: incense sticks
ahimsa: non-violence
almirah: cupboard
amla: a sour fruit, rich in vitamin C, a kind of gooseberry
amlaka: forest tree common in north Karnataka
areca: palms bearing nuts which are used in the preparation of paan
atta: plant used for medicinal purposes
ayah: nanny
Ayurveda: a traditional Indian system of medicine

baal mela: children's festival
badmash: wrongdoer
bajra: a cereal, a winter crop
bambool: a small tree
banias: businessmen
betta lands: semi-common land, the produce of which is used to serve the areca gardens in north Karnataka
bhandej: tie-dye method of colouring fabric
bhang: ganja-based drug, used in religious festivals
bhatti: furnace for firing pottery
bidi: Indian cigarette
bigar labour: corvee or forced labour
bighas: a measure of land area; 1 acre = 2.5 bighas
BJP: Bharatiya Janata Party, the Hindu communalist party which was in power in Uttar Pradesh at the time of the demolition of the mosque at Ayodhya and now governs Gujarat and Maharashtra
brinjal: aubergine
brown sugar: a derivative of heroin
BSP/SP: Bharatiya Samaj Party / Samajwadi Party, the Socialist coalition of lower castes and Muslims which came to power in the Northern State of Uttar Pradesh in November 1993.

215

bulbul: an Indian bird
bund: embankment
bustee: slum

casuarina: tree with feathery leaves, often found on sandy ground
chadar: bedsheet
chakunda: name of a coarse grass growing in Orissa
channa: chickpeas
chappals: sandals
charas: hashish
charpoy: wood-and-string bed
chaupari: meeting place
Chilika Bachao Andolan: Save Chilika Movement
chitti: a letter, official piece of paper
chowkidar: security guard, janitor
chulha: cooking stove, of brick or baked earth
chullu: alcohol distilled illegally in Calcutta
crore: 10 million

dacoit: bandit, outlaw
dalit: literally, the oppressed, a term referring to Untouchables in
   general, and members of lower Hindu caste-groups
darbar: a roadside snack-stall
daru: liquor distilled illegally
deshi: domestic
dharna: peaceful protest, a sit-in
dhokra: a shrub

gira: spices used in cooking
gharara oni: the upper and lower parts of a loose suit worn by
   women
gobar: cowdung
godown: a warehouse or storage building
goonda: a hoodlum, hired criminal
gulmohar: forest tree
gur: hardened molasses, rich in iron

haldi: spices used in cooking
hijara: a eunuch; formerly welcomed as a bringer of good fortune,
   now increasingly reduced to begging
Hindutva: Hindu hegemony
honala: forest tree common in north Karnataka

jaggery: molasses

jaghirdar: landowner
jamun: forest tree
Janata Dal: literally, People's Party, a Left-inclined party which
   holds power in Bihar and Karnataka
jhuggi-jopri: hut, slum shelter
jowar: a cereal, a crop grown in the dry season in northern India
JP Movement: the Gandhian/socialist movement of J.P. Narayan
jui: a small shrub

kachera: rubbish, offal
kahigirige: plant used for medicinal purposes
kakri: cucumber
kamiz: shirt or blouse
karanj: forest tree
kassaka: forest tree common in north Karnataka
kavla: forest tree common in north Karnataka
khazan: agricultural land on the shoreline of Goa
khati: an illegally brewed liquor
Koli: fishing community on the coast near Bombay
Konkani: the language of Konkan, around Goa
krait: a poisonous snake

lakh: 100,000 (numeral)
lathi: a stick wielded by police in India
loo: a hot wind that blows in the plains of India before the
   monsoon
lungi: a wrap-around garment for men tied at the waist

mahua: a shrub, the leaves and flowers of which are used in
   distilling alcohol
marada, panu, konga, bagada, genda, sahb: Oriya names for fish
   caught in Lake Chilika
masala: hot red chilli seasoning for cooking
masjid: mosque
matkis: stills
mela: a fair or festival
methi: coriander
mitti: earth, mud, used in construction of village buildings
MLA: member of State legislature
mungphali: peanut
mutti: forest tree common in north Karnataka

nalla: stream, small river
namkeen: salt

Naxalites: an insurgent Leftist movement which began in West Bengal, and spread to Andhra Pradesh which remains its stronghold, especially in the feudal rural areas
neem: a tree, the twigs of which are used for cleaning teeth in India; neem is also a powerful natural pesticide
nityapushpa: everlasting flower

paan: betel-nut mixed with spice for chewing
padayatri: a foot-march
padi: rice, including stalks and husks
paise: the lowest denomination of money in contemporary India
paisewala: a rich person
pakka: literally, cooked; used of buildings, it means of brick and cement
palamoore: migrant labour from Andhra Pradesh
panchayat: the governing body of the smallest administrative unit in India
panchpav: a measure of rice, 1.2 kilos
pangara: forest tree
papad: papadom
patta: deed (to land etc.)
patwari: local revenue official
pekora: vegetable pastie
peon: the most menial employee in an office
puja: Hindu worship

rishi: holy-men
roti: bread
RSS: the extreme wing of Rashtriya Swayam Sangham, the Hindu fundamentalist movement, a member of which assassinated Mahatma Gandhi in 1948

sadhu, Rishi: holy-man
sanjira: a herb
sarpanch: head of the panchayat
sarsoon: mustard
satyagraha: crusade, peaceful movement of protest
shankara: a flowering shrub
shirali: gourd
shunti: plant used for medicinal purposes
sudra: lowest level within the Hindu caste system, artisans
supa: a an open shallow basket in which women winnow rice
suran: a tuber eaten by Adivasis
svadeshi: self reliance

tallab: reservoir, pond, lake
taluka: a medium-size area of local administration
tehsil: an administrative area, local authority
tehsildar: local official
thikedar: contractor
togri, hessera: pulses used in the preparation of dal
tulsi: a sacred plant, like basil

urad: a small dark-coloured bean, a pulse crop

vanaspati: cooking oil
VHP: Vishwa Hindu Parishad, an extreme right-wing Hindu
  organisation

zari: embroidery

Index

Index by Judith Lavender